# Mastering the Possibilities

# Mastering the Possibilities
## A Process Approach to Instructional Design

R. Neal Shambaugh
Susan G. Magliaro
Virginia Polytechnic Institute and State University

Allyn and Bacon
Boston · London · Toronto · Sydney · Tokyo · Singapore

Copyright © 1997 by Allyn and Bacon
A Viacom Company
160 Gould Street
Needham Heights, Massachusetts 02194

Internet: www.abacon.com
America Online: keyword: College Online

ISBN 0-205-19795-7

Printed in the United States of America

10 9 8 7 6 5 4 3 2 1     00 99 98 97

# Contents

# Design Activities

# Preface

Originally we did not set out to write a textbook. Instructional design is a challenge to learn and teach. Early versions of this book were conceived and designed simply as guides to help students manage the requirements of a graduate course in instructional design.

Our stance is that the nature of the instructional design (ID) process is dynamic, systematic, iterative and frequently non-linear in practice. So the question of how to design a text for instructional design was a puzzling one. However, we found the linear form of a book was not altogether a disadvantage. This book gives you a chance to consider each aspect of ID before moving on. Correspondingly, designing with an actual project helps you to see the big picture of the process.

The book is organized around what we believe for the novice are ten distinct and somewhat predictive phases of design. Design Activities form the central basis for its content, supported by the accompanying text. In this way the learning of instructional design can be assisted by actually designing, usually through a project of your choice. Chapters 1 and 2 on Learning Beliefs and Design Tools are unique contributions to the ID field. We believe that they are important aspects of design thinking that are often either taken for granted or omitted completely. We have also included in the back of the book a fictional story that addresses the content in a way that frames the ID process as the adventure that we feel it is.

Although we have designed this book as a learner-centered text, *Mastering the Possibilities* remains a representation of our understanding of how we believe instructional design should be presented to those new to the field. Its learner-centered features have evolved out of our use of the text in the classroom. We would like to hear from you on your experiences with it.

# Plan for This Book—Main Ideas

| GETTING STARTED | Main Ideas |
|---|---|
| **Chapter 1**<br>**Learning Beliefs** | 1. Designing requires attention to learners, content, and context.<br>2. Your beliefs need to be examined.<br>3. Mission statements are tools to express and focus your beliefs. |
| **Chapter 2**<br>**Design Tools** | 1. Differences exist in what people define as instructional design.<br>2. Learning theories form the basis for many ID models.<br>3. Instructional design models can be compared along different lines.<br>4. Conceptual and procedural tools exist to help you in your designing.<br>5. Designing experience takes time to develop. |
| **ANALYSIS** | |
| **Chapter 3**<br>**Needs Assessment** | 1. Needs assessment examines the instructional problem.<br>2. There are three steps in the process: describe intent, gather information, summarize, and revise intent.<br>3. Needs assessment information helps you to write goals. |
| **DESIGNING** | |
| **Chapter 4**<br>**Sequence of Instruction** | 1. Understanding learning levels aids in sequencing content.<br>2. There are a number of ways to sequence content.<br>3. Flexible understanding involves both teacher and students.<br>4. Task analysis examines what it takes to learn something. |
| **Chapter 5**<br>**Assessment** | 1. There are multiple functions for assessment.<br>2. Match assessment methods to assessment purposes.<br>3. There are multiple ways to categorize assessment purposes.<br>4. Determine what it is that you are assessing.<br>5. There are multiple assessment methods. |
| **Chapter 6**<br>**Instructional Framework** | 1. Instructional frameworks support models appropriate to learners, content, and context.<br>2. Families of instructional models are based on learning theories.<br>3. Match instructional models to instructional purpose.<br>4. Models possess a syntax to help to learn them.<br>5. Designing an instructional framework can help to increase one's instructional repertoire. |
| **Chapter 7**<br>**Instructional Media** | 1. There are endless possibilities for instructional media.<br>2. Technology in instruction is a means to solve problems and construct products to assist in the instruction and learning.<br>3. Instructional technology exists to engage learners in learning.<br>4. Examine the instructional issues of media materials.<br>5. Different realities exist for purchasing, modifying and developing media. |
| **Chapter 8**<br>**Prototype** | 1. Instructional events influence mental processes and behavior.<br>2. Instructional events help instructors provide learners with learning opportunities.<br>3. Instructional models include ways to address instructional events.<br>4. The ID process can be used to prototype details that help to address your instructional problem. |
| **EVALUATION** | |
| **Chapter 9**<br>**Program Evaluation** | 1. Program evaluation is a systematic process that determines the effect of your instructional design on educational "programs."<br>2. There are numerous functions and purposes for program evaluation, one of which is the evaluation of instructional outcomes.<br>3. Formative program evaluation scrutinizes (who, what, how, when?) your design during its designing and implementation.<br>4. Summative program evaluation, in the context of instructional design, answers the question: Did the design accomplish its goals? |
| **Chapter 10**<br>**Self Evaluation** | 1. Reflection on your performance as a learner will serve you as a designer.<br>2. This book is an example of a design-in-action.<br>3. This "first pass" through the principles and processes of ID may influence your model of designing. |

# Plan for This Book—Design Activities

| GETTING STARTED | Design Thinking |
|---|---|
| 1. Design a Lesson<br>2. What is Learning?<br>3. Mission Statement of Learning Beliefs | 1. Approaching the design task from the learner's perspective.<br>2. Recognizing the impact of beliefs on the ID process.<br>3. Understanding connections between beliefs and actions. |
| 4. Your Learning Principles<br>5. Your Preliminary ID Model<br>6. Your Designer Competencies | 4. Understanding the intimate connection between educational psychology and instructional design.<br>5. Understanding concepts and principles of learning theories and their use as tools guiding our designs.<br>6. Appreciating the need to represent the complex ID process through models or some conceptual means of communication.<br>7. Articulating your stance as a designer of learning events.<br>8. Knowing your own limitations and capabilities as a designer. |
| **ANALYSIS** | |
| 7. Intent Statement<br>8. Needs Assessment Strategy<br>9. Learner Profile<br>10. Context Analysis<br>11. Goals & Revised Intent/Mission Statements | 9. Understanding complex relationships between learners, content, and context.<br>10. Understanding the political nature of design.<br>11. Being able to moderate or put aside personal stances to meet the needs of learners, content, and context. |
| **DESIGNING** | |
| 12. Matching Learning Goals with Learning Types<br>13. Content & Lesson Outline<br>14. Learning Task Analysis of a Key Task | 12. Appreciating the complexity of levels of learning across different learning domains.<br>13. Connecting the sequencing of instructional events to your stance on learning and the curriculum.<br>14. Understanding the critical relationship between the nature of learning and instruction. |
| 15. Your Assessment Purpose(s)<br>16. Instructional Sequence—Assessment Tools<br>17. Assessment Plan | 15. Understanding dimensions and methods for assessment.<br>16. Understanding connections between assessment purposes, learning, and instructional goals.<br>17. Appreciating ethical and moral responsibilities of assessment design and practice. |
| 18. How Do You Present Instruction Now?<br>19. Your Instructional Framework<br>20. Your Instructional Repertoire | 18. Connecting learning theories, instructional goals, and pedagogy.<br>19. Ensuring the instructional practice meets the needs of learners, content, and context.<br>20. Being able to explore new pedagogies to fulfill goals or meet the needs of learners, content, and context. |
| 21. Identify Media Possibilities<br>22. Your Instructional Media Plan | 21. Appreciating the range of media possibilities and their limitations.<br>22. Understanding connections between goals, and pedagogy.<br>23. Being resourceful to find, adapt, and create media to match instructional purposes. |
| 23. Instructional Events<br>24. Prototype<br>25. Design Syllabus or Brochure | 24. Synthesizing components of design into a coherent instructional event.<br>25. Communicating intentions clearly and concisely. |
| **EVALUATION** | |
| 26. Your Formative Plan<br>27. Your Summative Plan | 26. Understanding and embracing the need for formative and summative evaluation components in a design.<br>27. Knowing how to construct an evaluation plan that assesses your success in meeting your intended and unintended outcomes. |
| 28. Your Revised Instructional Design Model<br>29. Self Assessment of Your Learning<br>30. Feedback to Us | 28. Examining your thinking and actions in the design process.<br>29. Articulating and representing publicly your model for design.<br>30. Providing helpful feedback for another's design using the design thinking knowledge and skills shared in this book. |

# Acknowledgments

We'd like to thank, first of all, our students, who have willingly engaged in the design of an artifact for learning. These are the individuals who have helped to make this text a reality. It grew out of an intent to help students engage in learning in a different manner than traditional textbooks.

Although we feel our approach to instructional design is unique, we would like to acknowledge the contributions made to the instructional design field by its numerous advocates. We are a product of what these researchers have given to the field. It is our hope that this book extends this understanding based on what has been discovered about learning and learners and implemented in this text.

We would like to thank the blind reviews and comments from field testers at three universities, the student groups who examined early versions of the manuscript, and Cindy Beacham, Tom Hergert, and Eileen Moccia for their comments from their unique points of view. Our thanks to George V. Wills for his illustrations used in the stories.

A thank you to Nancy Forsyth at Allyn & Bacon for her willingness to publish this product and make it available to a wider audience.

An important acknowledgment must go to the collaborative process that helped to shape this book, as a book about "possibilities" cannot be done alone. A grateful thank you, as always, to our mates, Cindy and Terry, who supported us in this endeavor.

# Mastering the Possibilities

# Getting Started

- **Chapter 1 - Learning Beliefs**
- **Chapter 2 - Design Tools**

---

WELCOME TO MASTERING THE POSSIBILITIES. We hope that you enjoy your experiences in learning instructional design.

In these first two chapters we will try to prepare you for designing by examining your beliefs about learning, then explaining what we mean by the process approach and summarizing the features of this book. The tools of an instructional designer are presented in Chapter 2.

Good luck. Enjoy the adventure!

---

"To relate, to be connected, one must pay attention, and paying attention is what process is all about."

(Godfrey, 1992, p. 17)

"Dear Sophie, when you read this you may already have met Hermes. In case you haven't, I'll add that he is a dog. But don't worry. He is very good-tempered—and moreover, a good deal more intelligent than a lot of people. In any event he never tries to give the impression of being cleverer than he is."

(Gaarder, 1996, p. 60)

CHAPTER

# 1

You will not likely find a chapter like this in any other instructional design textbook. Learning beliefs are not usually considered a piece of this process. We believe that your beliefs about learners and learning are fundamental to this whole process. As such, we invite you to consider their importance in the design of instructional events.

# Learning Beliefs

*He calmly rode on, leaving it to his horse's discretion to go which way it pleased, firmly believing that in this consisted the very essence of adventures.*

(Miguel Cervantes Saavedra, 1993)

---

Let's begin with what you know! We will ask you to take stock of what you believe learning is, so that you can begin to see how your beliefs, ideas, and perceptions influence your instructional designing. We encourage you to review these beliefs, to discover the personal and psychological basis for them, and to decide if these beliefs are appropriate in what you design. In addition, we will explain what we mean by the "process" approach to instructional design (ID), and describe the chapters and learning aids in this book.

In this chapter you will:

1. Be provided with a trio of design activities to examine your learning beliefs.
2. Record what you believe instructional design to be.
3. Assess what you have learned thus far and record questions you may have regarding what was written in this chapter.

# Where Are You?

You can write in this space!
⇩

Everyone comes to a course in instructional design with different experiences, backgrounds, interests, and a wide range of instructional design competencies. Let's begin with a small slice of the process by examining your present understanding of instructional design.

> This activity is YOUR starting point!

↓

# DESIGN ACTIVITY 1

## "Design a Lesson"

1. Identify an activity, lesson, workshop, or some other type of learning event or setting that you are familiar with.

2. Based on what you know about your choice and as you imagine the problem, outline or sketch out (i.e., "design") some of the major features of this instructional activity. You will likely need more space than we have provided here. Use this space to get started.

 **Task Description**

The purpose of this Design Activity is to reveal what you know about instructional design through a task familiar to many teachers or trainers.

This activity is designed to prompt you to think about the issues in designing instructional activities, as well as to witness the influence your beliefs play in these features.

Depending on your intent, your learning beliefs, and your present understanding of the instructional design process, there may be many ways of designing a learning activity. At this point you may want a definition of instructional design. We believe that an examination of your learning beliefs is necessary first. However, the instructional design process, as presented in this book, is a systematic means to explore the major issues of designing and construct features that are responsive to instructional needs. We provide our definition on page 24.

# Why Learning Beliefs?

Learning is a human enterprise. With this understanding, we cannot dismiss or ignore the value of our beliefs about learning in the design of learning opportunities. Such a stance complicates designing, but it also opens the door for many possibilities. Examining these beliefs, whether personal or institutional, makes public those that are hidden or fuzzy, and acknowledges those that may influence the design process. Learning beliefs are *personalized understandings* that describe how you think and feel about learning, schooling, and education. Learning beliefs are frequently embedded in the complex contexts of real settings where the values and beliefs of schools, business, and communities must be considered.

The instructional design process can be used to identify *inconsistencies* and *contradictions* in our belief systems. By constantly comparing stated beliefs and emerging design components you remain vigilant that your intentions are addressed appropriately for the nature of the content, the needs of your learners, and the realities of the instructional setting.

Let's begin to examine your learning beliefs through writing.

↓

# DESIGN ACTIVITY 2

### "What Is Learning?"

**1.** In this task we would like you to answer two critical questions: *What is learning?* and *What is instruction?* Record your initial thoughts on learning and instruction and what they mean for you.

 **Task Description**

The purpose for this activity is to examine through writing what you believe learning to be.

This may be one of the most important tasks in this book!

Now, let's move your beliefs to ACTION!

↓

# Operationalizing Beliefs

**Institutions using mission statements:**

- Governments
- Companies
- Non-profit companies
- Support groups
- Schools
- Organizations

**Other labels for mission statements:**

- Creeds
- Principles
- Philosophies
- Mottoes
- Objectives
- Statement of Purpose
- Management Statement
- Foundations
- Guiding Principles
- Operating Principles
- Standards of Performance
- Our Commitments
- Beliefs
- Code of Conduct
- Thoughts
- Our Vision
- Core Values

Many institutions use **mission statements** to describe what their purpose is, who they are serving, and what values they practice to meet the needs of their constituents. Mission statements represent the character and personality of the institution and may indicate not only the institution's endeavors, but the direction the institution is aiming towards. As such, a mission statement can be a reflection of the people who direct the institution (Falsey, 1989).

Although mission statements have been identified with institutions, they also are useful in examining one's personal life (Covey, Merrill & Merrill, 1994), and may help people to leverage their learning beliefs in designing instruction. Whether they are being drawn up for institutions, personal use, or for designing instructional activities, mission statements address three major aspects of a mission: *overall purpose*, *relationships*, and *accountability*. See the chart on the next page for examples of questions one might ask to address these three aspects of a mission statement.

Within this book, a mission statement will be used to help you crystallize what you defined learning to be in **Design Activity 2** .

Mission statements require careful thought. Several versions may be needed before you feel comfortable with what you have written. Successive versions will, over time, reflect the principles you choose implementing your instructional design and moving your mission toward reality.

**Key Words**
- **Mission statement**

### Questions to Address in Mission Statements

| Institutional | Personal | Designing | |
|---|---|---|---|
| What is our business? What markets should we be in? | What is my role in the world? | What is learning? What are my learning beliefs? What learning principles support these beliefs? | **Purpose** |
| What are our constituencies? | How do I view and treat others? | What is my role as a designer? How do I view learners and teaching? Do I understand connections between learners, content, and context? | **Relationships** |
| How do we address profitability, service, quality, responsiveness, and work environment? | How do I judge what is ethical and appropriate thinking and behavior? | What is the purpose of assessment? Do I have a plan for program evaluation? | **Accountability** |

Here are the benefits of writing a mission statement:

♦ See **For Further Reading** for sources on Mission Statements.

### Benefits of Writing a Mission Statement

1. Record on paper learning beliefs and principles.
2. Provide an enduring, yet evolving statement of who you are and a means to communicate this to yourself and to others.
3. Position your thinking and ready yourself for instructional design (action).
4. Focus your design activities in ways that are consistent with your mission and the goals that you establish from a needs assessment (Chapter 3).

Let's examine a learning setting using institutional beliefs.

# ☆ SCENARIO

## Health Care Setting: Institutional Beliefs

It's not always possible or appropriate to bring your personal beliefs into the picture. Consider a health care setting featuring Lakeside Health Systems, a for-profit health care provider with facilities in several communities. Below is Lakeside's Mission Statement:

> **Our Service Mission**
>
> Our mission is to provide high quality, cost effective health care.
>
> **Supporting Principles**
>
> 1. We insist that each patient deserves dignity and respect.
>
> 2. We value the relationships between patients, staff, vendors, and the public.
>
> 3. We are dedicated to continuous improvement in services and ongoing training and evaluation of our staff.

The mission statement reveals not only the overall *purpose* of the institution, but begins to reveal the challenge of operationalizing the mission. For example, how does "high quality, cost effective" health care happen? The importance of people are also identified as qualitative issues regarding *relationships* between individuals. *Accountability* to these principles needs to be substantiated in supporting documents and behavior. For example, what does "cost effective" mean? How do these words become translated into reality?

A mission statement can be a working document for those who have to live or work by it. Most mission statements are lists of aspirations that people and organizations must continually work toward.

> Now, let's write your personal mission statement of learning beliefs.

↓

# DESIGN ACTIVITY 3

## "Mission Statement of Learning Beliefs"

**1. Write a paragraph below that summarizes your beliefs about learning.** Do this within a context that is meaningful to you; for example, write about a project you may have in mind, based on previous experiences or current needs.

**2. Cite any references that you have consulted.**

 **Task Description**

This is another challenging task, designed to help you focus your learning beliefs from **Design Activity 1** into a coherent and cohesive statement that summarizes your beliefs.

It might be helpful to first make a list of your learning beliefs and see which of these might be useful or appropriate.

These 3 **Design Activities** are challenging, but important tasks. They may help you to reflect on what you have written. For now, let's examine the process approach and how this book is structured.

↓

# What Is the Process Approach?

We would like to share with you our instructional strategy that we use in this book. We call it the "process approach." Our aim in discussing this is to make clear the strategy that we are using and also to give you a working example of how learning principles form the basis for a text. Learning principles are powerful foundations from which to construct instructional designs. Here are the three learning principles that serve as the foundation for this book:

---

### Learning Principles of This Book

**1.** Teaching and learning is a *human* enterprise.

**2.** Learning is facilitated through authentic tasks, which are *meaningful* to the learner and are relevant in light of current practice.

**3.** Teaching is a means to *assist* learners.

---

**Assistance in this book**
- Meaningful Tasks
- Structure
- Reflective Features

The means by which we try to achieve these learning principles is by providing (1) meaningful tasks, (2) structure, and (3) reflective opportunities.

**Meaningful tasks**. The process approach used by this book attempts to translate learning principles into action by providing *meaningful tasks* that will introduce basic instructional design concepts, *tools* to design with, and *opportunities* to design and reflect on your learning. One of the best ways to learn instructional design in an authentic way is to experience the design process through a project of one's choosing. It may be possible to learn the basic principles of instructional design, but it is impossible to appreciate the design

♦ See Schön (1987) in **For Further Reading** for a discussion of the need to immerse oneself in the designing process.

process and to master the possibilities without actual *hands-on* designing.

**Structure**. We don't throw you into the designing process without assistance! Each phase of the generic ID process is covered by its own chapter and set of Design Activities, which are designed to help you complete your own ID project. Each chapter also has "design tools" to assist you in understanding the chapter's major ideas, plus questions, tables, or forms to help you manage the details of a project. To assess your understanding of instructional design and the progress you are making on your design project, we have included prompting questions and a self-assessment at the end of each chapter. For additional assistance, we list references and suggestions for further reading at the end of each chapter.

While specific activities follow a predictable sequence in the instructional design process, some activities are iterative and require re-visiting at each step of the way. To assist this re-examination you will find in each chapter four design topics:

**Structure**
- Ch. 1 - Learning Beliefs
- Ch. 2 - Design Tools
- Ch. 3 - Needs Assessment
- Ch. 4 - Sequence of Instruction
- Ch. 5 - Assessment
- Ch. 6 - Instructional Framework
- Ch. 7 - Instructional Media
- Ch. 8 - Prototype
- Ch. 9 - Program Evaluation
- Ch. 10 - Self Evaluation

---

### Design Topics in Each Chapter

1. Relating your **learning beliefs** to the major ideas of each design phase.

2. Updating your own **instructional design model**.

3. Examining the possibilities of **instructional media**.

4. Engaging in **formative**, or ongoing, **evaluation** of your design as it is being constructed.

---

This chapter examines the influence of your *learning beliefs* and encourages you to examine them in the context of a design project chapter.

Related to this revisiting of beliefs is an ongoing examination of a *personalized instructional design model* that you will develop vis-à-vis this book. Beginning in Chapter 2 you will describe a preliminary version of your own instructional design model. The purpose of this task is to explain and model what you already know about designing. Throughout the book we will ask you to reflect on your model, modifying it to better meet your intentions. We will ask you to revise it in Chapter 10.

*Instructional Media* is an important feature in many instructional designs as they are powerful supporters to learning. While this is the focus of Chapter 7, each chapter will briefly discuss a media topic related to the topics of that chapter.

A fourth topic that will be re-visited each chapter is *formative program evaluation*. Formative evaluation examines ways to determine if your formative, or developing design, is on target and heading in the right direction. At the end of each chapter we will prompt you with questions and checklists to ensure that your project is staying consistent with your beliefs, mission, and goals.

**Reflection.** An important aspect of learning assistance is helping you to *reflect* on the ID process. We will encourage you to think about what you are learning as well as about your progress on the Design Activities and your design project. Use the space in the margins to record questions or ideas. At the end of each chapter you can record your accomplishment. Finally, Chapter 10 is devoted to Self Evaluation, which looks at what you have learned about the instructional design process.

**Reflective Features**
- Wide margins for notes.
- Prompting questions in the margin.
- Self Assessment at the end of each chapter.
- Chapter 10 - Self Evaluation chapter

This book features a number of learning aids.

↓

# Learning Aids in This Book

Each chapter has the following features to help you in your learning. They can be identified by the following symbols:

| Icon | Learning Aid |
|------|--------------|
| ✍ | Design Activity |
| ⚑ | Important Idea |
| **BOLD** | Key Word found in Glossary |
| ◆ | For Further Reading ... |
| ☆ | Scenario |
| **Talking About Media** | Talking About Media |
| 💡 | Conceptual Design Tool |
| ✏ | Procedural Design Tool |
| 📖 | Stories |
| **Food for Thought** | Enrichment Blocks |
| ∞ | Design Iteration |
| ✓ | Your Personal Learning |
| **Glossary Index** | Design Glossary and Index |

Here is a brief description of these learning aids:

✍ **Design Activity**. Within each chapter are Design Activities to give you hands-on design opportunities. Used in conjunction with a design project of your choosing, these activities can help move your ideas and your intentions to paper and eventually to enactment.

⚑ **Important ideas**. This icon "flags" an important idea. These ideas are summarized at the end of each chapter.

**Key words**. Within the text are key design words highlighted in bold and listed at the bottom of each page. These words can also be found in the Design Glossary.

◆ **For further reading**. During your reading you may see this "diamond" symbol in which we point out important references related to that section in the text. These sources are listed in **References** or **For Further Reading** at the end of each chapter.

☆ **Scenario.** Throughout the book we will profile three different learning settings that, although different in many ways, feature similar instructional design issues. The settings include (1) staff development in a health care setting, (2) curriculum within a middle school science class, and (3) training issues at a small consulting firm.

**Talking About Media.** In Chapters 2-9 we have included brief discussions of the instructional design implications of media within the context of that particular chapter.

💡 **Conceptual design tool.** The light bulb signals what we call a "conceptual design tool," which may help you to make sense of an idea or concept. These will be discussed in Chapter 2 , Design Tools.

⚘ **Procedural design tool.** These tools help to gather information about your design problem, as well as aids to manage the details of the design document. Examples of these tools include tables and charts in the text and the Design Activities. We will discuss these aids in Chapter 2.

> **Food for Thought.** Throughout each chapter are shaded boxes in the margins we call "enrichment blocks." These short ideas serve as "Food for Thought."

∞ **Design Iteration.** The infinity symbol signals a possible need to revisit and revise other components of your instructional design.

✓ **Your Personal Learning.** At the end of each chapter is a self-assessment section titled "✓ Your Personal Learning" to record what you have learned and what you would like to know more about. Checklists and criteria are available to check your performance on the Design Activities.

**Design Glossary and Index.** Words in BOLDFACE signify an entry into a Design Glossary found at the back of the book. We have found that learners appreciate a place for definitions of key terms. An index is also included to help you to find topics.

# Overview of Chapters

---

The book is divided into four major sections: *Getting Started*, *Analysis*, *Designing*, and *Evaluation*.

**Chapter 1: Learning Beliefs.** The first two chapters comprise *Getting Started* and introduce you to yourself and the instructional design process. This chapter will help you to come to grips with what you believe learning is. Without such an understanding, it will be difficult to design meaningful and responsive instructional activities.

**Getting Started**
- Ch 1. Learning Beliefs
- Ch 2. Design Tools

**Analysis**

- Ch 3. Needs Assessment

**Designing**

- Ch 4. Sequence of Instruction
- Ch 5. Assessment
- Ch 6. Instructional Framework
- Ch 7. Instructional Media
- Ch 8. Prototype

**Chapter 2: Design Tools.** This chapter includes several important tools for instructional designers: (1) definitions, that is, concise representations of what we mean by certain key terms and concepts; (2) learning theories, which form the basis for (3) instructional design models; (4) conceptual tools; (5) procedural tools; and (6) instructional design competencies.

**Chapter 3: Needs Assessment.** This chapter begins another major aspect of design—analysis! In the context of instructional design, analysis finds out what *really* needs to be done and what has *already* been done by others to address this instructional problem, *before* you begin designing. All of this is transformed into goals that provide structure and coherent guidance to your designing efforts.

The next major chunk of design activity is the actual *designing*, which includes phases for Instructional Sequence, Assessment, Instructional Framework, Instructional Media, and a Prototype of a component of your design.

**Chapter 4: Sequence of Instruction.** Is there some order or sequence to content or learning activities? This order is usually critical to achieve learning goals. If there is some flexibility, this may be articulated in this phase.

**Chapter 5: Assessment.** The assessment stage of design activity determines how learning will be measured. A survey of assessment methods will be examined.

**Chapter 6: Instructional Framework.** This chapter will survey a range of instructional models, in which learning opportunities are presented or made available to learners.

**Chapter 7: Instructional Media.** We would like you to think about a wide range of media possibilities, from chalk to computers. Chapter 7 is devoted to the design implications of choosing and integrating instructional media into your design.

**Chapter 8: Prototype.** Design features can be tried out in a sample component, or prototype. Here the major design features can be tested and evaluated against the goals established from the needs assessment. Lessons learned from a prototype can then be incorporated into the design before actual implementation.

The final chunk of activity considered after *Getting Organized*, *Analysis*, and *Design* is *Evaluation*.

**Chapter 9: Program Evaluation.** The Program Evaluation Plan describes how an instructional design will be evaluated as it is being developed and once it is finished and implemented.

**Chapter 10. Self Evaluation.** This chapter is a self-assessment of your experiences and learning of instructional design activities.

**Appendices.** After you finish each chapter in this book, you are invited to read *Touring Instructional Design*, a series of stories at the back of the book. In each chapter, you will notice a symbol of a small book that signals an idea addressed in the stories.

This serial of short stories involves two students who enter a very different kind of "design space," a fantasy design setting in which the only escape is to "design" their way out. The pair encounter quirky individuals who assist the two along their way. The stories address the content of instructional design in a different way, and give you a different perspective on many of the same issues facing novice instructional designers.

Another appendix is a *Design Glossary* listing words highlighted in the text and summarized at the bottom of each page.

**Evaluation**
- Ch 9. Program Evaluation
- Ch 10. Self Evaluation

*"I'll bet the two of you have never seen the likes of me."*

From Tour 1: Learning Beliefs

We're at the end of Chapter 1. It's time to examine your learning performance.

# Reviewing Design Activities

Below are criteria to help you gauge your performance on these tasks.

**Design Activity 1: Design a Lesson.**

☐ Selection of a "lesson" or other instructional activity.
☐ Description of major features.

**Design Activity 2. What Is Learning?**

☐ Definition of "learning."
☐ Definition of "instruction."

**Design Activity 3: Mission Statement of Beliefs.**

☐ Articulation of beliefs and principles.
☐ Clear connections of beliefs and principles to content, context, and learners.
☐ References consulted and cited.

# ᛒ **Summary of Important Ideas**

**1.** There are no clear right or wrong choices in instructional design, only more appropriate choices to meet the needs of the learner, the nature of the content to be taught, and the reality of the instructional setting. There also may be many ways to address these needs.

**2.** Examining one's learning beliefs can help to identify inconsistencies and contradictions in one's belief systems and help to determine if these beliefs are appropriate in instructional design activities.

**3.** Mission statements are useful tools for expressing and focusing your learning beliefs and providing a guiding statement in designing.

## ✓ Your Personal Learning

### Relating Your Beliefs to This Chapter:

Record here the learning beliefs you feel are important and any notes about beliefs that are fuzzy and need to be examined.

**Food for Thought**

Start thinking about an idea for a design project, something that you've always wanted to do or that you need to do, such as an upcoming course to be taught. Choose a project in an area or topic that you have some content knowledge and experience with, so you can concentrate on learning the instructional design process.

### What is the most important idea that you learned from this chapter?

### What questions do you have thus far?

# References

Cervantes, M. (1993). *Don Quixote*. Ware, Hertfordshire: Wadsworth.

Covey, S. R., Merrill, A. R., & Merrill, R. R. (1994). *First things first: To live, to love, to learn, to leave a legacy*. NY: Simon & Schuster.

Falsey, T. A. (1989). *Corporate philosophies and mission statements: A survey and guide for corporate communicators and management*. NY: Quorum.

Gaarder, J. (1996). *Sophie's World: A novel about the history of philosophy*. New York: Berkley.

Godfrey, J. (1992). *Our wildest dreams: Women entrepreneurs making money, having fun, doing good*. NY: HarperCollins.

# For Further Reading . . .

Connelly, F. M., & Clandinin, D. J. (1988). *Teachers as curriculum planners: Narratives of experience.* NY: Teacher's College Press.

> Examines the connection behind our life experiences and our design actions. Explains how we can help ourselves articulate and enact instruction from a more reflective perspective.

Covey, S. R., Merrill, A. R., & Merrill, R. R. (1994*). First things first: To live, to love, to learn, to leave a legacy.* NY: Simon & Schuster.

> Appendix A provides a "Mission Statement Workshop" to help you think and write through a personal mission statement.

Eisner, E. (1994). *The educational imagination* (3rd ed.). NY: Macmillan.

> Promotes connectedness behind our intentions and beliefs through the design of our programs.

Falsey, T. A. (1989). *Corporate philosophies and mission statements: A survey and guide for corporate communicators and management.* NY: Quorum.

> Provides facsimiles of actual corporate mission statements.

Graham, J. W., & Havlick, W. C. (1994). *Mission statements: A guide to the corporate and nonprofit sectors.* NY: Garland.

> Contains 622 mission statements.

Newman, D., Griffin, P., & Cole, M. (1989). *The construction zone: Working for cognitive change in school.* NY: Cambridge University Press.

> Discusses learning as constructing meanings through authentic activity.

Schank, R. C. (1990). *Let me tell you a story: A new look at real and artificial memory.* NY: Scribner.

> Schank says our memories are essentially scripts or stories. A good introduction to Roger Schank. Also see his *Connoisseur's Guide to the Mind* (1991).

Schön, D. A. (1987). *Educating the reflective practitioner.* San Francisco: Jossey-Bass.

> This book examines a design practice in the context of the architecture design studio, but Schön discusses learning processes where dialogue between student and teacher is essential within the context of actually doing the task.

Tharp, R. G., & Gallimore, R. (1991). *Rousing minds to life: Teaching, learning, and schooling in social context.* NY: Cambridge University Press.

> A detailed discussion of teaching as the process of assisting learners.

# What's Next?

In Chapter 2 we launch into the actual instructional design process and describe design tools to assist you in your designing efforts.

These tools will include definitions of design and instructional design and learning theories, which are the basis for instructional design models, another set of design tools. In addition, we describe conceptual and procedural tools to help learn instructional design and develop your own design project. We also will examine another critical design tool—your skills and experiences—by describing competencies of an expert instructional designer.

Take a break. See you soon in Chapter 2!

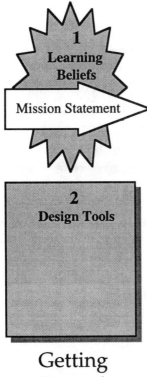

Getting
Started

# CHAPTER 2

Instructional design has at its disposal many "tools."

**W**e believe that your learning of the instructional design process will benefit from a careful consideration and use of these tools.

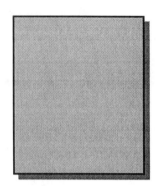

# Design Tools

*All of these tools, by the way, are optional. No one needs to know or use any of them to learn the necessary lessons .... As such, there's no need to struggle, thinking that if you don't master them your life will be a failure. Be easy, play with these techniques. Experiment. Play with them. Have fun.*

(Roger & McWilliams, 1991, p. 69)

Design tools help you to accomplish design tasks. Looking into the instructional designer's tool kit we can find six types of tools: definitions, learning theories, design models, conceptual and procedural tools, and designer expertise.

In this chapter you will:

1. Build on your learning beliefs by listing your principles of learning and identifying the theories of learning on which they are based.

2. Construct a preliminary version of your own instructional design model.

3. Examine your instructional designer skills and competencies.

Now, here is Design Tool #1:

# Definitions

---

"Definitions" are concise representations of what we know. You may have privately wished in a class or workshop that the instructor or facilitator would have defined some terms that were used. Each of the participants may have had different understandings of the meanings behind these words. We start off with examining what we and others define as instructional design to give you an idea of where we are coming from as well as other views based on their **definitions**.

The first question needs to be: What is **design**?

**What is Design?** Simon (1981) believes that design is a problem - solving process which is "aimed at changing existing solutions into preferred ones" (p. 180). Design from Simon's point of view deals with messy, ill-structured problems, and its goal to achieve the best possible solution using available information.

Rowland's (1993) definition is similar: "Design is a disciplined inquiry engaged in for the purpose of creating some new thing of practical utility" (p. 80). It involves exploring an ill-defined situation, finding—as well as solving—a problem and specifying change. The design process, according to Rowland, is affected by the designer's knowledge, skill, and experience. Also influencing the process is the nature of the design task, the designer's working environment, and the design methods and management techniques employed.

Because design is a goal-directed process to achieve a special purpose (Cross, 1982), it requires social interaction. According to Schön (1983), design is conducted within a reflective dialogue, a conversation between designer and situation, with a teacher acting

**Key Words**
- Definitions
- Design

as coach. This **reflection-in-action** guides the designer to continually reframe the problem and possible solutions.

**Our definition of instructional design.** We'd like to share our definition so that you have a clear idea of where we are coming from:

What do you think about this definition? How does it fit your current conception of instructional design?

---

### Our Definition of Instructional Design

**Instructional Design:** An intellectual process which systematically analyzes the needs of learners and provides features to assist designers construct structured "possibilities" to responsively address those needs.

---

Let's examine this definition closely. A *process* provides systematic *structure* to help guide your design decisions, whether you are a novice or an expert designer. There is no one right or wrong design process; however, some design processes may be more appropriate given certain content, contexts, and learner needs. Many models depict instructional design processes. We describe some in this chapter.

Describing instructional design as an *intellectual process* suggests that designing uses the same high-level thinking skills characteristic of problem solving and decision-making (Nelson, Magliaro, & Sherman, 1988). Instructional design is a challenge to learn and master, but it offers rich possibilities for addressing instructional problems. Teaching and learning, being complex activities, need a sufficiently robust process that can address their possibilities in a way that is *responsive* to learners and contexts and is useful to practitioners. Instructional design is that process.

**Other definitions.** Now, let's consider some other instructional design definitions which were developed by experts based on their experiences and research:

**Key Words**
- Instructional design
- Reflection-in-action

---

### Definitions of Instructional Design

1. Instructional systems development (ISD) is a process for determining what to teach and how to teach it (Dick, 1993, p. 12).

2. Instructional design can be defined as the science of creating detailed specifications for the development, evaluation, and maintenance of situations which facilitate the learning of both large and small units of subject matter (Richey, 1986, p. 9).

3. Instructional systems design is the systematic process of planning instructional systems, while instructional development is the process of implementing the plans. Together, these two functions are components of what is referred to as instructional technology (the systematic application of theory and other organized knowledge to the task of instructional design and development) (Gagné, Briggs & Wager, 1992, p. 20).

4. As a process it is the systematic development of instructional specifications using learning and instructional theory to ensure the quality of instruction. As an area of study it is that branch of knowledge concerned with research and theory about specifications for instruction and the processes for developing those specifications (Seels & Glasgow, 1990, p. 4).

5. The systematic process of translating principles of learning and instruction into plans for instructional materials and activities (Smith & Ragan, 1993, p. 2).

---

*While authors agree that instructional design involves a combination of rational and creative thought processes, they tend to accentuate one or the other extreme.*

(Rowland, 1993, p. 88)

What are your reactions to these definitions? How does each of these fit your conception of instructional design?

These definitions represent a range of views of what instructional design is—on one hand, instructional design is a technical process driven by rules and principles (e. g., Dick & Carey, 1996; Richey, 1986); on the other, instructional design is an iterative process that identifies and interprets learning needs within the context of the specific instructional situation (Rowland, 1993) where rules or procedures fail to adequately address real world problems. We embrace the latter view, since the situations dealt with by instructional designers involve human issues and are, therefore, complex, precluding the use of rules or procedures to cover all contingencies.

> Your learning beliefs may be based on several learning theories—Design Tool #2.

# Learning Theories

Models of instructional design are based on our knowledge of how humans learn. There are many different learning theories which you can draw upon to serve as foundational for your own models. But, over the past century, three theoretical approaches have provided the primary guidance for instructional practice: behaviorism, cognitive psychology, and constructivism. Mayer (1992) offered us three metaphors which parallel each of these approaches and provide ways of thinking about these theories. Recently, Wildman (1996) expanded these metaphors to articulate the theoretical assumptions and instructional design considerations that equip us with the tools we need as designers. In this section, we will blend the work of these authors to provide an overview of the major theoretical tools at our disposal.

**Learning as response acquisition.** Behavioral psychology dominated the study of human learning during the first half of this century. From a **behavioral** perspective, learning is seen as the acquisition of responses due to external contingencies of our environment (Mayer, 1992). The assumptions of this theory are clear and concise. In essence, behavior is a function of its consequences. Learning is achieved through the frequent responding and immediate reinforcement of appropriate behaviors. Humans acquire complex processes over time through the gradual shaping of the desired responses via the contingencies of reinforcement.

The specific instructional design considerations provided a very organized and systematic set of guidelines for design (Wildman, 1996). First, given that the value of the **reinforcement** is based on the individual learner's needs and interests, the designer must allow for individual pacing and progress. Subject matter has an inherent organization that must be programmed so that the learner can acquire knowledge in the appropriate sequence. Consequently, design decisions must follow the caveat, "Teach first things first." Specific objectives for the learner that take into account performance of the actual task to be mastered are articulated using a task analysis which breaks down the behavior into the correct sequence of observed actions. Learning is ascertained by objective measures in which behavior is operationally defined and measured according to some behavioral indicator.

**Learning as knowledge acquisition.** Mayer's (1992) second metaphor reflects the **cognitive** perspective, more specifically, the information processing model of human memory. Dominating the research during the sixties and seventies, learning theorists turned to studying the mental processes, such as thinking, remembering, and problem solving, and used the computer as the metaphor for the human memory system. Key memory structures and processes were identified. Memory and recall were seen as dependent on the quality of processing. New information is built on existing knowledge structures. And, internal executive control was required to enable the entire system to function efficiently.

With cognitive psychology, our instructional design considerations expanded (Wildman, 1996). Our primary goal begins with the identification of the ideal or expert knowledge structure(s). From here instruction is designed to promote processing activity toward that of an expert. Once appropriate mental

**Key Words**
- Cognitive
- Reinforcement

processes are identified, relevant processing activities are stimulated and specific strategies are taught to ensure that the learner efficiently acquires the information or solves the problem. As instructional aids, conceptual **organizers** are carefully constructed to facilitate how learners frame their understandings. Assessment practices rely on observable behavior and infer specific mental operations based on the design of the test.

**Learning as knowledge construction.** Since the 1980s, learning has been depicted as knowledge construction (Mayer, 1992). Here, construction replaces reproduction as the dominant metaphor (Wildman, 1996). Most frequently termed a constructivist framework, learning is understood as interpretative and emergent, and under the control of the learner. Consequently, unique understandings (i.e., constructions) are assumed to be natural and inevitable, and responsibility for learning resides heavily with the learner. Of particular importance is the assumption that all **cognition** is situated, and therefore must be understood in terms of the settings, purposes, tools and tasks in which the knowledge was or is to be learned.

There are many different kinds of **constructivism** in the current literature (Phillips, 1995). The various perspectives range from **radical constructivism** in which reality and understanding are totally individual (e.g., von Glaserfeld, 1984) to **social constructivism** (e.g., Vygotsky, 1978), which emphasizes the critical role of the social milieu to define reality and knowledge. While each of these perspectives offers us a different look at a learner and his/her needs, some very clear design considerations have been identified (Wildman, 1996). Of primary import is that the goal structures need to be negotiated within the teacher-learner interaction. Learners are at the center of the design activity, and their points of view are given primacy in dialogue. The curriculum centers around problems that are relevant to the learner and emerge

**Key Words**
- Cognition
- Constructivism
- Organizers
- Radical constructivism
- Social constructivism

during the course of inquiry. It is here that the notion of **communities of learners** emerge (Brown, 1994), in that teachers as well as the students are all learners in the instructional process. Teachers assume the role of facilitator, and the predominant pedagogy sees teaching as assisted performance (Tharp & Gallimore, 1988). The focus is on helping learners engage in **authentic activities** that are situated in real practice. These activity settings involve **reciprocal teaching** and **cooperative learning**, and rely on the more capable other to lead. Assessment practices are also designed to solve real-life problems and promote self-reflection to maximize the emphasis on learner responsibility.

**Theories to beliefs to action.** A challenge to novice designers is trying to process the above ideas in some meaningful, coherent, and cohesive way. You may begin to see that aspects of each of these perspectives contribute important directions for your designing efforts. A common view from those new to the field is that they think that they need to choose one or the other, or they struggle to choose one that "feels" or "fits" their beliefs most closely. A deeper understanding of these approaches and their implications for learning provides a firmer basis from which to design. We encourage you to explore these ideas in more depth (see *For Further Reading*).

> **Food for Thought**
>
> **Throwing out the babies with the bathwater.** It is a human trait that when faced with a set of items, we tend to select one over the other. This is sometimes the case when faced with learning theories. Novices to educational psychology feel an urgency to adopt only one. Although cognitive approaches are currently on center stage, there is much that all three theoretical approaches discussed in this section have to offer. Brown (1994) cautions against throwing out the babies with the bathwater when considering what many years of research have produced.

> With the above overview, you can build on the thinking and writing you did in the previous chapter when you answered the question, *"What is learning?* in **Design Activity 2**.

↓

> **Key Words**
> - Authentic activities
> - Communities of learners
> - Cooperative learning
> - Reciprocal teaching

# DESIGN ACTIVITY 4

### "Your Learning Principles"

✍ **Task Description**

This **Design Activity** will help you to see what theoretical approaches match your beliefs and how these beliefs might impact your design decisions.

Learning principles are statements which are based on learning theories.

It might be helpful to consult sources in **References** and **For Further Reading** to help identify learning principles identified in your Mission Statement (**Design Activity 3**).

1. List 10 learning principles that you value. See the examples we listed in Chapter 1 (p. 10).
2. Identify appropriate learning theories for each of your principles.
3. Make a brief statement as explaining why each principle is important to you.

# Design Models

**Uses of Models.** Another set of important design tools are models, which help us to understand the whole range of human existence, to clarify ways of *representing, communicating,* and *revealing* (Montuori & Conti, 1993).

**Representing reality.** Models help us to better understand our world by *representing* reality. This is the traditional conception of a model, a representation of something. Models can be used to analyze the features of something, explain how it works, or predict its performance. A model of an airplane design in a wind tunnel is an example. This is a very useful model, as long as it simulates reality adequately to provide designers with useful information. If such a model can be proven as reliable, designers can use it to predict performance. Reliable models give the green light to those who make and use the objects that the model is simulating.

Models can be used to explain complex systems of reality. Humans have a tough time actively storing the details of such complexity in our brain, so models help us retain and make sense of important features by providing representations of the complexity. Norman (1993) says that "We value what we can represent" (p. 53). We can extend this idea and say that *we better understand what we can represent.* Models that explain the weather and the economy, for example, have been proposed. Imagine the power of such models that could successfully and thoroughly explain the behavior of either of these. People probably represent the most complex systems of all. For the instructional designer, models can be used to represent one's understanding of the complex undertaking of designing instruction for humans.

**mod·el** (mòd'-l) *n., adj., v.*
1. A standard or example for imitation.
2. A representation, generally in miniature, to show the construction or appearance of something.
3. Serving as an example.
4. To give shape or form to.
5. To simulate a process, concept, or the operation of a system.

*The Random House Dictionary of the English Language.* (1987). p. 1235-1236.

**Communicating understandings.** Models also help us to make sense about the world and to share our understanding of it. If we did not need to *communicate* we would not need models. Models communicate our understandings of how we perceive the world. These representations can be physical, such as a mockup of a new product; visual, such as concept map; or mathematical in form.

Teachers and learners, trainers and trainees, parents and children can use models to communicate their understandings to each other. Parents have their own models of child rearing which are constantly changing to fit different needs, although some could say that models of child rearing break down during adolescence! Thus, one measure of modeling success is the degree to which the model provides a basis for *shared understanding*.

Instructional design models can be used to communicate to members of the design team or to clients the overall view of a particular design process, so that these individuals can understand how the design issues will be addressed.

**Revealing what is hidden.** Models also have the ability to bring out into the open what was once hidden, invisible, or unacknowledged. Thus, models help us *reveal* what we believe about ourselves as humans, and more specifically, what our views are about learning, teaching, or designing.

Marvin Minsky (1986) says that the **mental models** of our friends are clearer to us than the mental models we have of ourselves. We tend to assign a particular mental model of some quality to an individual and that quality seems to define them in our mind. For example, you might unconsciously view a person you know as being organized or creative, although your understanding of their other features is vague. Models of ourselves, on the other hand, are fuzzy and slippery and frequently contain erroneous representations; but these imprecise, sometimes faulty

**Key Words**
• Mental models

mental models, have the power to tell us something about the world and about ourselves.

**Misuses of models.** Models can take a long time to develop, longer to become accepted, and even longer to be modified. Initially, we are skeptical about a model, but after a model is adopted, we tend to place a lot of confidence in it.

A model needs to be re-examined if it fails to remain useful. All models benefit from a periodic evaluation of their ability to *represent*, *communicate*, and *reveal*. The models used in teaching and learning also change over time, and unless they are examined periodically, models in use may no longer be accurate or appropriate.

> Models have been developed to depict the scope of the ID process. Here are examples of some instructional design models.

**Profiles of ID models.** The ID models briefly profiled in this chapter include the following:

## Examples of ID Models

- Dick and Carey's model.
- Gagné and Briggs model.
- United States Air Force model.
- Kemp's model.
- Gerlach & Ely model.
- Layers of Necessity model.
- Rapid Prototyping model.
- The ASSURE model.

**Dick & Carey model.** This model is a procedural, step-by-step ID model that depicts a learning environment through "instructional goals," which act as the starting point (Dick & Carey, 1996). Analysis of needs, skills, and learners refines these goals. The model consists of one component's output as the input to the next. Although revision is noted in the model, this strict closure to each phase may be difficult to achieve in practice. In addition, resource limitations and other realities of the **instructional problem** have no way of figuring into this model.

## Dick & Carey Model (1996)

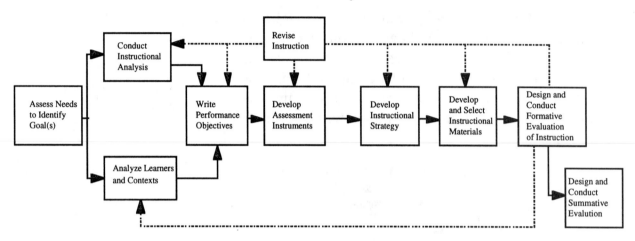

From THE SYSTEMATIC DESIGN OF INSTRUCTION, 4th ed., by Walter Dick and Lou Carey. Copyright © 1996 by Walter Dick and Lou Carey. Reprinted by permission of Addison Wesley Longman.

**The Gagné & Briggs systems model.** This model addresses more factors and stages than the previous model. Such a large systems approach is necessary for the planning of large scale curriculum efforts, which can involve the analysis of resources, constraints, alternate delivery methods, teacher preparation, and the implementation of new instructional methods and materials (Gagné, Briggs, & Wager, 1992). The model uses analysis to determine what the goals should be and designs prescriptive features to accomplish these goals. Despite its linear look this model is **iterative**—design phases must be revisited once new features are designed or new information is uncovered. This model classifies lesson objectives by learning type, allowing the designer to address a wide range of knowledge. At the lesson level, the model addresses the interactions and tasks involving teacher and student in each activity.

**Key Words**
- Instructional problem
- Iterative

**Gagné & Briggs Systems Model**

| System Level | 1. Analysis of needs, goals, and priorities |
| | 2. Analysis of resources, constraints, and alternate delivery systems |
| | 3. Scope and sequence of curriculum and courses; delivery system design |

| Course Level | 4. Course structure and sequence |
| | 5. Analysis of course objectives |

| Lesson Level | 6. Performance objectives |
| | 7. Lesson plans or modules |
| | 8. Selecting materials and media |
| | 9. Assessment |

| System Level | 10. Teacher preparation |
| | 11. Formative evaluation |
| | 12. Field testing and revision |
| | 13. Summative evaluation |
| | 14. Installation and diffusion |

Tables adapted from PRINCIPLES OF INSTRUCTIONAL DESIGN, Fourth Edition by Robert M. Gagné, Leslie J. Briggs, and Walter W. Wager, copyright © 1992 by Holt, Rinehart and Winston, Inc., reproduced by permission of the publisher.

**Air Force model.** The United States military has been very successful at implementing systematic design models for training. Such models have been rigorously applied across all training needs, which are clearly identified with standardized outcomes. Up-front analysis of learner needs and environmental requirements are conducted, so that goals are clearly known before any designing begins. Relationships between the steps of the model are more clearly specified than other design models; thus, changes in one phase signal possible revisions in other aspects of the model. The five-step process of this model includes the following:

**Steps in the USAF Model (1975)**

1. Determine job performance requirements.
2. Determine training requirements.
3. Write behavioral objectives and test items.
4. Design instructional procedures and materials.
5. Conduct and evaluate the instruction.

From U. S. Air Force. (July 31, 1975). *Instructional system development.* Washington, DC: UF Manual 50-2.

One strength of this model is the significant up-front analysis of learning needs and resources and the degree to which revisions are specified. Feedback and interaction are central elements of the model (USAF, 1975).

### USAF Model (1975)

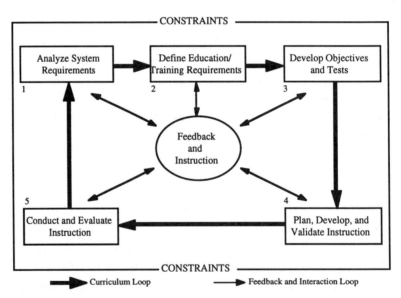

U. S. Air Force. (July 31, 1975). *Instructional system development.* Washington, DC: UF Manual 50-2.

**Kemp model.** This model is visually much different than previous models. It features learner needs and goals at the center, while describing instructional resources and support services on the outside (Kemp, Morrison & Ross, 1994).

## Kemp Model (1994)

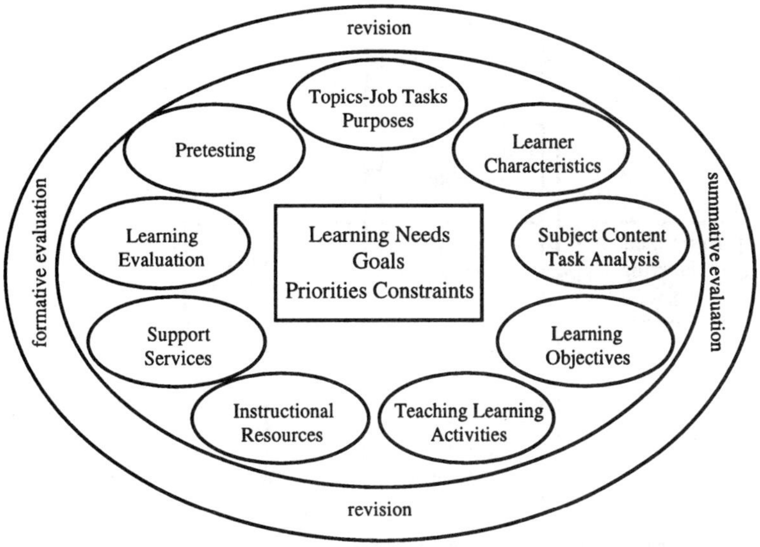

Diagram showing concentric ovals. Outer labels: revision (top and bottom), formative evaluation (left), summative evaluation (right). Inner ovals: Topics-Job Tasks Purposes, Pretesting, Learner Characteristics, Learning Evaluation, Subject Content Task Analysis, Support Services, Learning Objectives, Instructional Resources, Teaching Learning Activities. Center box: Learning Needs Goals Priorities Constraints.

DESIGNING EFFECTIVE INSTRUCTION by Kemp, © 1994. Adapted by permission of Prentice-Hall, Inc., Upper Saddle River, NJ.

This flexible model addresses any of the component concerns as long as they relate to learning needs and goals. There is also interdependence among the elements, although the exact nature of these relationships are not addressed visually by the model. The model is appropriate for the teacher or designer who is comfortable with the responsibility of judging exactly how to use the model or to adapt it. Edmonds, Branch, and Mukherjee (1994) also cite business as benefiting from this model.

**Gerlach and Ely model.** This model was written for the teacher who is a novice designer, but who possesses content expertise and can specify objectives, or specific outcomes of instruction (Gerlach & Ely, 1980). This systematic model prompts teachers to specify entering behaviors or to what extent students achieve these objectives.

**Gerlach & Ely Model (1980)**

From Gerlach, V. S., & Ely, D. P. *Teaching and Media: A Systematic Approach,* 2nd Edition © 1980 by Allyn and Bacon. Reprinted by permission.

Designing with this model includes determining an instructional strategy, accomplishing the objectives, organizing students into groups, determining how much time and space to allocate to activities, and selecting instructional materials. The model further specifies design tasks to evaluate performance, both teacher and student, as well as an analysis of feedback on whether or not the objectives were met. This model, suitable for teachers in both K-12 and in higher education, also integrates instructional media into the design process.

**Layers of Necessity model.** This model represents a "practitioner's model of instructional design," which taps a *layer* of design and development activities that is appropriate to the time and resources available to the designer (Wedman & Tessmer, 1990). This model is suitable for experts who can pull from their experiences and use whatever approaches are appropriate, depending on the *necessities* of the design challenge. Each layer is a self-contained ID model, which accommodates additional layers of design features to enhance (rather than just revise) previous work. Each layer uses two sets of guidelines: the first governs the selection of appropriate activities; the second determines their implementation. Consistency within each layer is an important evaluation feature.

**Layers of Necessity Model (1990)**

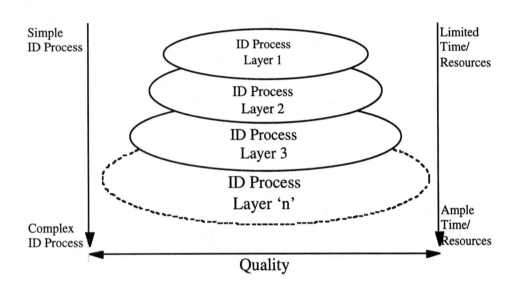

Wedman, J., & Tessmer, M. (1990). A layers-of-necessity instructional development model. *Educational Technology Research & Development, 38*(2), 77-85. Reprinted with permission from the Association for Educational Communications and Technology, Washington, D. C.

This model is described by the authors as "what can be done in the situation, not what ought to be done" (Wedman & Tessmer, 1990, p. 81). Thus, this model requires the expertise to know what questions to ask in order to target for development a particular layer of designing and how to make informed decisions about design efforts that are still appropriate for the situation. This model can be personalized to the user, as well as to the situation.

**Rapid Prototyping model.** Instructional design is frequently presented through idealized ID process models; however, Broadbent (1973) regards these as decision models rather than design models. Rapid prototyping is based on studies of designers in action (Carroll & Rosson, 1985) and the notion that the design process is complex and unpredictable. Rapid prototyping was first used in software development, in which the feasibility and current situation is studied, followed by a continual design and testing of a **prototype**, so that construction and testing are parallel processes.

Tripp and Bichelmeyer (1990) have examined the uses of this approach in instructional design. An assumption of the model is that the designer must address learner needs, content, and context throughout the designing, while other models view these issues as inputs to the system. The involvement of intended users in the prototyping is one of the strengths of this model.

### Rapid Prototyping Model

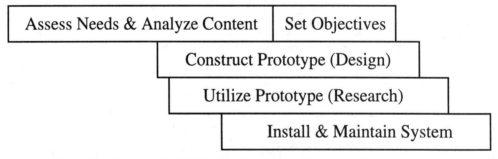

Tripp, S. T., & Bichelmeyer, B. (1990). Rapid prototyping: An alternative instructional design. *Educational Technology Research & Development, 38*(1), 31-44. Reprinted with permission from the Association for Educational Communications and Technology, Washington, D. C.

Tripp and Bichelmeyer (1990) state that "alternate, even contradictory designs" may result from the use of this model. It is intended for (1) complex instructional situations where no one right way exists to design a response to an instructional problem, and where flexibility is necessary to respond to unique situations;

**Key Words**
- Prototype

(2) situations where the designer may have some experience but is unsatisfied with a linear feel that does not approximate the actual design process; and (3) new situations with limited experience to guide the design (Tripp & Bichelmeyer, 1990). Designs that require the ongoing analysis of the effects of new instructional media frequently use this model.

Here is a model that addresses the development of instructional media.

# Talking about Media

**The ASSURE model.** This model selects and implements media within learning activities (Heinich, Molenda, Russell & Smaldino, 1996). The authors stress that this model assumes that instructional issues inherent to the use of the media materials, such as needs assessment, task analysis, and assessment of learning have been addressed.

The six stages of the ASSURE media development model denote a linear, input-output nature, with decisions made in the first stage contributing to decisions for succeeding stages.

## 1. Analyze learner characteristics.

The analysis is conducted in terms of general characteristics of the learners and the specific competencies needed by these individuals, such as knowledge, skills, and attitudes.

## 2. State objectives.

The second step is to state the learning objectives in terms of what the learner will know or be able to do as a result of the instruction.

## 3. Select, modify, or design materials.

Three options exist to bridge learners and objectives: select materials that currently exist, modify materials in some way, or design new materials.

## 4. Use materials.

It is now necessary to plan how the materials will be used, gathering the necessary materials together, and using them in instruction.

**5. Require learner response.**

This stage requires activities and time for adequate practice and reinforcement of performance.

**6. Evaluate.**

The model specifies evaluation in terms of learner achievement, evaluation of media materials and methods, and evaluation of the entire instructional process before, during, and after instruction.

From INSTRUCTIONAL MEDIA AND TECHNOLOGIES FOR LEARNING, 5/E by Heinich, Molenda, Russell & Smaldino, © 1996. Adapted by permission of Prentice-Hall, Inc., Upper Saddle River, NJ.

How would you model the ID process?

# DESIGN ACTIVITY 5

## "Your Preliminary ID Model"

### ✍ Task Description

As we mentioned earlier in our discussion of models, by constructing a model you begin to understand what you represent, as well as value and take ownership of what you can represent in a personalized way.

We will be asking you to review the features of your model throughout this text and **Design Activity 28** in Chapter 10 will ask you to review and revise it.

**1.** Describe what you know about instructional design by representing it with your own instructional design model. Draw a picture if this helps to explain your model.

**2.** As you represent your model of instructional design think about how you will address the following issues:

- learner needs
- realities
- teaching and learning goals
- assessment
- instructional strategy
- instructional media
- program evaluation

### Food for Thought

*We value what we can represent.*
(Norman , 1993, p. 53)

*Metaphor is horizontal, reminding us that it is one's vision that is limited, and not what one is viewing.*
(Carse, 1986, pp. 130-131)

# Conceptual & Procedural Tools

In addition to the representational, communicative, and revealing power of models, the instructional design field can draw on numerous conceptual and procedural tools to help construct appropriate design features.

**Conceptual design tools.** Conceptual tools are means to help you to construct meanings to ideas. Conceptual tools are necessary because, although concepts can be shared, each of us has a unique understanding of what something means. Taxonomies, discussed in Chapter 3, are conceptual tools that help designers understand the learning task. Other examples of conceptual design tools include many of the Design Activities in this book. The Mission Statement task in **Design Activity 3** is a conceptual tool to help you integrate your learning beliefs into an operational statement that will serve as a point to design from.

**Procedural design tools.** Procedural tools are procedures, techniques, or methods to complete a particular designing task, such as task analysis or media selection. The self assessment at the end of each chapter is a procedural tool. Another example is the Formative Program Evaluation Plan, which we introduce here because it will be useful to you in designing during the formative, or growth stages of your instructional design. A chart provides a procedural tool to summarize its essential features.

**Formative evaluation.** Chapter 9 addresses Program Evaluation, which is a phase of designing that determines if your design is heading in the right direction *during* designing (**formative evaluation**), and if your design produced the changes you had intended *after* its implementation (**summative evaluation**).

**Key Words**
- Conceptual design tool
- Formative evaluation
- Procedural design tool
- Summative evaluation

Who, When, What, and How? The Formative Evaluation Strategy Grid on this page summarizes information about *who* evaluates, *when* to evaluate, *what* gets evaluated, and *how* the evaluation might be done. This chart is a procedural design tool to collect formative evaluation data.

**Formative Evaluation Strategy Grid**

| Who? | When? | What? | How? |
|---|---|---|---|
| **Designer** | End of each stage of design | Content Technical quality Learnability | Checklists Design teams |
| **Experts** | During needs assessment Consult suitable expert after phase is designed | Subject matter | Checklists Panel Interviews Think aloud |
| **Learners** | Early in design End of design Finished design | Content Technical quality Learnability | 1-to-1 Groups Field testing |
| **Generalists** | After goals have been determined (End of Needs Assessment) Sample lesson | Overall design elements | Panel Interviews |

The first formative evaluator is *you*, the designer. Can you stand back and be self-critical? Sometimes you are so close to the details that this is difficult. Although formative evaluation may tap others to do the evaluating, it's the designer or design team who still makes many of the ongoing revisions.

A second candidate for your formative evaluation team are *experts*. Call in experts to give your design details a review of content, language, media, pedagogy, and instructional design.

The *target audience* is the most frequently forgotten formative evaluation group. Here you can involve the actual people who will benefit from the design. End users are frequently cited in media projects where typical users try out prototype versions of the media materials. Why not in other design projects?

The *generalist* is someone who may not be an expert or a member of the target learning audience, but one that has experience in other areas and might see something that others miss. Their insights could be quite useful and can be another source of valuable feedback.

Under the "What" section of the chart, criteria need to be specified that accurately address how content, technical quality, and learnability is evaluated. Each of the formative evaluators may have a basis for evaluating a design. You should know what these criteria are.

Finally, here is Design Tool #6.

# Designer Expertise

Yet another design tool is the designing skills and abilities of yourself and the collaborative expertise of others.

**Competencies.** In recent years the design field has been considering competencies for instructional designers. The National Society for Performance and Instruction (NSPI, now the International Society for Performance and Instruction or ISPI) and the Division of Instructional Development of the Association for Educational Communications and Technology (AECT) appointed a task force, which proposed a list of 16

1. Definitions
2. Learning theories
3. Design models
4. Conceptual tools
5. Procedural tools
**6. Designer expertise**

competencies for possible certification of instructional designers (Bratton, 1984).

*Experience, it is said, is the best teacher—providing, of course, we become the best students. But who, really, is the teacher?*

*The real teacher is you.*

(Roger & McWilliams, 1991, p. 23)

---

## Competencies for Instructional Designers

1. Determine appropriate projects.
2. Conduct needs assessment.
3. Assess learner characteristics.
4. Analyze jobs, tasks, and content.
5. Determine learner outcomes.
6. Analyze setting.
7. Sequence outcomes.
8. Specify instructional strategies.
9. Sequence learner activities.
10. Determine instructional resources.
11. Evaluate instruction/training.
12. Produce materials.
13. Monitor projects implementation.
14. Communicate.
15. Demonstrate interpersonal, group process, and consulting behaviors.
16. Promote diffusion and adoption.
17. Exhibit design thinking.
18. Scrutinize learning beliefs.

#1-16 Copyright © 1984. International Society for Performance Improvement. Reprinted with permission from *Performance Improvement* (formerly *Performance & Instruction*). The International Society for Performance Improvement (ISPI) is a 6,000 member professional association dedicated to improving human performance for more than 30 years. For more information, contact ISPI at (202) 408-7969.

#17-18 From Shambaugh, R. N., & Magliaro, S. G. (1996).

---

*Every cell of the human body carries a blueprint of the way all the other cells are constructed. So there is 'something of everything' in every single cell. The whole exists in each tiny part.*

(Gaarder, 1986, p. 38)

**Key Words**
• Design thinking

**Design thinking.** Competency #17 includes higher level thinking skills, such as solving messy, real world problems (Nelson, Magliaro & Sherman, 1988; Wallington, 1981); the ability to use design tools (e.g., interviewing, task analysis, and learning taxonomies) to facilitate data gathering and decision-making; an ability to break a project into smaller pieces yet retain the overall picture; iteration of changes made in one design phase that influences others; consideration of contextual factors; and drawing upon one's knowledge base, personal heuristics, and prior experiences. Design thinking also includes an ability to be creative and flexible in order to address the inherent complexity and conundrums characteristic of instructional problems (e.g., Nelson et al., 1988; Sachs, 1981).

**Learning beliefs**. Competency #18 inevitably influences how one designs. Tapping learning beliefs requires that one acknowledge their existence and examine their implications in terms of the **learning principles** that apply to them, and to what extent, if any, these beliefs are appropriate influences in a design project.

Below is a scenario of another learning setting.

## ☆ SCENARIO

### Consulting Firm: Developing and Sharing Expertise

The purpose of these scenarios is to identify instructional issues that are similar across instructional settings.

In this chapter we consider your expertise, the range of competencies listed above, as a design tool. Consider in this scenario a second learning setting: a consulting firm, Rockford & Associates, which specializes in customized training packages. Like many other firms, Rockford has found itself in the position of growth, and the consulting partners in the firm want to be able to attract new talent and provide a good place to work.

An acquaintance of one of the partners has been brought in to provide some outside consultation to help manage the firm's rapid growth and providing a good place to work. The first recommendation was to identify what the business is and identify the firm's key principles supporting this mission. The second was to involve people at all levels in this effort. This required making changes in the mission statement and supporting principles that address the needs of these people resources. The following was proposed:

**Key Words**
- Learning principles

### The Business of Rockford & Associates

Our mission is to provide our clients with products that meet their needs in a responsive manner.

### Supporting Principles: Staff

1. As a consulting firm we believe that our major strength is tapping the core capabilities of our staff.

2. We will emphasize in hiring, evaluations, and daily interactions respect for the individual and different styles of work and acknowledge the competencies that each bring to the firm.

3. We will stress open communications among staff to keep everyone briefed on progress and their support needs.

Many firms are realizing that their human capital requires investment and a different stance than before. In this regard, firms are adopting a worker-centered approach, rather than a hierarchical top-down approach. This is analogous in many ways with learner-centered approaches in instruction, where the role of the teacher is a facilitator for the learner.

By involving everyone in these discussions, the following suggestions resulted:

- Develop networking technology so that everyone can have access to needed information on clients and the firm's databases. This will increase the efficiency of the consultant work teams who are responsible for each client.

- Pair up of new hires with existing staff so the new hires can quickly learn the culture of the firm and client companies.

The consultant suggested to everyone the reality of self-mentoring; each person needs to make autonomous decisions about self improvement in addition to the efforts made by the firm.

The next Design Activity gives you an opportunity to assess your design abilities.

# DESIGN ACTIVITY 6

## "Your Designer Competencies"

How would you rate your abilities in the following list of designer competencies?

✍ **Task Description**

The purpose of examining your design competencies is to impress upon you the skills that an instructional designer needs to have. These are developed over time, particularly through actual designing over a wide range of instructional problems.

## Quick Self-Assessment of Competencies

### 1. Determine appropriate projects.

Determine if project is an instructional problem.
Determine if project is appropriate for instructional design.

1. Weak  1  2  3  4  5  Strong

### 2. Conduct needs assessment.

Develop a needs assessment plan that increases one's understanding of the instructional problem.
Conduct needs assessment and use information to suggest courses of action.

2. Weak  1  2  3  4  5  Strong

### 3. Assess learner characteristics.

Identify the range of learning characteristics within intended participants.

3. Weak  1  2  3  4  5  Strong

### 4. Analyze jobs, tasks, and content.

Use design tools to analyze the characteristics of a job, task, or content.

4. Weak  1  2  3  4  5  Strong

### 5. Determine learner outcomes.

Specify learning goals and supporting objectives.

5. Weak  1  2  3  4  5  Strong

### 6. Analyze setting.

Analyze setting characteristics of the learning environment, including a determination of resources and constraints.

6. Weak  1  2  3  4  5  Strong

### 7. Sequence outcomes.

Determine a method of sequencing learning outcomes appropriate to the instructional problem.

7. Weak  1  2  3  4  5  Strong

### 8. Specify instructional strategies.

Select strategies appropriate to the learner, content, and context of the instructional problem and provide a rationale for their selection.
Determine purposes of learning assessment and select appropriate assessment methods.

8. Weak  1  2  3  4  5  Strong

9. Weak 1 2 3 4 5 Strong

10. Weak 1 2 3 4 5 Strong

11. Weak 1 2 3 4 5 Strong

12. Weak 1 2 3 4 5 Strong

13. Weak 1 2 3 4 5 Strong

14. Weak 1 2 3 4 5 Strong

15. Weak 1 2 3 4 5 Strong

16. Weak 1 2 3 4 5 Strong

17. Weak 1 2 3 4 5 Strong

18. Weak 1 2 3 4 5 Strong

### 9. Sequence learner activities.

Specify a sequence of learner activities appropriate to the intended learner outcomes.

### 10. Determine instructional resources.

Determine media and instructional materials needed for instructional strategies.

Evaluate resources, provide rationale for their use, and determine issues in their development and use.

### 11. Evaluate instruction/training.

Construct a formative and summative plan of program evaluation.

### 12. Produce materials.

Determine components of course, training, workshop packages.

Determine production and management system for material production.

### 13. Monitor projects implementation.

Construct a plan to monitor the development of the instructional design plan appropriate to the instructional problem and realities of the setting.

### 14. Communicate.

Communicate effectively using visual, listening, oral, and written skills.

### 15. Demonstrate interpersonal, group process, and consulting behaviors.

Be able to work with key participants and groups and adopt professional consulting behaviors, including responsiveness, efficiency, resourcefulness, timeliness, attention to budgets, time, and details.

### 16. Promote diffusion and adoption.

Select strategies to promote the adoption and use of the proposed instructional design.

### 17. Design thinking.

Use the systematic features of the design process (structure and interrelationships of phases), design tools, and iteration of design features. Think in terms of the big picture while maintaining awareness of the details of the design project.

### 18. Learning beliefs.

Select and scrutinize one's learning beliefs and the appropriateness for instructional problem.

Which competencies are your major strengths? Which ones need improvement?

# Reviewing Design Activities

### Design Activity 4: Your Learning Principles

☐ Made a list of 10 learning principles.
☐ Identified learning theories for each principle.
☐ Identified reasons for choosing each principle.

### Design Activity 5: Your Preliminary ID Model

☐ Constructed an ID model that depicted and described how you design instruction based on what you now know.
☐ Explained relationships between major components.

### Design Activity 6: Your Designer Competencies

☐ Rated yourself on the 18 competencies.
☐ Identified your strengths and areas to address.

**Food for Thought**

**Certification for Instructional Designers.** Despite efforts at drawing up a possible set of competencies for instructional designers, no progress has been made at establishing these in some form of certification program.

- How do you feel about this issue? Should the field have a certification program?

- Should competencies be specified?

- How would these competencies be determined?

# 🏳 Summary of Important Ideas

1. The differences that exist in how people define instructional design reveal their design orientation.

2. Learning theories form the basis for ID models.

3. Instructional design models can be compared along several characteristics, the purpose of which is to assist you in selecting models appropriate to your designing needs.

4. Conceptual and procedural tools can be used to help you in an instructional design.

5. Your designing expertise includes a wide range of competencies that require time and designing experiences to develop.

*We humans spend our lives in systems: in the family, the classroom, the friendship group, the team, the organization, the task force, the church, the community, the bowling league, the nation, the ethnic group. We find joy and sadness, exhilaration and despair, good relationships and bad ones, opportunities and frustrations. So much happens to us in system life, yet system life remains a mystery. There is so much we don't see.*

(Oshry, 1995, p. xi)

## ✓ Your Personal Learning

---

### *Relating Your Beliefs to This Chapter:*

This is a key phase of the design process in which learning beliefs can play a major role in your instructional design. Understanding how your beliefs relate to learning theories and models helps you to take advantage of what research has found out about learning and how we can use models and design tools to systematically address learning needs.

At this point in the text can you describe the "feel" of your emerging stance towards learning and designing? Do this task for *you*. Try to capture your own stance at this time.

See **Tour 2: The Learning Cafe** in "Touring Instructional Design" at the back of the book.

---

## References

Bratton, B. (1984). Professional certification: Will it become a reality? *National Society for Performance & Instruction Journal, 23,* 4-7.

Broadbent, G. (1973). *Design in architecture.* London: Wiley.

Brown, A. L. (1994). The advancement of learning. *Educational Researcher, 23*(8), 4-12.

Carroll, J. M., & Rosson, M. B. (1985). Usability specifications as a tool in iterative development. In H. R. Hartson (Ed.), *Advances in human-computer interaction* (1-28). Norwood, NJ: Ablex.

Carse, J. (1986). *Finite and infinite games.* NY: Ballantine.

Cross, N. (1982). Designing ways of knowing. *Design Studies, 3*(4), 221-227.

Dick, W. (1993). Enhanced ISD: A response to changing environments for learning and performance. *Educational Technology, 33*(2), 12-16.

Dick, W., & Carey, L. (1996). *The systematic design of instruction* (4th ed.). NY: HarperCollins.

Edmonds, G. S., Branch, R. C., & Mukherjee, P. (1994). A conceptual framework for comparing instructional design models. *Educational Technology Research & Development, 42*(4), 55-72.

Flexner, S. B. (Ed.). (1987). *The Random House dictionary of the English language* (2nd ed.). NY: Random House.

Gagné, R. M., Briggs, L. J., & Wager, W. W. (1992). *Principles of instructional design* (4th ed.). Fort Worth, TX: Harcourt Brace Jovanovich.

Gaarder, J. (1996). *Sophie's world: A novel about the history of philosophy.* NY: Berkley Books.

Gerlach, V. S., & Ely, D. P. (1980). *Teaching and media: A systematic approach* (2nd ed.). Englewood Cliffs, NJ: Prentice-Hall.

Heinich, R., Molenda, M., Russell, J. D., & Smaldino, S. E. (1996). *Instructional media and the new technologies of instruction* (5th ed.). Englewood-Cliffs, NJ: Prentice-Hall.

Kemp, J. E., Morrison, G. R., & Ross, S. M. (1994). *Designing effective instruction*. Columbus, OH: Merrill.

Mayer, R. E. (1992). *Cognition and instruction: Their historic meeting within educational psychology*. Journal of Educational Psychology, 84(4), 405-412.

Minsky, M. (1986). *The society of mind*. New York: Simon & Schuster.

Montuori, A. & Conti, I. (1993). *From power to partnership: Creating the future of love, work, and community*. San Francisco: HarperCollins.

Nelson, W. A., Magliaro, S. G., & Sherman, T. M. (1988). The intellectual content of instructional design. *Journal of Instructional Development*, 37(3), 81-94.

Norman, D. A. (1993).*Things that make us smart: Defending human attributes in the age of the machine*. Reading, MA: Addison-Wesley.

Oshry, B. (1995*). Seeing systems: Unlocking the mysteries of organizational life*. San Francisco: Berrett-Koehler.

Phillips, D. C. (1995). The good, the bad, and the ugly: The many faces of constructivism. *Educational Researcher, 24*(7), 5-12.

Richey, R. (1986). *The theoretical and conceptual bases of instructional design*. London: Kogan Page.

Roger, J., & McWilliams, P. (1991). *LIFE 101: Everything we wish we had learned about life in school, but didn't*. Los Angeles: Prelude.

Rowland, G. (1993). Design and instructional design. *Educational Technology Research & Development, 41*(1), 79-91.

Sachs, S. G. (1981). Practicing the art of instructional development. *NSPI Journal 20*(7), 8-10.

Schön, D. A. (1983). *The reflective practitioner: How professionals think and act*. New York: Basic Books.

Seels, B., & Glasgow, Z. (1990). *Exercises in instructional design*. Columbus, OH: Merrill.

Shambaugh, R. N., & Magliaro, S. G. (1996*). Teaching instructional design in a constructivist learning environment: Lessons learned*. Paper presented at the Annual Meeting of The American Educational Research Association, New York.

Simon, H. A. (1981). *The sciences of the artificial* (2nd ed.). Cambridge, MA: MIT Press.

Smith, P. L., & Ragan, T. J. (1993). *Instructional design*. New York: Merrill.

Tharp, R. G., & Gallimore, R. (1988). *Rousing minds to life: Teaching, learning, and schooling in social context*. Cambridge: Cambridge University Press.

Tripp, S. T., & Bichelmeyer, B. (1990). Rapid prototyping: An alternative instructional design strategy. *Educational Technology Research & Development, 38*(1), 31-44.

U. S. Air Force. (July 31, 1975*). Instructional system development*. Washington, DC: UF Manual 50-2.

von Glaserfeld, E. (1984). An introduction to radical constructivism. In P. Watzlawick (Ed.), *The invented reality* (pp. 17-40), NY: Norton.

Vygotsky, L. S. (1978). *Mind in society: The development of higher psychological processes*. Cambridge, MA: Harvard University Press.

Wallington, C. J. (1981). Generic skills of an instructional developer. *Journal of Instructional Development, 4*(3), 28-33.

Wedman, J., & Tessmer, M. (1990). A layers-of-necessity instructional development model. *Educational Technology Research & Development, 38*(2), 77-85.

Wildman, T. M. (1996). *Learning: New understandings and imperatives* (White paper). Blacksburg, VA: VPI&SU, Center for Excellence in Undergraduate Teaching.

# For Further Reading ...

## Behaviorism

Skinner, B. F. (1968). *Technology of teaching*. Englewood Cliffs, NJ: Prentice-Hall.

Translating behaviorist principles for instructional settings.

Watson, J. B. (1930). *Behaviorism* (2nd ed.). Chicago: University of Chicago Press.

The initial American treatise on behavioral psychology.

## Cognitive psychology

Anderson, J. R. (1990). *Cognitive psychology and its implications*. NY: W. H. Freeman.

An information-processing orientation.

Ausubel, D. P. (1968). *Educational psychology: A cognitive view*. NY: Holt, Rinehart and Winston.

The seminal text which first articulated a new perspective on learners and learning cognitive psychology.

Bransford, J. (1979). *Human psychology: Learning, understanding, and remembering*. Belmont, CA: Wadsworth.

A classic and readable treatment of cognitive psychology different from the information processing viewpoint.

Bruer, J. T. (1993). *Schools for thought: A science of learning in the classroom*. Cambridge: MIT Press.

A current treatment of cognition embracing the information processing perspective (e. g., memory via computer metaphor, expert-novice characteristics, task analysis, and how cognitive research provides a basis for instruction in mathematics, science, reading, and writing.

Bruner, J. S. (1966). *Toward a theory of instruction*. NY: Norton.

Learning as reorganizing what one knows.

Bruner, J. (1983). *In search of mind: Essays in autobiography*. New York: Harper & Row.

A look at cognitive psychology through autobiography by one of the principal minds behind the "cognitive revolution."

Newell, A., & Simon, H. A. (1972). *Human problem solving*. Englewood Cliffs, NJ: Prentice-Hall.

A classic writing on the information processing, problem-solving approach to cognition.

Piaget, J. (1972). Intellectual evolution from adolescence to adulthood. *Human Development, (15)*1-12.

An example of a schema-based theory of cognitive research in which knowledge is represented in mental structures called schemata.

Rumelhart, D. E., & Norman, D. A. (1978). Accretion, tuning, and restructuring: Three modes of learning. In J. W. Cotton & R. L. Klatzky (Eds.). *Semantic factors in cognition*. Hillsdale, NJ: Erlbaum.

A schema (long-term memory) and information processing view of learning describing the structures and mechanisms used to process information.

Wittrock, M. C. (1979). The cognitive movement in instruction. *Educational Researcher, (8)*5-11.

A generative learning model based on constructing connections between old and new knowledge.

## Social constructivism

Fosnot, C. T. (1996) *Constructivism: Theory, perspectives, and practice* (Ed.). NY: Teachers College Press.

> A recent set of articles on implementing constructivist principles in learning settings.

Moll, L. C. (1990). *Vygotsky and education.* New York: Cambridge University Press.

> A collection of articles on neo-Vygotskian thought.

Newman, D., Griffin, P., & Cole, M. (1989). *The construction zone: Working for cognitive change in school.* Cambridge: Cambridge University Press.

> A well documented study that tested and implemented the concepts of principles of the sociohistorical-sociocultural framework of Vygotsky.

Tharp, R. G., & Gallimore, R. (1988). *Rousing minds to life: Teaching, learning, and schooling in social context.* Cambridge: Cambridge University Press.

> A theory of education including a view of teaching as a means to assist learners.

## Instructional design models

Andrews, D. H., & Goodson, L. A. (1980). A comparative analysis of models of instructional design. *Journal of Instructional Development, 3*(4), 2-16.

Edmonds, G. S., Branch, R. C., & Mukherjee, P. (1994). A conceptual framework for comparing instructional design models, *Educational Technology Research & Development, 42*(4), 55-72.

Gustafson, K. L. (1991). *Survey of instructional development models* (2nd ed.). Syracuse University: ERIC Clearinghouse on Information Resources. (IR-91)

> Three articles comparing instructional design models.

# What's Next?

---

*Getting Started* examined learning beliefs and design tools. The next chapter begins a shift in design thinking and activity, that of *Analysis*. Chapter 3, Needs Assessment, is a set of design tools that examines in detail the instructional needs of learners, the nature of instructional content, and the reality of the context of the instructional setting.

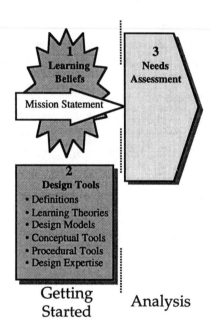

# Analysis

- **Chapter 3 - Needs Assessment**

---

SO, WHERE ARE YOU IN THE DESIGN PROCESS? In Chapter 1, **Learning Beliefs**, you examined your beliefs about learning. In Chapter 2 you were introduced to **Design Tools**—definitions, learning theories, design models, conceptual and procedural tools, as well as your existing knowledge, skills and experiences. These chapters were aimed at getting you ready to learn the instructional design process.

Now it is time to move to the next major aspect of instructional design: **Analysis**, which, if used well, will contribute to informed and responsive design decisions, no matter what learning setting interests you. This phase of instructional design is covered by Chapter 3, **Needs Assessment**.

---

"We forget that living rooms are made only in the living .... The more living rooms I see, the more I know this: It's the messy bits that make a home."

(Kalins, 1988, p. 8)

# CHAPTER 3

In the big scheme of things, being skilled at needs assessment will serve you well, whatever your field.

From a design point of view, this chapter is about data gathering and how you as the data gatherer will have a stake and a viewpoint that will affect the data collection.

# Needs Assessment

*Those who omit this step risk developing instruction that may be unnecessary or inappropriate.*

(Smith & Ragan, 1993, p. 27)

This chapter will explain what a needs assessment is, what designers learn from this process, and how to conduct a needs assessment using data collection and data summary tools.

In this chapter you will:

1. Identify a problem as an instructional or administrative problem and describe your intent to solve it.

2. Draw up a needs assessment strategy.

3. Learn more about your learners.

4. Examine the context surrounding your problem-solution.

5. Draw up goals to design towards and make revisions to your Intent and Mission Statements.

# Moving into Analysis

---

Needs assessment is common across a wide range of learning settings. In education needs assessment can be used to identify educational needs and make judgments about ways to address these needs. Funding agencies frequently request a needs assessment to justify a proposed project.

Staff development is frequently conducted with workshops as the instructional setting. Personnel responsible for these activities use needs assessment to review the effectiveness and suitability of the workshops for the needs of participants.

Firms now tie performance levels to business success and prefer to leverage people's capabilities in light of downsizing and restructuring efforts. To do this, people in these firms are examining their mission and strategic vision, and using **analysis** as a tool to determine what training or instructional experiences are necessary before they try to implement a new organizational strategy.

**Analysis Words**
- Needs assessment
- Organizational analysis
- Organizational audit
- Stakeholder analysis

To better understand and appreciate how valuable needs assessment is, you should have an instructional problem to tackle.

↓

**Key Words**
- Analysis

# DESIGN ACTIVITY 7

## "Intent Statement"

### Task Description

The purpose of this Design Activity is to record the essential features of your idea for a design project.

Designing with a real project provides an authentic experience and improves the learning of the ID process.

**1. Write an intent statement about a project in an area with which you are familiar.** Describe the major features of your project along the following areas as best you can:

1. Instructional problem
2. Intended setting
3. Participants
4. Intended change you are expecting or desiring
5. Supporting details

# What is Needs Assessment?

Needs assessment is an analysis activity that examines the instructional problem, intended learners, and learning context (Smith & Ragan, 1993). Although any meaningful activity takes time and effort, a needs assessment is an *investment*, which provides useful information so that optimal efforts can be spent on responsive designs.

Needs assessment is primarily conducted before designing begins. However, we learn that in **authentic contexts** with real instructional problems, a needs assessment is an *ongoing* process. Within the instructional design process, new information is constantly being collected from **formative evaluation** and **prototyping** of materials.

The Design Activities in this chapter will give you practice conducting a needs assessment and understand why needs assessment is necessary.

## Functions of Needs Assessment

1. *Confirm* that a design intent is an instructional problem or opportunity.
2. *Discover* the nature of what is to be learned.
3. *Learn* more about the learners within the context.
4. *Understand* the realities of the instructional context.
5. *Explore* the issues surrounding the instructional problem and proposed solution.
6. *Generate* goals that will guide designing.

**1. Confirm the instructional problem.** Not every problem can be solved by instruction. Is your idea a *real* need that can be addressed by instruction, or is it

**Key Words**
- Authentic contexts
- Formative evaluation
- Prototyping

Is your project idea
an instructional problem?

only a *perceived* need? If your idea is based on a lack of knowledge or skills, then you have an **instructional problem** (Seels & Glasgow, 1990). However, if the need stems from organizational issues such as rewards, work conditions, and work procedures, then you have an organizational problem, one that is not suitable or appropriate to the ID process. Maybe your perceived need is really just a communication problem. Your problem might be better addressed with a change in procedure, policy, or management intervention.

Not all instructional problems require the scope of effort involved in the systematic design of learning opportunities. Needs assessment may reveal new information about it, so reworking an already existing plan or activity may adequately address the problem.

Do you need to shift your
instructional design intentions?

A needs assessment also provides data that helps you to decide whether to proceed. Does your idea, your intent, have a realistic chance of being addressed considering the realities of the problem? Is the focus of your intent the correct problem? A needs assessment may reveal that you need to shift your priorities or discover that a completely different instructional approach exists than your original intention.

You may want to examine learning needs as *opportunities*, rather than as problems, something "important enough to be attempted and interesting enough to trigger a definite commitment" (Davis, 1974, p. 35). Frequent projects for students are staff development activities, because their professional practice may be implementing such activities. Needs assessment is a tool suitable for both problem solving and opportunity exploration.

Is there a solution
embedded in your idea?

**2. Discover the nature of what is to be learned.** What are you asking your participants to learn? Is it knowledge? Is it a new set of skills? Is it a change of attitude or a new of way of thinking or working together? Is it some combination of these? Needs assessment is the time to think through the "content,"

**Key Words**
• Instructional problem

of what you'll be teaching *or* what participants will be learning. Needs assessment frequently uncovers a complexity to the content that may help you to design features that better teach it or help learners to learn it. A needs assessment also gathers data on how others have approached this type of learning in a learning setting that may be related to your problem.

**3. Learn more about your learners.** In addition to analyzing the learning task and content, needs assessment examines the learner who is to benefit from the instruction. Discovering more about the participants gives you valuable insights into the range of their backgrounds, previous experiences, competencies, developmental level, as well as their expectations and motivations. Ultimately, you may learn from your participants and incorporate this into your design as you shift its details to fit the reality of your participants.

Do you know all there is to know about your learners?

**4. Understand the instructional context.** What do we mean by context? Generally, we are referring to the major physical and use features of your instructional setting and factors that support this setting (Tessmer, 1990), including the politics influencing the players within the setting. We will examine what we mean by **physical** and **use factors** later in this chapter. Reality has a way of messing up the best of intentions and the most elaborate of up-front analysis. Every instructional problem has a unique context that will ultimately shape your design. Needs assessment provides data to help you address these realities.

What are the realities surrounding the instructional problem (or opportunity)?

**5. Exploring the instructional problem and solution.** A strict **systems approach** to needs assessment would avoid including a solution, because doing so would limit one's options (Kaufman, 1988b). This may be appropriate in large design projects, such as curriculum or whole educational system designs. However, design project ideas, which are meaningful based on your interests and prior experiences, are part problem, part solution. Look back to **Design Activity 7** and read through what you wrote. What statements

What are possible solutions?

**Key Words**
- Physical factors
- Systems approach
- Use factors

are part problem, part solution? Needs assessment can analyze not only issues of need, but issues of resolution. You should not eliminate other possibilities, but your initial data gathering efforts may identify some of the relevant issues of the whole picture.

Needs assessment helps to uncover what is already known about the problem and explore what has already been done to address it. This information can be gained through the experiences of others in practice, talking with learners about the problem, and talking to experts. We will spend much of this chapter suggesting ways to explore your instructional problem and how to make sense of the information you obtain from a needs assessment.

Based on this data, what should be done?

**6. Generate goals.** What you learn from analyzing the learning task or content, learners, and context needs to be summarized so that you can generate goals which address your revised intent. Along with your Mission Statement, goals provide guidance for designers by acting as benchmarks throughout the design process. As the design plan unfolds and new information about the content, learners, and context is discovered, your goals may need to be revised.

Instructional problems and possible solutions are complex, considering the interconnections between learning task and content, learner, and context. Without an up-front analysis through a needs assessment, it is unlikely that you can bring to the design solution what is known about the full nature of the instructional problem. You may believe that you do not have enough time to conduct a needs assessment. Unfortunately, this is almost always the case in practice. However, you do need to conduct as comprehensive a needs assessment as you can in the time that you do have. Remember, that needs assessment is an ongoing process, one that can continue even when you need to move on to the next stage of design.

# Doing a Needs Assessment

Needs assessment has traditionally been viewed as a means to identify the gaps between current results and needed results (Kaufman, 1988b). Another way of looking at needs assessment is to negotiate what we would like to see occur, the **ideal**, with what is possible, or the **reality**. The outcome of needs assessment, if it is to support future designing efforts, is a list of goals, which guide subsequent designing.

Needs assessment can be handled in a number of ways, depending on your particular instructional problem (Kaufman, 1988a; English & Kaufman, 1975) and the way you view it. Provided in this chapter is a three-step approach to conducting a needs assessment.

**Food for Thought**

The notion of a gap in results is used by institutions that conduct stakeholder analysis. In this type of needs assessment a firm examines the various groups that depend on it, such as community, customers, employees, and shareholders. The analysis looks at the impact the firm has on each group and determines the differences between the outcomes desired by each group and actual performance. The firm attempts to narrow this performance difference. Understanding stakeholder needs is critical.

**Steps to Conduct a Needs Assessment**

Step 1: Describe your intent: the **Ideal**.

Step 2: Gather information: **Reality**.

Step 3: Summarize & revise your intent: **Goals**.

The needs assessment chart on the next page is a procedural design tool that helps to manage your conceptual understanding of this process. The chart summarizes the information categories, where to find this information, and ways to make sense out of what you discover. The challenge is knowing what information to look for, where to find it, and how to make sense of it.

**Key Words**
- Ideal
- Reality

Needs Assessment Strategy Chart

| *What* information do you need?<br><br>Information Categories | *Who* and *Where* are your sources of information?<br><br>Information Sources | *How* will you evaluate this information?<br><br>Information Processing Tools |
|---|---|---|
| **1. Describe the Ideal** | Personal beliefs, existing experience, and knowledge<br>Literature | Intent Statement<br>Literature review |
| **2. Gather information**<br><br>*What is known about the learning task?* | On-site records, interviews, observations of learners, and key participants<br>Interviews and surveys from experts<br>Library resources | Task analysis<br>Ethnography<br>Structured Questions<br>Protocol Analysis<br>Displays<br>Statistics<br>Document analysis |
| *Who are your learners?* | Your experience and knowledge<br>Interviews and surveys from experts and learners<br>Potential participants | Data analysis tools<br>Learner Profile |
| *What are your resources and constraints?* | Your experience/knowledge<br>Interviews with key informants | Context analysis |
| **3. Summarize & Revise** | All of the above | Summary of problem<br>Description of solution<br>Goals for design |

# Step 1: Describe Your Intent

See
**Design Activity 3:**
Mission Statement
**Design Activity 7:**
Intent Statement

**Key Words**
• Intent statement

The primary source of information for a description of the ideal, what you would like to see happen, is recorded in an **intent statement**, which summarizes your initial view on the instructional problem. The intent statement usually includes statements on a possible solution. Also reflected in your intent statement are personal or institutional beliefs and prior knowledge and experiences, which can be recorded and examined in the Mission Statement. From these documents you can make a list of the information you need in order to have a clearer understanding of content, learners, and context.

# Step 2: Gather Information

The purpose of Step 2 is to find out more about an instructional problem or opportunity. Writing an intent statement records your initial understanding of the problem and may influence issues which will require additional analysis. It is unlikely that this statement will include all of the relevant information on learning task or content, learners, and learning context. What appears as a simple problem may reveal, upon further examination, complexity and richness. Learning problems *are* complex. Using observations, on-site data, interviews, surveys, and research data will enhance your designing efforts. This new understanding could also influence decisions on priorities or identification of the problem (or opportunity) that should really be the focus of your designing efforts.

**What is known about your problem/solution?** What do you want people to learn? What information already exists that examines the learning tasks inherent to the instructional problem? If your intent statement proposes an approach or a list of possible solutions then these can be researched at the same time. Sources of information on the learning task include site-specific sources, experts and novices, and research.

*Site-specific* sources provide details that are closest to addressing your instructional problem. These on-site sources include records, observations, and interviews with teachers and students, teacher aides,

> **Food for Thought**
>
> It's OK to acknowledge your own expertise and viewpoints. Make this clear in your design document, so that readers of your design document will know the source of ideas is you.

parents, administrators, managers, and other key participants. These primary sources will provide much of the detail on the instructional setting as well.

Interviews and surveys of *experts* provide specialized insights. The range of experts include specialists in content, teaching, media, psychology, guidance, health, and government. Interviews provide individualized responses to specific questions and may shed light on the real problems. Drafting questions and conducting the questioning, listening, and record keeping is challenging (Carin & Sund, 1978), while data analysis requires time and systematic procedures to summarize (Miles & Huberman, 1994; Spradley, 1980). Consider asking these same experts to review representative samples of your design through a pilot test or **prototype**.

**Task analysis** is a research tool that is used to identify the problem solving performance of people, ranging from novices to experts. Bruer (1993) captures the value of performing a task analysis: "What I know about the task and about your problem-solving behavior allows me to figure out how you must have understood the task" (p. 34). Thus, task analysis, in addition to identifying **learning prerequisites**, helps to "reveal our cognitive architecture" (Bruer, 1993, p. 49). Knowing these prerequisites and the knowledge representations that both experts and novices use to solve problems, provide teachers with ways to teach and assess learning progress in problem-solving domains. Task analysis helps to reveal an expert's or a learner's problem solving knowledge and skills and how these are revealed in their unique knowledge structures and representations.

Data gathering involves recording the problem solving—the knowledge structures, representations, and strategies of learners. **Protocol analysis** is another tool that records the "think aloud" details of how one performs a task. Key aspects of these transcriptions are analyzed for differences in ways that one represents existing knowledge, encodes processes, and notes

**Key Words**
- Learning prerequisites
- Protocol analysis
- Prototype
- Task analysis

detail of the instructional or real world environment. As Bruer (1993) notes, the task environments that reveal expert behaviors are the instructional environments that we should be using to enhance learning. Instructional environments and the instructional frameworks that create these environments, will be the subject of Chapter 5.

♦ See Ericsson & Simon (1993) in **For Further Reading** for more discussion on protocol analysis.

*Surveys* offer a cost-effective data source, but require careful construction to ensure that you are sampling an accurate cross-section of data sources and that the questions are structured appropriately for the information you are seeking. For example, questions should make sense for those being surveyed and should return the data you need. Data analysis of surveys is also a challenge, so please consult references on survey design and data analysis (Fink, 1995). Survey results should be supported by observations (Goetz & LeCompte, 1984). While surveys are useful as sources of the judgments individuals make about people and settings, they may be inaccurate data sources for indicators of learning progress.

The *library* is a third source of data on the learning task. University libraries provide reference librarians who are specialists in helping you find the information you need. They can show you how to use the library's specialized references, such as physical and electronic catalogs, indexes, abstracts, and databases, as well as library services, including interlibrary loans (Bliss, 1992). It's one thing to conduct a *literature search*, a process that requires its own unique strategy, but it is the *literature review* that summarizes and synthesizes the results of the search in such a way that it informs your needs assessment. Sternberg (1993) provides advice on searching the literature and writing up what you discover.

## ☆ SCENARIO

# Consulting Firm: Discovering "What's the Real Problem?"

Remember the consulting firm in our scenario is Rockford & Associates, who produces customized training materials. As the firm grew the partners worried that their vision was not the same as their staff. Somehow they just have not communicated their vision to a staff that is increasing each week to handle the growing number of client projects. In addition, they perceive a spotty record in client service, a key feature of their competitive strategy.

The partners decided to conduct a needs assessment of their own. In the business world such an analysis is known by many words, one of which is an "organizational audit." With such an audit, the partners hoped to discover where the gaps in performance are.

The partners assembled everyone together to solicit feedback on staff concerns. During the meeting a piece of paper was distributed to everyone. This was an activity in which everyone ranked the degrees of control they believed were exhibited by project leaders and partners. This ranking activity addressed control of others, control of information, control of standards, and focus on short term goals at the expense of the firm's Mission.

The partners realized from the open meeting that to develop shared values everyone needed to be involved in their development. From this understanding the group had a basis for communication, which contributed to the development of ways to determine and enact these shared values, one of which was client service.

Needs assessment can be found in many different settings. In all cases, its purpose is to analyze the current situation to uncover opportunities for improvements and also to discover what has already been learned about the problem from outside sources.

---

In the next Design Activity decide on a strategy to help guide your needs assessment.

# DESIGN ACTIVITY 8

## "Needs Assessment Strategy"

**1. What is your needs assessment strategy?** In other words, *what* information do you need about learning tasks: content, learners, and learning context; *where* will you find it; and *how* will you make sense out of it?

 **Task Description**

Having a needs assessment strategy keeps you from over-researching the topic and helps you make a plan before "walking out the door."

Always remember, as you read more about your learners and the instructional context, you may need to revise this strategy.

| Information | Sources | Tools |
| --- | --- | --- |

**Who are your learners?** In addition to gathering information on the learning task, a needs assessment should also include information on the intended participants and beneficiaries of the instructional design. This is a **learner profile**. Learner characteristics include age, sex, educational level, development and achievement level, prerequisite knowledge and skills needed, socioeconomic background, learning style preferences, motivation, attitudes, and expectations (Seels & Glasgow, 1990). The range and depth of this information will differ from project to project and are based partly on the type of instructional problem, availability and reliability of information, and time available to obtain this information.

Learner information can be obtained from the setting itself, from records, teachers, and administrators in an educational setting, or from company information and managers in a business setting. Experts may provide some insight to your learners. Students are frequently forgotten as sources of information in the needs assessment, as well as sources of ongoing, or **formative evaluation**, during designing. Talking with the intended participants during planning may give you some insight to the dimensions of your instructional problem and may suggest ideas for your instructional design.

> The following Design Activity is a procedural design tool to assist in gaining greater understanding of your learners.

**↓**

**Key Words**
- Formative evaluation
- Learner profile

# DESIGN ACTIVITY 9

## "Learner Profile"

**1. Identify characteristics of your learners and try to describe the range of learners.** Consider these characteristics, if appropriate.

- Age
- Sex
- Educational level
- Achievement level
- Prerequisite knowledge and skills
- Socioeconomic background
- Learning style preferences
- Motivation
- Attitudes
- Expectations

 **Task Description**

A learner profile is a tool to summarize the characteristics and range of learners in your setting.

Some of this information may be difficult to obtain, particularly if the intended participants are unknown to you and cannot be researched easily. The answers to these questions may then be uncovered when the instructional activity begins.

**What are the realities of your instructional setting?** Learning problems do not exist in a vacuum. They are embedded in some fascinating and complex, but messy settings we call "context." A procedural design tool, called **context analysis**, can reveal the resources and the constraints to this context. Tessmer (1990) provides an organizing structure to examine the resources and constraints inherent to any instructional setting.

**Key Words**
- Context analysis

**Context Analysis (Tessmer, 1990)**

| Physical Factors | Use Factors |
|---|---|
| Instructional environment | Instructional environment |
| Support Environment | Support Environment |

Reprinted with permission from the Association for Educational Communications and Technology, Washington, D. C.

### Food for Thought

Examining these issues of context *before* you design can save time, money, and headaches. However, this context analysis is a good example of the iterative nature of designing. Context can be re-examined throughout the designing process as more information becomes available from other aspects of the needs assessment or through **prototyping** (Chapter 8) and **formative evaluation** (Chapter 9). If goals established by a needs assessment become modified, it may be necessary to take another look at your context analysis to see if critical factors change.

### Key Words
- Formative evaluation
- Physical factors
- Prototyping
- Use factors

Context analysis, as articulated by Tessmer (1990), examines two categories of factors: **physical** and **use**. The physical factors address how your design creates and supports your instructional setting, while the use factors deal with how the setting is used for instructional purposes. Within each category are issues of the instructional and support environment. The instructional environment deals with the physical and use characteristics of the setting, while the support environment is the overall system in which the instructional environment operates—the facilities, administration, departments, organizations, or governmental units.

**Physical factors** in the *instructional environment* include facilities, equipment, and instructional lifespan. *Facilities* provide a major factor in the choice of instructional strategy. In addition to the fundamental needs of a safe and secure setting, having the proper *equipment* that is safe and appropriate to the task, and to the developmental level of the participants is essential. The *instructional lifespan* of the content being presented as well as the lifespan of the instructional materials may be an issue. Presentation materials may contain outdated information if the nature of the content changes rapidly (e.g., current events, computer software, technology and learner interest). Some instructional materials may have a short shelf-life (living plants) or can be used only once (dissection specimens).

The support environment within these physical factors includes site distribution, management, and times of the year. Will your instructional design be implemented at more than one *location* or will the instruction be centralized, but distributed to many sites. A design may specify additional *personnel*, such as audiovisual support, parent-as-aides, or guest speakers. Does your design specify field trips or research that requires particular *weather* conditions?

### Resources & Constraints (Tessmer, 1990)

| 1. Physical Factors | 2. Use Factors |
|---|---|
| **Instructional Environment**<br>Facilities<br>Equipment<br>Instructional lifespan | **Instructional Environment**<br>Patterns of use<br>Reasons for use<br>Student-user characteristics<br>Administrator characteristics |
| **Support Environment**<br>Site distribution<br>Management and coordination<br>Seasons and climate | **Support Environment**<br>Production services<br>Storage and delivery services<br>Dissemination resources<br>Support resources |

Tessmer, M. (1990). Environmental analysis: A neglected stage of instructional design. *Educational Technology Research & Development, 38*(1), 55-64. Reprinted with permission from the Association for Educational Communications and Technology, Washington, D. C.

**Use factors** in the instructional environment include patterns of use, reasons for use, and student and instructor characteristics. *Use patterns* include the rate of use (e. g., continuous, sporadic, as needed or self-directed); size of group (e. g., individual learning, groups or work teams); and the schedule (fixed or flexible). *Student characteristics* include entry skills, attitudes, perceptions, physical or psychological handicaps, anxiety levels, and expectations. Use

**Key Words**
- Use factors

characteristics for those who *administer* the instruction include job descriptions, required skills, and turnover in personnel. Information from administrator characteristics will tell you personal dispositions to innovation and requirements for administrator support. You also may need to design features that assist the teacher in some fashion, learn new content or teach new knowledge or skills.

Use factors within the support environment include those services that make the instructional product available for end users. These services include production services, storage and delivery capabilities, mail or computer dissemination, and other support services (e. g., audiovisual, computer support, maintenance, health).

## Talking about Media

**Media Needs.** Needs assessment is a good time to look at the possibilities for media in your design project. We view media materials as ranging from chalk to computers, so don't restrict your media possibilities. For now, record ideas on materials that will support your intent. The context analysis can be used to examine the resources you have available to you and the limitations or constraints placed upon their use.

What materials are already available and what may need to be purchased? Some materials may need to be adapted for your particular application, while others may need to be developed, particularly if they are key elements in your project.

**Media selection charts.** General selection criteria for your media materials (Heinich, Molenda, Russell & Smaldino, 1996) include:

(1) Characteristics of the learner
(2) Nature of the objectives
(3) Instructional approach
(4) Limitations of the instructional setting

More specific criteria can be applied through the use of media appraisal checklists adapted for a particular media format (See Heinich et al., 1996). You may need to modify these checklists to add criteria that fits your media needs.

Now, here's a **Design Activity** to analyze the context of your project.

# DESIGN ACTIVITY 10

### "Context Analysis"

Tessmer (1990) suggests three questions to guide you in analyzing the context of the learning setting:

**1.** What aspects of the instructional and support environments are critical to the success of your design?

**2.** Within each category (e.g., facilities, site distribution, patterns of use, and support resources) what are the most important factors?

**3.** What conflicts exist between categories that will affect the success of the design?

**4.** In addition, include a statement on how stable this analysis is and if there is a possibility of re-visiting the context analysis if goals change.

 **Task Description**

You can use the context analysis chart described earlier as a procedural design tool. You are looking for details of the instructional setting that provide or limit your intended teaching strategies, media use, and assessment.

Use the Tessmer (1990) outline to guide your context analysis. Add whatever categories make sense to your needs.

# ☆ SCENARIO

## All Settings: Needs Assessment Outline for a Workshop

Workshops are common instructional settings in all three scenario settings (hospital, school, and business). People have particular expectations about workshops since most of us have attended several. Workshops also are frequent topics for ID projects, because they represent a finite and achievable instructional activity. Workshops have unique characteristics in terms of their resources and constraints, participants, and content. They are also intense instructional activities, as they must address multiple details in limited time.

Below is a generalized outline that attempts to cover the major needs assessment issues.

### Identifying and Organizing Content

- Topic(s)
- Participant needs
- Distinctive feature

### Identifying Learners

- Participant profile
- Participant concerns
- Participant knowledge (about content)
- Participant experience (with other workshops)

### Context of Workshop

- Institutional support for workshop
- Institutional history behind workshop
- Number expected
- Mandatory or voluntary attendance
- Supporting materials
- Possible involvement strategies
- Managing details
- Constraints

# Step 3: Summarize and Revise

Step 3 recommends that you summarize the research you have conducted on the three aspects of the instructional problem or opportunity (i.e., the learning task or content, the learners, and the instructional setting) and the possible solution or approach.

---

**Outline of a Needs Assessment Study**

1. **Summarize your instructional problem.**
   Confirm instructional problem.
   Describe major issues that characterize the problem.
   Cite the sources of information and tools used.
2. **Describe your instructional solution.**
   List features addressing learning task or content.
   Include a learner profile.
   Include a context analysis.
3. **Identify major goals that address the problem.**
   Identify and prioritize goals.

---

**1. Summarize your instructional problem.** Now it's time to revisit the instructional problem question again. Is your perceived need an instructional problem? The needs assessment should provide convincing evidence that your need is a problem or opportunity that can be addressed through instruction and that you have a realistic chance to achieve or construct a workable plan.

In addition to validating the instructional problem, summarize the major issues that characterize the problem or opportunity. These issues will focus primarily on what you discovered about the learning task or content and the learners. Cite the sources you consulted so that your summary is validated and that you have a record of those you consulted. Others reading your needs assessment summary may want to know where you got your information. It also will be helpful to specify the tools you used to process your data. The data itself can be a separate document or placed in an appendix to the summary.

**2. Describe your instructional solution.** Based on what you have learned from the needs assessment, you might need to revise your original intent statement. Describe the major features of your instructional solution that address the tasks or content to be learned. Include what you have discovered about the participants from the learner profile and the critical factors and conflicts from the context analysis. The context analysis summary you made earlier will greatly facilitate this step.

**3. Identify your goals.** Make a list of the major goals of your instructional design. This list should be based on your new understanding of what really needs to be done to address your instructional problem. Original intentions may need to be modified to fit the new realities you have discovered. Some of these goals may also involve the instructor or facilitator or workshop leader. A long list of goals will have to be prioritized. Decide what can be accomplished reasonably within time available and using available resources.

 In "Touring Instructional Design," see Tour 3: The Gatekeeper.

It's time to re-examine your intent and mission statements, based on what you have learned from a needs assessment.

# DESIGN ACTIVITY 11

"Goals & Revised Intent/Mission Statements"

From your needs assessment:

**1.** List your prioritized goals for your design project.

**2.** Revise your Intent Statement to more accurately reflect your instructional problem or opportunity.

**3.** Revise your Mission Statement if you have changed or made additions to your learning beliefs, particularly in the context of your project.

 **Task Description**

One of the realities of any kind of design work, including instructional design, is the need to revise what one has designed based on new understandings or trial runs or prototypes.

Goals identified from the Needs Assessment as well as your Intent and Mission Statements are key documents to help keep you on track with your designing efforts.

# Reviewing the Design Activities

## Design Activity 7: Intent Statement

☐ Clear statement of project purpose.
☐ Clear delineation of target audience.
☐ Clear delineation of time length.
☐ Clear description of content.

## Design Activity 8: Needs Assessment Strategy

☐ Outlined information you need.
☐ Provided sources of information.
☐ Described how information will be evaluated and summarized.

## Design Activity 9: Learner Profile

☐ Identified range of learners.
☐ Identified essential and supporting prerequisite skills and knowledge.

## Design Activity 10: Context Analysis

☐ Outlined resources and constraints.
☐ Explained how critical resources and constraints will be addressed.

## Design Activity 11: Goals and Revised Intent/Mission Statements

☐ Validated project as an instructional problem.
☐ Articulated goals for project.
☐ Iteration of goals, intent, and mission statements.
☐ Identified data sources.

# ⚑ Summary of Important Ideas

---

**1.** Needs assessment is an analysis activity that engages you in an indepth examination of an instructional problem, intended learners, and learning context. The needs assessment helps you to:

- **Confirm** that your design intent is an instructional problem.

- **Discover** more about the content, skills, or what your learners will learn.

- **Understand** the realities of the instructional context.

- **Discover** more about your learners.

- **Explore** the issues surrounding the instructional problem and your proposed solution.

- **Generate** goals that will guide you in designing.

**2.** Three steps in the needs assessment process include:

- **Step 1:** Describe your intent

- **Step 2:** Gather information

- **Step 3:** Summarize and revise your intent

**3.** A needs assessment summary helps you to generate design goals. Possible topics include:

- Summary of instructional problem

  ✓ Determination of instructional problem
  ✓ Major issues that characterize the problem
  ✓ Sources of information and tools used

- Description of instructional solution

  ✓ Include learner profile and context analysis

- Identification of major goals that address problem

  ✓ Prioritize goals

# √ Your Personal Learning

*What constitutes an educational need depends on the educational values one holds. . . the influence of the values one brings to a situation is manifest in how one describes that situation.*

(Eisner, 1994, p. 177)

## Relating Your Beliefs to This Chapter:

- What do you think about needs assessment?
- Do you think it is a worthwhile activity?
- Have you learned something about your instructional problem or opportunity?
- Do you have a needs assessment approach different from the three-step process suggested in this chapter?

## Any revisions to your personal ID model:

- Did a needs assessment or some analysis of learning needs figure into your preliminary ID model?
- How would you represent it now?

## What questions do you have about this chapter?

# References

Bliss, P. (1992). Library resources: Using a university library to aid in your research and your search for a publisher. In A. Allison and T. Frongia (Eds.). *The grad student's guide to getting published*. NY: Prentice-Hall.

Bruer, J. (1993). *Schools for thought: A science of learning in the classroom*. Cambridge: MIT Press.

Carin, A., & Sund, R. B. (1978). *Creative questioning and sensitive listening techniques: A self-concept approach* (2nd ed.). Columbus, OH: Merrill.

Davis, L. N. (1974*). Planning, conducting, evaluating workshops*. Austin, TX: Learning Concepts.

English, F. W., & Kaufman, R. A. (1975). *Needs assessment: A focus for curriculum development*. Washington, D.C.: Association for Supervision and Curriculum Development.

Fink, A. (Ed.). (1995). *The survey kit*. Thousand Oaks, CA: Sage.

Goetz, J. P. & LeCompte, M. D. (1984). *Ethnography and qualitative design in educational research*. San Diego: Academic Press.

Heinich, R., Molenda, M., Russell, J. D., & Smaldino, S. E. (1996). *Instructional media and the new technologies of instruction* (5th ed.). Englewood Cliffs, NJ: Prentice-Hall.

Kalins, D. (1988, September). *Metropolitan Home*, p. 8.

Kaufman, R. A. (1988a, July). Needs assessment: A menu. *Educational Technology*, 21-23.

Kaufman, R. A. (1988b). *Planning educational systems: A results-based approach.* Lancaster, PA: Technomic.

Miles, M. B., & Huberman, A. M. (1994). *Qualitative data analysis* (2nd ed.). Thousand Oaks, CA: Sage.

Seels, B. & Glasgow, Z. (1990). *Exercises in instructional design.* Columbus, OH: Merrill.

Smith, P. L., & Ragan, T. J. (1993). *Instructional design.* NY: Merrill.

Spradley, J. P. (1980). *Participant observation.* Fort Worth, TX: Harcourt Brace Jovanovich.

Sternberg, R. J. (1993). *The psychologist's companion: Edition III: A guide to scientific writing for students and researchers.* Cambridge: Cambridge University Press.

Tessmer, M. (1990). Environmental analysis: A neglected stage of instructional design. *Educational Technology Research & Development, 38*(1), 55-64.

# For Further Reading ...

Ericsson, K. A., & Simon, H. A. (1993). *Protocol analysis: Verbal reports as data* (2nd ed.). Cambridge, MA: MIT Press

> A revised edition to this important design tool reference which examines situations and appropriate protocols.

Seels, B., & Glasgow, Z. (1990). *Exercises in instructional design.* Columbus, OH: Merrill.

> A complementary treatment of needs assessment. Chapter 4 discusses basic skills in collecting information and using verbal and visual methods to summarize information.

Gross, R. (1982). *The independent scholar's handbook: How to turn your interest in any subject into expertise.* Reading, MA: Addison-Wesley.

> Chapter 3 examines how to uncover information through the library, interlibrary loan, and electronic databases. Chapter 4 and 5 discuss the benefits of researching with others and matters of intellectual craftsmanship, such as managing one's research project. However, the real value of this book is how it infuses the joy of research in people who want to find out more about something.

Sharp, P. A. (1993). *Sharing your good ideas. A workshop facilitator's handbook.* Portsmouth, NH: Heinemann.

> Down-to-earth, easy-to-read and good advice and pointers about leading educators in workshops.

# What's Next?

---

The next five chapters address the designing phases:

- Chapter 4: Sequence of Instruction
- Chapter 5: Assessment
- Chapter 6: Instructional Framework
- Chapter 7: Instructional Media
- Chapter 8: Prototype

In Chapter 4, we determine the sequence of instruction. Here we will take another look at tasks and content, or what you are asking your participants to learn, and trying to determine what pieces of this "content" should come first, second, etc.

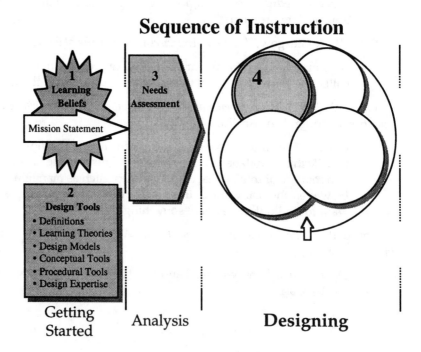

# Designing

IT IS TIME TO MOVE INTO DESIGNING. Now that you have determined your goals and have a sense for what you really want your learners to achieve, you are ready to move into the design component of the instructional design process. This is the real action component of instructional design where decisions are made on the instructional issues of your goals. The major components in instructional design that address these issues are covered by Chapters 4-8.

"Design ... is a tool for understanding as well as for acting.... [It] is concerned with how things ought to be, with devising artifacts to attain goals."

(Simon, 1981, p. 133)

"Human design process is inherently synthetic, requires the human feedback mode, and often transcends the knowledge of any one discipline."

(Kline, 1995, p. 90)

# CHAPTER 4

What content comes first, what comes second, what comes third? That's what this chapter is about. This may not be so difficult at first glance, but is this sequence truly right for your learners?

Sequencing may challenge your beliefs on learning. Challenging these beliefs is our way of asking you to consider what is appropriate and possible!

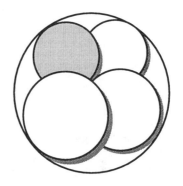

# Sequence of Instruction

*... although a larger design problem can be broken into parts, the total solution is not a sum of the smaller ones.*

(Schön, 1987, p. 159)

This chapter examines how to organize content within your instructional event, whether it is a course, unit, activity, tutorial, workshop, or other instructional opportunity. We will discuss sequencing principles based on two very different goals. If your goal is to transmit a body of information, which can be characterized by concepts, procedures, or principles, then the structure and ordering of the content follows a fairly predictable sequencing pattern. However, if one of your goals is that students develop flexible understandings of subject matter or processes, then sequencing is much more elaborate.

In this chapter you will:

1. Identify learning types for each goal you developed from your needs assessment.

2. Draw up a sequence of instruction based on some stated sequencing rationale.

3. Conduct a task analysis of a key task identified in your instructional activity.

# What is Sequencing?

---

**Sequencing** involves "the selection and organization of the knowledge, skills, and attitudinal factors of any topic" (Kemp, 1977, p. 44). Learners benefit when material is structured and sequenced appropriately (Brophy & Good, 1986). Cognitive research explains this by pointing out that the short-term memory of humans can easily be overloaded with new material and that careful pacing, structuring, and sequencing assists the learner with processing new information. So then, how does one structure and sequence content in such a way that accomplishes the goals that you determined from a needs assessment? The first step is to carefully examine the learning implications of your goals. This can be done through learning taxonomies.

# Taxonomies

---

A **taxonomy** is a means of classifying complex things. For biologists and naturalists, taxonomies are used in systematics, a science of naming organisms based on their natural relationships. All life is classified into a hierarchy of groups of related organisms with each organism being assigned a two-word Latin name designating its generic (genus) and specific (species) name. Characteristics are made on structural grounds, since physiological and behavioral criteria are absent when taxonomists handle dead specimens (Medawar, 1977).

Another example of a taxonomy is the periodic table in which the chemical elements are arranged in order of their atomic numbers and their properties are

**Key Words**
- Sequencing
- Taxonomy

classified in a two-dimensional matrix of rows (periods) and columns (groups). From its position in the table, the properties of elements can be predicted with a good degree of accuracy, and in fact, some undiscovered elements were predicted to exist because of their position in the table.

Other domains have less elaborate taxonomies. Those in the social sciences (e.g., history, political science, economics, psychology, sociology, and anthropology) are less obvious and tend to have fuzzy boundaries (Kline, 1995). Abraham Maslow's (1970) hierarchy of human needs, ranging from survival and safety at the bottom level to self-actualization, a realization of one's potential at the top, is an example of a hierarchical means to classify the range of human needs. Another example within educational psychology and instructional design are learning taxonomies.

Learning taxonomies are conceptual design tools that label and describe the learning capacities of what learners are able to do, think, and feel. These taxonomies can be useful in understanding and accounting for a wide range of human capabilities that may need to be addressed by your instructional design. In addition, they are useful in sequencing content, depending on the sequencing principle used, as well as assessing learning progress, based on learner behavior. We will address these sequencing principles later in this chapter.

Learning taxonomies have been developed to address cognitive, or thinking skills; psychomotor, or movement skills; and affect, or attitudes. Within Bloom's (1956) taxonomy for **cognitive skills**, the main ordering principle is the degree of complexity of thinking processes. The categories are organized in hierarchies with the simplest category at the lowest level and the more complex at the top. This ordering implies that each level requires mastery of the skill level below it (Bloom, 1956).

- See Bloom, 1956
- See Krathwohl et al., 1964
- See Harrow, 1972
listed in **References**

**Key Words**
- Cognitive skills

**Cognitive Taxonomy (Bloom, 1956)**

| Learning type | Behavior examples |
|---|---|
| ⇧<br>Evaluation | To argue, decide, compare, consider, and contrast |
| ⇧<br>Synthesis | To write, produce, plan, design, derive, and combine |
| ⇧<br>Analysis | To distinguish, detect, employ, restructure, and classify |
| ⇧<br>Application | To generalize, develop, employ, and transfer |
| ⇧<br>Comprehension | To transform, paraphrase, interpret, reorder, infer, and conclude |
| ⇧<br>Knowledge | To recall, recognize, acquire, and identify |

**Organizing Principle**
- Degree of complexity

From THE TAXONOMY OF EDUCATIONAL OBJECTIVES: HANDBOOK 1: COGNITIVE DOMAIN, Bloom, et al. Copyright © 1956, renewed 1984. Reprinted by permission.

The **psychomotor domain** is organized on the degree of physical coordination required in a task (Harrow, 1972). Think about the possibilities of physical movement learning from activities in your design. For example, how "hands-on" are hands-on activities? Some activities may require manual dexterity to handle laboratory glassware or living things; other activities may require the ability to coordinate hand-eye movements when using computers and other physical tasks.

Another type of learning that has frequently been ignored by designers is the **affective domain**. The affective domain includes attitudes, interests, and values. It is organized according to the degree of internalization, a process where a person's attitude shifts from general awareness to an attitude that consistently guides one's behavior (Krathwohl, Bloom & Masia, 1964).

**Key Word**
- Affective domain
- Psychomotor domain

**Organizing Principle**
• Degree of physical coordination
        **Psychomotor Taxonomy (Harrow, 1972)**

| Learning type | Physical Behavior examples |
|---|---|
| ⇧ <br> Non-discursive Communication | Body postures, gestures, and facial expressions |
| ⇧ <br> Skilled Movements | Skilled activities such as in sports, recreation, and dance |
| ⇧ <br> Physical Activities | All activities which require strenuous effort, muscular exertion, wide range of motion, and quick, precise movement |
| ⇧ <br> Perceptual | Coordinated movements such as jumping rope, punting, and catching |
| ⇧ <br> Basic Fundamental Movement | Walking, running, pushing, twisting, gripping, grasping, and manipulating |
| ⇧ <br> Reflex Movements | Flexion, extension, stretch, and postural adjustments |

From Harrow, A. J. (1972). *A taxonomy of the psychomotor domain*. NY: McKay.

Krathwohl et al. (1964) who developed this domain cite three reasons why affective objectives are not frequently used: (1) there is less grading of students' achievement on affective objectives, which has been due to inadequate assessment methods; (2) achievement and competence have traditionally been regarded as a public matter, while affective learning is regarded as a private matter; and (3) results in this taxonomy take time.

The affective taxonomy, however, helps you to be more precise when trying to specify affective goals. "The evidence suggests that affective behaviors develop when appropriate learning experiences are provided for students much the same as cognitive behaviors develop from appropriate learning experiences" (Krathwohl et al., 1964, p. 20).

**Affective Taxonomy (Krathwohl et al., 1964)**

| Learning type | Affective examples |
|---|---|
| ⇧<br>Characterization by Value or Value Set | To revise, require, be rated high in value, avoid, resist, manage, and resolve |
| ⇧<br>Organization | To discuss, theorize, formulate, balance, and examine |
| ⇧<br>Valuing | To increase measured proficiency in, relinquish, subsidize, support, or debate |
| ⇧<br>Responding | To comply with, follow, commend, volunteer, spend leisure time in, or acclaim |
| ⇧<br>Receiving | To differentiate, accept, listen for, or respond to |

**Organizing Principle**
• Degree of internalization

From TAXONOMY OF EDUCATIONAL OBJECTIVES: BOOK 2: AFFECTIVE SKILLS, Krathwohl, et al. Copyright © 1984. Reprinted by permission.

Yet another taxonomy is Gagné's **learned capabilities**, which incorporates cognitive, affective, and psychomotor aspects. The previous taxonomies were characterized by their particular behavior, while Gagné's learning taxonomy specifies the learning outcome requirements of five kinds of learned capabilities: intellectual skills, cognitive strategies, verbal information, attitude, and motor skills.

By organizing learning around learning outcomes, similar instructional strategies can be used, and thus, can be easier to translate into practice than the three other taxonomies (Seels & Glasgow, 1990). This framework, however, concentrates primarily on intellectual skills. Note that there is no differentiation within the attitude and motor skill aspects. Gagné

**Key Words**
• Learned capabilities

recommended that designers refer to Krathwohl et al. (1964) and Harrow (1972) for breakdowns of these domains.

## Gagné's Learned Capabilities (Seels & Glasgow, 1990)

**Organizing Principle**
- Learning outcomes

| Learning type | Conditions for Learning |
|---|---|
| **Intellectual Skills** | |
| Problem Solving | Generating rules, and trial and error |
| ⇧ Rule Using | Applying rules to new situations and relating concepts |
| ⇧ Concrete Concept | Recognizing similarities among a particular class of objects, people, or events |
| ⇧ Discrimination | Seeing essential differences between things |
| **Cognitive Strategy** | Self-assessing and self-regulating and forming mental frameworks to knowledge |
| **Verbal Information** | |
| Labels and Facts | Naming things and recall |
| Bodies of Knowledge | Recall of interconnected information |
| **Attitude** | Internal state that affects choice of action |
| **Motor Skills** | Body movements |

From EXERCISES IN INSTRUCTIONAL DESIGN BY Seels/Glasgow, © 1990. Adapted by permission of Prentice-Hall., Upper Saddle River, NJ.

**Assigning learning domains to goals.** By matching your learning goals to learning types within these taxonomies, you can begin to design instructional features to accomplish them. Taxonomies are not perfect tools, but they give us a means to talk about the complexities of human learning.

> An example might be helpful.

**Example.** If you wanted to construct a unit to help students learn about the lifestyles of the people who live in northern Africa, you might write up the following goals:

**Learners will:**

1. Know the countries that comprise the geographical region of northern Africa and be able to describe important features that characterize these countries in terms of geography, economy, political, and culture.

2. Understand the major issues facing citizens of these countries and be able to summarize them in writing.

3. Appreciate the differences between these people and ourselves and present to the class how these differences can be mutually supportive of each other.

Let's examine each of these goals in terms of their cognitive requirements and try to uncover the layers of learning included in each. For this example, we will be using Bloom's (1956) taxonomy of cognitive skills.

Refer to the box on the next page listing the learning types that have been matched up with the above learning goals:

1. The purpose of the first goal is to recall or identify important features of each country, a *knowledge* goal. However, we are also asking students to decide on the important features. This involves *analysis*, a higher level of learning than knowledge. Analysis involves the ability to distinguish and to detect Because the learner must also prioritize the information and make comparisons, as well as careful reflection on these decisions, a higher level than analysis, *evaluation*, is called upon.

## Matching Learning Goals with Learning Types

**Learners will:**

**1.** Know the countries that comprise the geographical region of northern Africa and be able to describe important features that characterize these countries in terms of geography, economy, political, and cultural.

**Cognitive:**
KNOWLEDGE—acquire, identify
ANALYSIS —distinguish, detect
EVALUATION—decide, compare

**2.** Understand the major issues facing citizens of these countries and be able to summarize them in writing.

**Cognitive:**
KNOWLEDGE—understand
ANALYSIS—summarize
SYNTHESIS—write

**3.** Appreciate the differences between these people and ourselves and present to the class how these differences can be mutually supportive of each other.

| **Cognitive:** | **Affective:** |
| --- | --- |
| ANALYSIS—differences | RECEIVING—appreciate |
| EVALUATION—decide | RESPONDING—supportive |
| SYNTHESIS—present | |

**2.** The second goal also includes *analysis*. Learning goals or objectives frequently specify that the students understand, but what does this really mean? For this goal students need to be able to identify and outline important issues as well as separate important issues from each other. Once again, this is an *analysis* learning level. But look closer. You are asking for more than analysis. Writing requires that one can synthesize parts to form a new whole. Composing and organizing involves *synthesis*, another level on the cognitive domain (Bloom, 1956).

**3.** The third goal extends across both cognitive and affective domains. When intellectual skills are to be learned, there is usually some affective component built in. As one masters these, one also achieves competency in *receiving, responding,* and *valuing*. The word appreciate signals learning on an affective level. Students must be able to identify and select cultural differences (cognitive) and also be sensitive to cultural differences (Krathwohl et al., 1964).

From the cognitive domain, being able to present one's findings once again taps a *synthesis* learning level. To construct this understanding one must also be able to evaluate how cultural differences can contribute to another culture.

> Now let's assign learning types to the goals
> you identified in the needs assessment.

**↓**

# DESIGN ACTIVITY 12

## "Matching Learning Goals with Learning Types"

1. **List the goals from your needs assessment.**

2. **Identify for each goal the type(s) of learning.** Consult the taxonomies for assistance.

 **Task Description**

By matching each of your goals with the types of learning you are expecting from your participants, you can begin to get a better idea of how to design what content goes first, second, and so on. This is the subject of the next section.

Identifying these learning types also assists you in coming up with ways of assessing learning and methods of instruction.

> Now, let's use taxonomies to help you sequence content!

**↓**

# Sequencing on Learning Types

The question now is: How does one structure and sequence content in such a way that accomplishes the goals that were determined from the needs assessment? We will use Gagné's learned capabilities taxonomy as a framework to examine sequencing principles and related factors (Gagné, Briggs, & Wager, 1992).

**Sequencing on intellectual skills.** Most of the literature on content sequencing involves the sequencing of intellectual skills. A major sequencing principle for intellectual skills is based on moving from the simple to the complex. A fundamental idea is first presented then more detailed ideas, which elaborate on the fundamental concept, procedure, or principle, are added. The initial idea is then reviewed and the relationships between the fundamental idea and new information are studied (Reigeluth and Stein, 1983). Sequencing *concepts*, *procedures*, and *principles* involve this simple-to-complex direction, but each are sequenced along different rationales.

*Conceptual goals.* These goals address the "what" and are sequenced via the relationships between the concepts, moving from generalized concepts down to specific concepts. Present the easiest, most familiar organizing concepts first. Concept maps are useful organizing structures to visualize these relationships (Novak & Gowin, 1984). The psychological process at work while learning conceptual goals is moving these goals to long-term memory. Concept maps are examples of cognitive tools that help us encode and store conceptual relationships.

*Procedural goals.* These are "how" goals, which are sequenced on the steps required to complete the goal. Present the steps in the order they are performed. It is sometimes helpful to identify the simplest version of the procedure and use simplifying assumptions before introducing more complex versions of the procedure. Learning the procedure may be primarily a cognitive, thinking set of processes, although a procedural goal may involve psychomotor aspects.

*Principles.* Sequencing on principles addresses the "why" and moves from basic and observable principles to more detailed and complex ones. Psychologically, learning with principles is based on an understanding of cause and effect or historical development. In many instances all three of these are at work. An overall sequencing guideline for concepts, procedures, and principles is to group coordinate concepts together and teach a principle, or a meaningful understanding of processes, before a related procedure (Reigeluth & Stein, 1983).

**Sequencing on cognitive strategies**. Students possess different cognitive strategies, some of which are automatic. Helping students become aware of the strategies they use will further support other learning, such as the development of intellectual skills. Sequencing may range from the use of verbal reminders to explicit instruction on study skills strategies, such as the use semantic maps, **concept maps** or knowledge vee diagrams (Novak & Gowin, 1984). Instructional time may be required to introduce students to new strategies, along with guided practice and opportunities to test out these new skills. Sequencing on cognitive skills, because they transfer over a long period of time, may not reveal learning improvements in students in brief instructional activities, such as a lesson, session, or tutorial. **Cognitive strategies**, however, are not adopted wholesale and represent personalized learning characteristics of individual learners. Your sequencing and instructional efforts, however, can present to learners a wide range of appropriate strategies, ones which may be adopted or adapted as the learner sees fit.

**Key Words**
- Cognitive strategies
- Concept map

**Sequencing Principles Related by Learning Type (Gagné et al., 1992)**

| Learning Outcome | Major Sequencing Principles | Related Sequence Factors |
|---|---|---|
| Intellectual skills | Presentation of learning situation for each new skill should be preceded by prior mastery of subordinate skills. | Verbal information may be recalled or newly presented to provide elaboration of each skill and conditions of its use. |
| Cognitive strategies | Learning and problem-solving situations should involve recall of previously acquired, relevant intellectual skills. | Verbal information relevant to the new learning should be previously learned or presented in instructions. |
| Verbal information | For major subtopics, order of presentation is not important. New facts should be preceded by meaningful content. | Prior learning of necessary intellectual skills involved in reading, listening, etc. is usually assumed. |
| Attitudes | Establishment of respect for the source is an initial step. Choice situations should be preceded by mastery of any intellectual skills involved. | Verbal information relevant to choices should be previously learned or presented in instructions. |
| Motor skills | Provide intensive practice on partial skills of critical importance and practice on total skill. | First of all, learn the executive subroutine (rule). |

Tables adapted from PRINCIPLES OF INSTRUCTIONAL DESIGN, 4/E by Robert M. Gagné, Leslie J. Briggs, and Walter W. Wager, copyright © 1992 by Holt, Rinehart and Winston, Inc., reproduced by permission of the publisher.

**Sequencing on verbal information.** According to Gagné, Briggs, and Wager (1992), sequencing on verbal information differs somewhat based on whether the information is a name or label, individual facts, or organized information.

For learning *names* or *labels* the most important sequencing issues for learners is that they possess meaningful ways of encoding and storing information, which are themselves cognitive strategies. *Facts* require encoding based on their relationships to other pieces of knowledge and can be supported by (1) presenting general information first followed by more specific information (Ausubel, 1968), and (2) the use of questions or statements about particular facts before they are presented in some activity (Gagné, Briggs, & Wager, 1992). *Organized information* also benefits from encoding and personalized memory structures. Sequencing involves the structuring of information by the teacher in ways that facilitate learning, such as relating to the learner's prior information.

**Sequencing on the affective domain.** Aspects of the affective domain are inherent in most learning, particularly as supporting the learning of intellectual skills. Developing a positive attitude towards a skill, for example, is dependent on success in learning the skill. One way of establishing affective capabilities is to provide models of such capabilities by teachers or peers. Like cognitive strategies, development of aspects of this domain occur over time.

**Sequencing on motor skills.** Depending on the complexity of the skill, sequencing on psychomotor skills involves the mastery of a subskill followed by the executive skill which may incorporate all of these subskills. Later in this chapter we will discuss prerequisites, the skills needed before moving to a more complex skill.

# Sequencing for Flexible Understanding

The previous sequencing principle of simple-to-complex is appropriate if your goals call for the accruing of information and skills; however, if they are designed to help students gain a flexible understanding of subject matter then your sequencing will differ. McDiarmid, Ball and Anderson (1989) have outlined the characteristics of flexible understanding and what learning along this stance means for both students and teachers.

**Characteristics of Flexible Understandings for Students and Teachers**

| Characteristic ⬇ | Flexible Understanding for Students | Flexible Understanding for Teachers |
|---|---|---|
| Content | Understand fundamental concepts and draw relationships within subject. | Comprehend fundamental ideas and relationships of content. |
| Representations | Understand unique value of one's own representations and ownership of knowledge; basis for learner control. | Represent ideas, information, and procedures of content; relate to other disciplines; develop criteria for assessment; and acceptance of student representations. |
| Transferability | Make connections of content to the world. | Provide range of examples. |
| World View | Adopting a critical perspective based on understanding of heritage of knowledge construction over time. | Know how content knowledge is generated and verified. |
| Cognitive Strategy | Use individual strategies. | Instruct range of strategies; provide guided practice and time; and provide meaningful tasks. |
| Reflection | Engage in reflective activities. | Provide opportunities for reflection. |
| Sharing Control | Diverse knowledge, experiences, expectations, values. | Acknowledge student knowledge and experiences and values. |

Reprinted from McDiarmid, G. W., Ball, D. L., & Anderson, C. W. Why staying one chapter ahead doesn't really work: Subject-specific pedagogy. In M. C. Reynolds (Ed.), *Knowledge Base for the Beginning Teacher*, Copyright © 1989, pp. 193-205, with kind permission from Elsevier Science Ltd, The Boulevard, Langford Lane, Kidlington OX5 1GB, U.K.

**Characteristics of flexible understanding.** To address sequencing for flexible understanding, it is essential that teachers know what their student's know and help learners to build upon their representations. Teacher representations, the basis for traditional instruction, may not be appropriate for learners, either due to their developmental level, prior experiences, relevance, or lack of exposure to teacher-developed strategies. Teachers will need to develop criteria to assess student representations for conceptual accuracy. In terms of content both students and teacher must have an understanding of a subject's fundamental concepts and be able to draw relationships between concepts. According to Ball (cited in McDiarmid et al., 1989), appropriate representations are:

## Criteria for Suitable Representations

1. Those that correctly and appropriately represent the substance and nature of the content.
2. Comprehensible to the student.
3. Helpful to learning.
4. Reasonable and appropriate considering the context.

From McDiarmid, G. W., Ball, D. L., & Anderson, C. W. (1989). Why staying one chapter ahead doesn't really work: Subject-specific pedagogy. In M. C. Reynolds (Ed.), *Knowledge base for the beginning teacher* (193-205). NY: Pergamon.

## Food for Thought

**Interactions as a sequencing issue.** The nature of the interactions between teachers and students contains implications for the structuring and sequencing of new information.

- Interactions require that both teachers and students attend to what each is saying and that teachers offer appropriate responses to student performance on tasks and what students say about the task. These interactions take time, whether or not this responsiveness is carried out on a one-on-one basis or during a class session.

- Interaction patterns provide ways of discussing content with students and affect how one structures content in meaningful ways for learners. It becomes essential to know when to provide verbal guidance or introduce appropriately structured and sequenced materials

♦ See in **References** Rowe, 1974; Cazden, 1986; and Doyle, 1986).

Being able to match the content to other problems is another characteristic of flexible understanding. Teachers can assist students by providing meaningful examples. Teachers who teach for flexible understanding must also know how content knowledge is generated and verified, so that they understand more about the discipline itself, as well as providing students with opportunities to make use of the information. In this teaching of a world view students come to adopt a critical perspective based partly on their understanding of the heritage of knowledge construction as well as its context.

The teaching of cognitive strategies is another feature of flexible understanding. However, such instruction requires that teachers provide a range of strategies for different learning styles, and provide guided practice and time with meaningful tasks that are related to the subject they are taking. Another issue to consider is deciding when to introduce these techniques.

Yet another characteristic of flexible understanding is students engaging in reflective activities to develop comparing-and-contrasting skills, thought, and decision making, all of which contribute to unique ideas and problem-solving responses (Norman, 1993). To achieve this teachers need to provide opportunities for reflective activities, both in and out of the classroom. However, these activities take time and assistance from the instructor. Sequencing issues include how reflectivity supports goals and when such activities should be introduced and developed.

As was mentioned earlier, teaching from a stance of promoting flexible understanding requires that the instructor be willing to acknowledge students' beliefs and experiences and view the content from a student's point of view; essentially, to share control.

## Talking about Media

**Sequencing hypermedia.** Hypermedia challenges traditional notions about sequencing. If you are thinking about using hypermedia in your "lessons," think about the sequencing issues. Hypermedia is a set of computer-controlled, non-linear links between nodes of information. This information is contained in various forms of media representations, such as text, graphics, video, audio, simulations, or animations. Because of this non-linear feature, the learning environment is exploratory and interactive, and sequencing is based on the control of the user. Users choose what they want to see or hear in the time they want it. The sequence between information may or may not be fixed, depending on how much control is given to the users within the product. The time spent at each information node or which nodes are accessed varies between users (Thompson, Simonson, & Hargrave, 1992). Some hypermedia designing issues include the following:

• How much of the learning paths should one design?

• Should users be allowed to choose their own paths or a portion of these paths? Hypermedia programs that adapt to one's learning needs have been found to be superior to those that give the user total control (Tennyson, Christensen & Parks, 1984).

• What type of strategies are needed to instruct learners how to learn from hypermedia?

• Learners have been found to become lost in hypermedia programs without some structure, such as a comprehensive index (Marchionini, 1988), a map (Heller, 1990), or navigational tools (Morariu, 1988).

## ☆ SCENARIO

## Health Care: Patient-Centered Instruction

Lakeside Health Systems is moving towards providing services outside of the traditional hospital and clinic and sending health care workers out to the community. As a result, health care providers will be placed in new roles that are quite different than those they followed in a traditional hospital setting.

♦ See in **References**, Manning, Curtis & McMillen (1996) on building work communities.

One of the supporting principles identified in the first Scenario in Chapter 1 was "continuous improvement in services and ongoing training and evaluation of our staff." To support this principle Lakeside is thinking of developing ways to provide "high quality, cost effective health care" for patients in the community.

New services include preventive education for families in areas of nutrition, pre-natal care, immunizations, annual checkups, exercise, and in-home diagnosis of common ailments. Questions raised on providing this "patient-centered instruction" include the following:

**Content:** What are the top priority topics that we should address?

**Learners:** What is the range of cultures and families in the service area so that we begin to understand the community? (a learner profile)

**Context:** What can we learn from other institutions and communities?

Identifying the priorities to content, knowing more about your participants, and exploring the realities of the learning context suggests ways to structure and sequence this information.

Now, let's sequence your content.

# DESIGN ACTIVITY 13

## "Content/Lesson Outline"

**1.** List the content in whatever order makes sense to you and that is appropriate to the topic or subject of your project.

**2.** Examine your goals and learning types drawn up from **Design Activity 12** and sketch a first attempt to organize the content based on your overall goals.

• Label each part of the sequence with conceptual titles or other ways to help communicate what you mean to do with each part.

• Identify steps or objectives that you believe are necessary in order to achieve the goals.

**3.** What is the rationale behind your sequencing plan?

• Does your sequencing plan resonate with what you wrote in your mission statement?

Now that you have a clearer idea of the nature of your content, you may come across aspects of the content that are critical to the learning you have expressed in your goals. Some of these critical learning tasks may need further analysis.

This can be accomplished through a design tool known as **learning task analysis**.

# Analysis of a Learning Task

The needs assessment confirms that your idea is an instructional problem and gives you data to list a set of goals to address the problem. Now you need to know what a learner should know or be able to do after "instruction." You also need to translate these goals into objectives that describe what learners should know or be able to do and the required knowledge and skills needed to achieve these objectives. **Learning task analysis** is the process that provides this information. It consists of four major steps:

> **Steps for a Learning Task Analysis**
>
> **Step 1:** Determine a target objective.
>
> **Step 2:** Conduct an analysis of the learning task.
>
> **Step 3:** Write performance objectives.
>
> **Step 4:** Analyze the requirements that instruction will have to address to meet the performance objectives.

**1. Determine a target objective.** What is it that you want students to know or do at the end of a lesson or task? Determining this **target objective** is the first step in conducting a learning task analysis. These target objectives are operational statements that clearly communicate what students need to know or do (Mager, 1975). Target objectives support the broad goals you have established from the needs assessment.

**Key Words**
- Learning task analysis
- Target objective

## 1. Determine a Target Objective

- Write your list of goals established from the needs assessment.
- Write a target objective that supports the above goals. Ask yourself: "What is it that you want students to do as a result of a unit or lesson?"
- Determine the types of learning (from the various learning taxonomies) that apply to your target objective.

Use the learning taxonomies to determine the types of learning that apply to your target objective. Knowing the learning types from these taxonomies will help you to unlock the types of learning (i.e., the complexity) that the target objective may contain. Knowing this information is helpful to the designer who can then more carefully design appropriate instructional activities that address each learning level.

**2. Conduct an analysis of the learning task.** This step involves breaking down the task into subtasks. List the steps in the order it takes to do them or think them through, and the required skills or thinking that would be necessary to master the task. Actually doing the task can help to reveal the performance that is needed. A combination of physical and mental steps may be appropriate for some tasks. Think also about the content knowledge needed to perform the task, as well as any affective or social requirements.

## 2. Conduct the Task Analysis

- List procedural steps, knowledge, and skills needed.
- List mental steps and skills needed.
- Determine the essential and supporting prerequisites and the learning type for each.

There is no one way to record a task analysis as the situation is likely to determine the procedure (Seels & Glasgow, 1990). Here is a list of other ways:

---

### Documenting Task Analysis

• For motor tasks and procedural tasks flowcharts can be used to document the process and to create a set of instructions or procedures to perform a task.

• For mental operations an information processing analysis identifies the cognitive requirements in each step. This consists of listing the mental steps that one uses to perform a skill. Conducting **think-alouds** is a way of supporting this.

• Tables are useful to document the tasks involved in higher level skills, such as problem solving, rule learning, and concept learning.

• For verbal information outlines are common data gathering formats.

• Attitudes use any format that documents the behavior and demonstrates that an attitude is learned.

---

In many lessons it may be necessary that some knowledge and skills be acquired before new learning can take place. After identifying the procedural and mental steps, outline these prior learning requirements by identifying essential prerequisites and supporting prerequisites (Gagné et al., 1992).

**Essential prerequisites** are skills that *must* be mastered in order to learn the new material or the desired objective. These skills may include understanding of concepts, procedures, and principles. **Supporting prerequisites** are useful to learning, but not absolutely essential. These conditions may make learning easier or faster; for example, a willingness to learn and attending to new material that relates to one's previous experiences can enhance the learning. Examples of essential and supportive prerequisites for the various learning levels are on the next page:

**Key Words**
- Essential prerequisites
- Supporting prerequisites
- Think-alouds

**Learning Levels & Learning Prerequisites (Aronson & Briggs, 1983)**

| Learning Level | Essential Prerequisites | Supporting Prerequisites |
|---|---|---|
| Intellectual skill | Rules, concepts, discriminations | Attitudes<br>Cognitive strategies<br>Verbal information |
| Verbal information | Structured information | Language skills<br>Cognitive strategies<br>Attitudes |
| Cognitive strategies | Specific intellectual skills | Intellectual skills<br>Verbal information<br>Attitudes |
| Attitudes | Intellectual skills and verbal information (sometimes) | Other attitudes<br>Verbal information |
| Motor skills | Part skills (sometimes) | Attitudes |

From Aronson, D. J., & Briggs, L. J. (1983). Contributions of Gagné and Briggs to a prescriptive model of instruction. In C. M. Reigeluth, (Ed.) *Instructional design theories and models: An overview of their current status* (75-100). Reprinted with permission of Lawrence Erlbaum Associates, Inc.

**3. Write performance objectives.** Knowing the steps, or subskills that make up the target skill, allows a designer to write **performance objectives**, statements that explicitly describe what the student needs to be able to do. Performance objectives need to be observable, measurable, and specify a level of performance. This detailed articulation guides you in the development of learning activities and serves as a basis for ongoing or final assessment by the instructor. The purpose of performance objectives is to clearly spell out what you want learners to learn from instruction (Smith & Ragan, 1993).

**3. Write Performance Objectives**

- Write performance objectives for each of the prerequisite skills.

**4. Analyze instructional requirements for learning.** Now it is time to take the above information and specify the *learning requirements* for each of these performance objectives. In other words, what does the instructor need to know in order to facilitate the learning of these performance objectives? This step is sometimes referred to as **instructional analysis** (Seels & Glasgow, 1990). The issues raised in this step include the following:

---

### Instructional Requirements for Learning

1. What are the predictable learning and performance difficulties?

2. What are the consequences of not learning the skill?

3. How frequently will the skill be used?

4. How immediate is the performance?

5. Is any assistance required to learn the skill?

6. What do instructors need to learn to make this happen?

7. How much time is needed to learn the skill?

8. What is the decay rate of the skill?

From EXERCISES IN INSTRUCTIONAL DESIGN by Seels/Glasgow, © 1990. Adaptaed by permission of Prentice-Hall, Inc., Upper Saddle River, NJ.

---

Analysis of the learning requirements also helps to (1) point out tasks that are not instructional problems and can be left out of your design, and (2) specify what subtasks of the task you want students to know going in to each lesson: what behaviors, what knowledge, what attitudes, and what motor skills. Determining these entry levels tells you at what level of learning you need to design activities and instruction for.

**Key Words**
• Instructional analysis

---

### 4. Analyze Instructional Requirements

- Examine the instructional realities that affect your performance objectives.
- Determine if some tasks should be excluded from instruction.
- Determine the entry requirements.

---

Determining the entry level for instruction reduces the problem of mismatching the level of instruction for your audience. The information from a learning task analysis, consisting of how should a task be done and the learning requirements, may suggest an ordering of lessons and improve your lesson sequence.

**Summary.** A learning task analysis determines (1) how a student should perform a task after instruction and the (2) instructional requirements of the task. Conducting a task analysis examines a skill closely so that you can sequence teachable subskills and identify related physical and affective aspects.

This analysis also is useful for instructional designs with flexible understanding goals by determining what experts know and how they represent what they know. These representations are restructured by teachers with versions that match their students' learning levels and that may feature different contexts.

> Identify a key task in your project and apply it to a learning task analysis.
>
> ↓

Check out Tour 4: The Director, in "Touring Instructional Design."

# DESIGN ACTIVITY 14

## "Learning Task Analysis of a Key Task"

**1. Select a key task within your project.**

**2. Identify the target objective.** What type of learning task is it?

**3. Specify the steps or thinking procedure needed to complete the task.** Identify the essential prerequisites and supporting prerequisites for each step.

**4. Write performance objectives for each step.** Describe what is to be done and the level of learning performance.

**5. Analyze the instructional requirements for this task.**

 **Task Description**

You will appreciate the value of a task analysis once you actually do one, particularly if that task or skill is a critical one in your instructional design.

A key task is one in which learning cannot proceed without its mastery or one in which a lesson or activity hinges. Ask yourself the question: "If I eliminated this task, what would happen?"

## Instructional Requirements

1. Learning-performance difficulties

2. Consequences of not learning the skill

3. Frequency of skill use

4. Immediacy of performance

5. Learning assistance

6. Teacher-learning needs

7. Time requirements

8. Decay rate

From EXERCISES IN INSTRUCTIONAL DESIGN BY Seels/Glasgow, © 1990. Adapted by permission of Prentice-Hall, Inc., Upper Saddle River, NJ.

# Reviewing the Design Activities

---

**Design Activity 12: Matching Learning Goals with Learning Types**

☐ Identified and matched up goals from the needs assessment with appropriate learning types.

**Design Activity 13: Content/ Lesson Outline**

☐ Sequenced content outline.
☐ Labeled sequence pieces with learning goals.

**Design Activity 14: Learning Task Analysis of a Key Task**

☐ Conducted a task analysis of a key task or skill.
☐ Conducted an instructional analysis providing details on the requirements of the learner within the lesson or activity.

# ⚑ Summary of Important Ideas

---

**1.** Understanding learning types via taxonomies helps to sequence content.

**2.** Simple-to-complex sequencing is appropriate for ordering concepts, procedures, and principles.

**3.** Sequencing for flexible understanding requires attention from both teacher and student to content, representations, transferability, world views, cognitive strategies, reflection, and mutual sharing of control.

**4.** Learning task analysis is a procedural design tool that examines what is necessary to learn something, thus providing insight on designing learning activities.

# √ Your Personal Learning

## *Relating Your Beliefs to This Chapter:*

Sequencing "content" is based on a rationale that you must choose. What rationale have you used in the past? Being aware of this choice allows you to sequence appropriately, saving you time in the long run, particularly when you begin to design learning activities.

## *Any revisions to your personal ID model?*

- Did you make any provisions for sequencing in your first ID model?

- How do you view sequencing in the context of this project?

- How will you represent it within your model?

## *What questions do you have about the information presented in this chapter?*

# References

Aronson, D. J., & Briggs, L. J. (1983). Contributions of Gagné and Briggs to a prescriptive model of instruction. In C. M. Reigeluth (Ed.), *Instructional design theories and models: An overview of their current status* (75-100). Hillsdale, NJ: Erlbaum.

Ausubel, D. P. (1968). *Educational psychology: A cognitive view.* NY: Holt, Rinehart & Winston.

Bloom, B. S. (Ed.) (1956). *Taxonomy of educational objectives: Handbook I: Cognitive domain.* NY: McKay.

Brophy, J., & Good, T. (1986). Teacher behavior and student achievement. In M. C. Wittrock (Ed.), *Handbook of research on teaching* (3rd ed., 328-375). NY: Macmillan.

Cazden, C. B. (1986). Classroom discourse. In M. C. Wittrock (Ed.), *Handbook of research on teaching* (3rd ed., 432-463). NY: Macmillan.

Doyle, W. (1986). Classroom organization and management. In M. C. Wittrock (Ed.), *Handbook of research on teaching* (3rd ed., 392-431). NY: Macmillan.

Gagné, R. M., Briggs, L. J., & Wager, W. W. (1992). *Principles of instructional design* (4th ed.). Fort Worth, TX: Harcourt Brace Jovanovich.

Harrow, A. J. (1972). *A taxonomy of the psychomotor domain.* NY: McKay.

Heller, R. S. (1990). The role of hypermedia in education: A look at the research issues. *Journal of Research on Computing in Education*, 431-441.

Kemp, J. E. (1977). *Instructional design: A plan for unit and course development* (2nd ed.). Belmont, CA: Fearon-Pitman.

Kline, S. J. (1995). *Conceptual foundations for multidisciplinary thinking.* Stanford, CA: Stanford University Press.

Krathwohl, D. R., Bloom, B. S., & Masia, B. B. (1964). *Taxonomy of educational objectives: Handbook II: Affective domain.* NY: McKay.

Mager, R. F. (1975). *Preparing objectives for instruction* (2nd ed.). Belmont, CA: Fearon.

Manning, G., Curtis, K., & McMillen, S. (1996). *Building community: The human side of work.* Cincinnati, OH: Thompson Executive Press.

Marchionini, G. (1988). Hypermedia and learning: Freedom and chaos. *Educational Technology, 28*(11), 8-12.

Maslow, A. (1970). *Motivation and personality* (2nd ed.). NY: Harper & Row.

McDiarmid, G. W., Ball, D. L., & Anderson, C. W. (1989). Why staying one chapter ahead doesn't really work: Subject-specific pedagogy. In M. C. Reynolds (Ed.), *Knowledge base for the beginning teacher* (193-205). NY: Pergamon.

Medawar, P. (1977). Biosystematics. In A. Bullock and O. Stallybrass (Eds.), *Harper Dictionary of Modern Thought.* NY: Harper & Row, 64-65.

Morariu, J. (1988). Hypermedia in instruction and training: The power and the promise. *Educational Technology*, 17-20.

Norman, D. A. (1993). *Things that make us smart: Defending human attributes in the age of the machine.* Reading, MA: Addison-Wesley.

Novak, J. D., & Gowin, D. B. (1984). *Learning how to learn.* NY: Cambridge University Press.

Reigeluth, C. M., & Stein, F. S. (1987). The elaboration theory of instruction. In C. M. Reigeluth (Ed.), *Instructional theories in action: Lessons illustrating selected theories and models* (335-381). Hillsdale, NJ: Erlbaum.

Rowe, M. B. (1974). Wait time—is anybody listening? *Journal of Psycholinguistic Research, 3*, 203-224; and *Journal of Research in Science Teaching, 11*, 81-94.

Schön, D. (1987). *Educating the reflective practitioner.* San Francisco: Jossey-Bass.

Seels, B. & Glasgow, Z. (1990). *Exercises in instructional design.* Columbus, OH: Merrill.

Simon, H. A. (1981). *The sciences of the artificial* (2nd ed.). Cambridge: MIT Press.

Smith, P. L., & Ragan, T. J. (1993). *Instructional design.* NY: Merrill.

Tennyson, R., Christensen, D., & Park, S. (1984). The Minnesota adaptive instructional system: An intelligent CBI system. *Journal of Computer-Based Instruction, 11*(1), 2-13.

Thompson, A. D., Simonson, M. R., & Hargrave, C. P. (1992). *Educational technology: A review of the research.* Washington, D. C.: Association for Educational Communications and Technology.

# For Further Reading ...

Ausubel, D. P. (1968). *Educational psychology: A cognitive view.* NY: Holt, Rinehart & Winston.

> This book addresses a general-to-detailed sequencing, or "subsumptive" sequencing, of concepts, in which instruction begins with general knowledge that "subsumes" the content that follows. Meaningful assimilation of concepts to memory and the advance organizer, another example of a simple-to-complex sequencing scheme, are discussed in this book.

Bruner, J. S. (1960). *The process of education.* Cambridge, MA: Harvard University Press.

> Source of Bruner's "spiral curriculum" with implications for the sequencing of principles.

# What's Next?

In Chapter 5 we will present an overview of assessment possibilities. Note in the visual below that designing requires periodic re-visiting and updating.

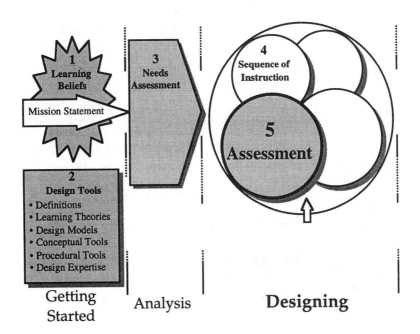

# CHAPTER 5

**H**ow will you know if your learners are learning anything?

**A**ddressing assessment issues holds your design accountable to learners, content, and context.

# Assessment

*The concept of assessment is new in American educational discourse. It represents an effort to develop fresh ways of thinking about what has been historically regarded as "evaluation."*

(Eisner, 1994, p. vi)

Assessment is where the rubber meets the road. An understanding of the task requirements through learning task analysis discussed in Chapter 4 provides data to answer the question: *What must learners do to achieve the objectives established for them or that the learners have established for themselves?* In this chapter we will look at three ways to look at assessments and profile common assessment tools and the issues you confront in selecting and using them.

In this chapter you will:

1. Determine the purpose(s) for assessment in the context of your project.

2. Determine the assessment tools for your sequence of instruction.

3. Summarize your assessment plan.

# What Is Meant by Assessment?

**Definitions.** First, let's provide some definitions to get started. **Assessment** deals with ways to determine what changes have taken place in instructional programs, instructor performance, and learner performance as a result of instruction yielding information that may be used for evaluative purposes. Our emphasis in this chapter will be on the assessment of learner performance. **Evaluation** uses assessment information and makes judgments and decisions about learners. **Program Evaluation**, the subject of Chapter 9, is a set of design tools that appraises the success of an instructional program and to what extent your instructional design contributed to that success.

**as·sess** (e-sès) *verb, transitive*
**as·sessed, as·sess·ing, as·sess·es**
1. To estimate the value of (property) for taxation.
2. To set or determine the amount of (a payment, such as a tax or fine).
3. To charge (a person or property) with a special payment, such as a tax or fine.
4. **To determine the value, significance, or extent of; appraise. See synonyms at ESTIMATE.**

[Middle English *assessen*, from Old French *assesser*, from Latin *assidêre*, *assess-*, to sit by as an assistant judge : *ad-*, ad- + *sedêre*, to sit.]

*The American Heritage Dictionary of the English Language* . (1992). Houghton Mifflin, p. 79.

---

### Operational Definitions

#### Assessment
*Determine changes in learner performance.*

#### Evaluation
*Make judgments and decisions about learners.*

#### Program Evaluation
*Appraise the success of your program.*

---

We address assessment before an instructional strategy, because one needs to determine the purpose and nature of assessment *before* one proposes an instructional method to facilitate the desired learning.

**Key Words**
- Assessment
- Evaluation
- Program evaluation

Now, stop and think about the purpose(s) for assessment in your design project.

# DESIGN ACTIVITY 15

## "Your Assessment Purpose(s)"

 **Task Description**

The purpose of this activity is to think through and record what you want assessment to accomplish in your project.

**1.** Identify and describe the purposes of assessment within the context of your project.

In the following section we will take a look at three ways to organize or classify assessments.

There are numerous functions to assessment. In this book we offer three ways of categorizing them: (1) Gronlund and Linn's classification, (2) level of inference, and (3) process or product.

**1. Gronlund & Linn's Classification.** According to Gronlund and Linn (1994), there are three ways to classify classroom assessment methods: (1) by nature of measurement, (2) how it is used in the classroom, and (3) how results are interpreted. The chart below visually demonstrates that assessment methods are useful based on the purposes they serve.

Classification as a
Conceptual Tool

## Classification of Assessment Types & Purposes (Gronlund & Linn, 1994)

| Classification Basis | Assessment Type | Purpose of Assessment | Examples |
|---|---|---|---|
| Nature of Measurement | *Maximum Performance* | Find out what learners can do when performing at their best. | Aptitude tests Achievement tests |
| | *Typical Performance* | Find out what learners can do under natural conditions. | Attitude, interest, and personality inventories; observational techniques; peer appraisal |
| Use in Classroom Instruction | *Placement* | Find out prerequisite skills, degree of mastery, and the best mode of learning. | Readiness tests, aptitude tests, pretests, self-report questions, observations |
| | *Formative* | Find out the learning progress. What's needed to reinforce learning? Correct learning errors. | Teacher-made tests, ready-made tests, observations |
| | *Diagnostic* | Find out causes of learning difficulties. | Published diagnostic tests, teacher-made diagnostic tests, observations |
| | *Summative* | Determine rationale for assigning grades or certifying mastery of objectives. | Teacher-made survey tests, performance rating scales, product scales |
| Method of Interpreting Results | *Criterion-referenced* | Assesses learner according to pre-determined task level. | Teacher-made tests, tests from publishers, observations |
| | *Norm-referenced* | Assesses learner according to relative position in a group. | Standardized aptitude and achievement tests, teacher-made survey test, interest inventories, adjustment inventories |

From MEASUREMENT AND EVALUATION IN TEACHING, 6/E by Gronlund © 1985. Adapted by permission of Prentice-Hall, Inc., Upper Saddle River, NJ.

One way to look at an assessment is whether it determines one's best performance or one's typical performance. Aptitude and achievement tests are used to assess maximum performance when learners are performing at their best. An **aptitude test** attempts to measure one's learning ability in the future, while **achievement tests** measure what one already knows. Typical performance, meanwhile, is what one will do under normal conditions. A range of methods are needed here as the use of attitude, interest, personality inventories, observations, and peer appraisal methods alone cannot accurately determine typical performance (Gronlund, 1981).

A second way to look at assessments, according to Gronlund and Linn (1994), is the way they are used in the classroom. Assessments for placement purposes prior to instruction help to identify prerequisite knowledge and skills, mastery of content, or some evidence that demonstrates a student's placement in a particular instructional setting, such as small groups or individual work. Assessments for placement include tests of readiness, aptitude tests, pretesting, and observations by teachers or guidance counselors. Teacher-made tests frequently assess student learning during instruction, while existing diagnostic tests and careful observations provide the basis for determining learning difficulties. Final measurements of student learning include teacher-made tests and results from performance activities (e.g., hands-on projects and lab work) and from products (e.g., portfolios, essays, and demonstrations).

A third way that Gronlund and Linn (1994) look at assessment is the way in which the results of assessments are interpreted. This can be accomplished either through **criterion-referenced** assessment, in which learning performance is based on mastery of subject matter identified by criteria, or **norm-referenced** assessments, which are designed to rank students based on some outside group. In both cases the group being measured and the comparison group

**Key Words**
- Achievement tests
- Aptitude tests
- Criterion-referenced
- Norm-referenced

need to be specified. Criterion-referenced assessments include any method where criteria for performance have been identified, while norm-referenced assessments are usually standardized aptitude and achievement tests.

**2. Level of inference.** Another way of looking at assessment methods is the level of inference that is required when scoring them. Once you determine your instructional purpose then you can select tasks that will help you to infer how well students achieve this purpose. Assessment tasks provide the data needed to make inferences about learner performance. The teacher must make a judgment about the degree to which one must make, what Popham (1995) calls an "inferential leap." The level of inference is how much judgment or variance is inherent in the scoring or rating process. Assessment methods have a level of inference, which ranges from low to high. Assessment methods vary in the amount of inference required to match judgments about performance. Inference within any method varies based on how specific the designer or evaluator has identified what quality performance is like, and how valuable each element of the performance is related to the whole score or judgment.

A low-inference assessment method requires you to make only a low amount of inference about a learner's performance. If you were assessing whether or not a student could bend glass tubing in a chemistry class, then a combination of observation and the finished product would clearly reveal whether a student's performance was acceptable. Specific criteria for the behavior could be identified and measured. The teacher would require very little inferencing to make this judgment.

On the other hand, a high level inference assessment method requires a greater amount of judgment—a greater leap—to draw conclusions about the extent of achieving the desired learning performance. Measurement of critical thinking, for example, requires a high level of inferencing, because

### Process Assessments

- Oral exams
- Interviews
- Observations
- Journals and logs
- Self-assessment
- Behavioral checklists

### Product Assessments

- Portfolios
- Essays
- Reports
- Projects
- Deliverables
- Formal performances
- Self-assessment
- Demonstrations
- Expositions
- Constructed response
  questions
- Aptitude tests
- Achievement tests

Adapted from Herman, J. L., Aschbacher, P. R., & Winters, L. The National Center for Research on Evaluation, Standards and Student Testing (CRESST). *A Practical Guide to Alternative Assessment.* Alexandria, VA: ASCD. Copyright © 1992 by The Regents of the University of California and currently supported under the Office of Educational Research and Improvement (OERI), U.S. Department of Education.

### Key Words
- Process assessment
- Product assessment

of the complexity of the learning and the multiple learning levels (e.g., cognitive, verbal, and affective) addressed.

**3. Process and product assessments.** Yet a third way to examine assessments for learner performance is by examining the form of the assessment—an assessment process, an assessment product, or both. **Process assessment** is a method which examines performance over time. This provides students and teachers with information on how they are performing. A **product assessment** reveals learning in a summarizable form, such as a science fair project, a folder of writing samples, an essay examination, or objectives tests. The product can be an actual performance, such as a persuasive speech, demonstration, simulation, acting out of a drama, or reading a story.

Although it is convenient to list assessments as a process or product, it is frequently the case that one can be both. Self-assessment, for example, can occur as a process of assessing one's own learning over time, but it can also assume a product form when the self-assessment is transformed into a written self-evaluation, a journal, or a log that is handed in. To ensure the effectiveness of these assessments, their purpose in the overall assessment plan must be identified along with measurable criteria to judge the quality of the performance.

> Now, let's examine more closely the assessment of learner performance.

# Learner Performance

This chapter examines assessment of learner performance. In the context of instructional design, this assessment function determines what changes have occurred in students and teachers as a result of instruction. Before we profile a number of assessment tools, you need to decide what it is that you are assessing. What information do you need to determine learner performance?

**What should you assess?** One way to answer this question is to look carefully at the broad goals you established during your needs assessment, as well as the supporting objectives behind the activities in your sequence of instruction. If you are faced with implementing your design project in a few months, you might develop many precisely-worded objectives, which may create an unwieldy design, one that is difficult to implement. According to Popham (1995), "the trick in conceptualizing instructional objectives that help rather than hinder is to frame those objectives broadly enough so that the objectives are still measurable" (p. 80). Having a manageable number of "broad yet measurable objectives" will motivate you rather than demoralize you as you move forward to construct useful and achievable assessment tasks.

Another way to decide what to assess is to examine your goals and objectives for the level of learning (see **Design Activity 12**). These goals and objectives may be learning within the **cognitive, affective, psychomotor domains**, or some mix of these as revealed by the learning taxonomies introduced in Chapter 4. When we asked you to identify learning levels for each of your goals, we were also giving you a means to determine appropriate assessment tools.

*My favorite gunky instructional objective of that era [1960's and 1970's] was one I ran across in a state-level language arts syllabus:* "The student will learn to relish literature." *After that time I keep on the lookout for an objective such as* "The student will mayonnaise mathematics." *I haven't encountered one —yet.*

(Popham, 1995, p. 79)

∞

**Key Words**
- Affective domain
- Cognitive domain
- Psychomotor domain

Bloom and others who constructed the learning taxonomies also suggested "illustrative verbs" which could help to construct assessment tasks. For example, if one of your objectives to a learning activity is to synthesize information to solve a problem, then consulting Bloom's (1956) suggestions of appropriate activities and illustrative verbs for synthesis objectives may prove helpful:

---

### Activities & Illustrative Verbs for "Synthesis"

| Suggested Activities | Illustrative Verbs |
| --- | --- |
| Write organized theme | Categorizes, combines, |
| Propose a plan | compiles, creates, devises, |
| Integrate learning from | designs, organizes, plans, |
| different areas | rearranges, reconstructs, |
| Formulate a scheme for | relates, reorganizes, revises, |
| classifying objects | rewrites, summarizes, tells, |
| | writes |

Bloom, B. S. (1956). *Taxonomy of educational objectives: Handbook I: Cognitive domain.* NY: McKay.

---

These illustrative verbs can be used as "indicators" in your assessment plan as you devise ways of scoring or evaluating your assessment tasks.

In the previous chapter we discussed sequencing issues for knowledge learning and learning for flexible understanding. If the focus of your goals and objectives is knowledge, the recall of previously learned material (and the lowest level of the cognitive domain) is your primary concern, and assessment tools need only match this instructional purpose. If, however, your intent is at the higher cognitive levels, then your assessment purpose is to evaluate **intellectual skills**. Examining the nature of the intellectual tasks through **task analysis** of key tasks, what experts know, as well as what you know from previous experiences, can help you to search for appropriate ways to measure whether these intellectual skills have been learned.

**Key Words**
- Intellectual skills
- Task analysis

**Flexible understanding**, as discussed in Chapter 4, addresses the learning needs of both students and teachers. Activities and assessment for designs that focus on these learning goals need to be constructed so that learners have opportunities to reveal these capabilities. A portion of an assessment plan may consist of an ongoing assessment in which you are looking for the development of these flexible understanding characteristics.

Below we profile some assessment tools.

# Assessment Possibilities

For most assessment purposes, there is no single right answer. Here, the evaluation system must be flexible to accommodate this stance.

Assessment possibilities can be divided into two types: asking your learners to choose from among choices or to provide their own responses. These two options are **selected response assessments** and **constructed response assessments**.

**Selected response assessment.** Selected response assessment methods require that students select from a choice of answers. Common examples of these include multiple choice, matching, and true-false questions. These assessments can be used to determine a student's mastery of a large body of content, and with careful construction, can be useful to assess a wide range of cognitive capabilities (Popham, 1995).

♦ See Popham, 1995, in **References** for a discussion of the issues involved in using these assessments as well as ways to construct them.

**Key Words**
- Constructed response assessment
- Selected response assessment

---

### Selected Response Assessments

- Multiple choice

- Matching

- True-False

---

The obvious advantage to selected response assessments is the ease with which they can be scored, so they are frequently used in situations with a large number of learners must be taught and/or when there is little time for scoring. Another advantage is that an adequate number of questions can be asked to assess a large amount of skills and knowledge. This reduces any success from merely guessing. The major disadvantage is that the student must make a choice rather than produce their own answer.

**Multiple choice.** One of the strongest selected response assessments is multiple choice, because one can construct selection options, or alternatives, that vary in their correctness, as compared with matching and true-false. Two ways in which multiple choice items are constructed are through a direct question or an incomplete sentence. Students are asked to select the correct answer or the best answer.

**Matching.** Matching assessments consists of two lists with the student attempting to match items from one list to another depending on the operating premise described in the assessment's directions. Items in each list are similar or homogeneous to each other, so that items in the first column, for example, are all dates, while items in the second column are all historical events. Matching items are frequently used in conjunction with other assessment options.

**True-False.** True-false assessments measure a student's ability to discern right-wrong answers. Increasing the number of items reduces the likelihood that guessing will produce a large number of correct answers. True-false questions require a short time to answer, so they can be used to cover a lot of content. Constructing them requires that they not be worded so that they are obviously true or false.

**Constructed response assessment.** While selected response tests require that students select responses, constructed response tests are ones, such as short answer and essay, that ask the student to supply or construct an answer. Such questions may have one right answer, such as a "fill-in-the-blank" question or more open-ended, such as an essay, where a range of responses may be correct based on some criteria; thus, the inference level can vary across these type of tests.

If you are looking for the learner to produce a correct answer to a question, then constructed response tests are the choice. They become more difficult to score as the response lengthens, such as short answer and essay. A **rubric** that specifies criteria for an acceptable response must be constructed to ensure scoring reliability. The trade-off here is scoring accuracy versus a better match between the assessment method and the desired skills.

---

### Constructed Response Assessments

- Short Answer and Essays
- Portfolios
- Projects
- Interviews
- Self Assessment

---

**Short answer and essays.** These are constructed-response assessments that attempt to assess understanding through writing by describing, analyzing, explaining, and summarizing (Gronlund, 1982). In fact, essays can be used to assess learning at all levels of Bloom's (1956) cognitive taxonomy. Essays can also be used to assess understanding,

**Food for Thought**

Traditionally, assessment has been viewed as testing, with tests being the principal way that students are evaluated. Wiggins (1989, May) recommends that we not shy away from "testing,"—the test is central to instruction—but that we must carefully decide on what is a true test of learning.

- What is the *purpose* behind this true test? Determining the true test depends on what it is that your students need to know and do or what they themselves determine they need to know or do.

- *Task analysis* can provide an understanding of how a task needs to be performed at a particular competency or performance level. By examining how experts and practitioners perform tasks in practical settings, an assessment method can be chosen or designed that reveals student achievement on knowledge and skills and also "reveals actual challenges and standards of the field" (Wiggins, 1989, May, p. 704).

Thus, testing, along with other forms, can be viewed as "techniques serving assessment. . . . Tests may contribute to the [assessment] program, but they should not define it" (Chittenden, 1990, p. 24).

**Key Words**
- Rubric

communication, and self-reflection skills. In addition to Bloom's cognitive skills, essays help to assess how one organizes responses and communicates them to an intended audience. The subskills of composition are also criteria for assessment. These include spelling, syntax, grammar, and sentence and paragraph structure, as well as mastering various essay forms, such as informative or persuasive essays.

Essays can be used to record and examine one's affective dimensions, such as being open to new views, responding to needs, valuing one's own ideas and the ideas of others, and being able to resolve conflicts of inner speech and transforming the results into writing. Good items for essays can be difficult to prepare and their scoring is subjective, difficult, and less reliable than objective tests (Gronlund, 1982).

**Portfolios.** According to Arter and Spandel (1992), portfolios are "a purposeful collection of student work that tells the story of the student's efforts, progress, or achievement in an area" (p. 36). The portfolio is a record of a student's accomplishments over time, making a broad-based rather than a narrow assessment of the learner. Although they are primarily product forms of performance assessment, portfolios also have process features in that they act as works-in-progress and self-reflective pieces that document how the learning has developed.

Portfolios generally take a physical form, such as files or folders of writings, pictures, or papers, or a box of objects, models, artistic creations, or specimens. Portfolios can also be electronic, either text or hypermedia works of papers, presentations, databases, visuals, or stories. They may also contain links to external media, books, or other files on electronic networks. Portfolios can include samples, systematic observations, and in the case of young children, screening tests, which are used to identify skills and strengths of learners. Samples of work depend on the task and content area, but can include drawings, writings, photographs, and projects.

**Key Words**
• Portfolios

Portfolios can also be used to collect and communicate evidence of performance of tasks. Portfolios can be critiqued not only on what they contain but also by how the materials have been adapted or restructured within the portfolio to create a unique product that essentially becomes a teaching and learning product (Norman, 1993). The skills of portfolio construction are additional criteria to include into these as assessments.

The purpose of the portfolio, as in the case of any assessment method, must be identified. Portfolios are suitable means to motivate students, to promote learning through reflection and self-assessment, and the assessment of student thinking and performance (Murphy & Smith, 1990). Challenges to portfolios include the time it takes to score or evaluate them, efforts needed to achieve consistency over their repeated use, the need for multiple measures over a single one, the need for long-term implementation, and an emphasis on viewing portfolios as developmental rather than final or summative.

**Projects.** Projects are assessment products that are comprehensive demonstrations of skills or knowledge. They usually address a broad range of competencies and scoring can be conducted by teacher, panel, or self-assessment (Rudner & Boston, 1994). Projects can be individual or group efforts and thus can include objectives for social skill development. Students need to select meaningful subjects for investigation, relevant to their interests, and suitable to address the goals of the instructional activity.

In group projects participants learn about the dynamic nature of group problem solving and communication. Students in a group tackling an authentic task re-create many of the same problems and challenges found in real life, such as misreading what one means or says, the different motivations between participants, and navigating the sometimes rough waters of power and partnerships. These authentic learning opportunities model real-world

### Food for Thought

Observations are not frequently thought of as ingredients to a portfolio, but they can be useful in assessing young children alone or in small groups (Bertrand & Cebula, 1980).

Observations of spontaneous events can take the form of anecdotal records, which are "factual, nonjudgmental notes of children's activity" (Northwest Regional Educational Laboratory, 1991). Observations can also include activity-performance checklists based on objectives, rating scales, questions and answers.

team building, social interaction, and responsibility for assigned work.

The challenges facing portfolios also confront projects. Scoring can be improved through the use of clear criteria that support learning goals and objectives, and that are clearly and frequently communicated to learners. Completing projects is usually conducted out-of-class; however, in-class time may be needed to introduce particular aspects of the content or skills supporting a project, or to give the instructor an opportunity to observe individual or group performance.

**Interviews**. Interviews are process forms of performance assessments that can be conducted prior to, during, and after instruction. Although infrequently used prior to instruction, interviews can provide a learning profile on participants and can help to adjust learning activities to match the needs of a learner or the group as whole.

During instruction, interviews can be conducted with individuals or in groups, depending on the structural details of the instructional event. Interviews can be either informal or formal. They can be held as needed during instructional sessions or scheduled with a list of questions that help instructors to structure the sessions and to obtain consistent range of responses. These sessions give learners feedback, advice, encouragement, and prompting for further understanding. In addition, teachers have information from which to make adjustments to subsequent instruction. They may also provide insight as to the real reason behind competencies and learning difficulties.

Learning debriefing sessions give a teacher information not usually obtained from other assessment methods. Students verbalize on how they solved problems and managed class requirements. They reflect on what they have learned and what they would like to learn, and provide feedback on the instructional methods and materials used. Interviews can also be used to elaborate on portfolios and projects.

**Self-assessment.** This form of assessment, which can be both process and product, gives students the opportunity to assess themselves. Self-assessment can take the form of logs and journals, while self-evaluations (oral and written) include debriefing interviews on student demonstrations, investigations, and projects. All of these require rating criteria for scoring purposes. Instructional time may be needed to introduce learners to this type of activity, as well as time in-class to record their responses.

**Observations.** As mentioned earlier, teacher observations can be a component of student portfolios. Tools for collecting these data range from low to high inference, based on the specificity with which target behaviors have been identified. In addition to other assessment methods, teachers can look for patterns of learner behaviors that are indicative of whatever they are promoting. Observations are rich sources of information but sometimes time-consuming and challenging to record. They do help to create a dialogue that will provide a learning opportunity for both the learner and teacher.

> Now that you've read about some assessment tools, dig out your Instructional Sequence (**Design Activity 13**) to help you make assessment choices.

# Design Activity 16

 **Task Description**

This Design Activity will help you to see whether or not your original view on content and tasks reflects your assessment purposes.

It is common at this stage of the designing process to be making minor adjustments in content, activities and choice of assessment methods.

∞

## "Instructional Sequence—Assessment Tools"

1. Refer to the sequencing order you developed in the previous chapter (**Design Activity 13**).

2. Identify the assessment purposes needed for each piece in your sequence and list appropriate assessment tools.

| Sequence Component | Assessment Purpose | Assessment Methods |
| --- | --- | --- |

## Talking about Media

**Media as assessments.** Some media materials, normally thought of as supporting instruction, are also ingredients to assessment. Art, design, music, public speaking, labs, and physical activities are other examples where the assessment can be tied to the performance required.

**Media as embedded assessments.** Some media materials provide an instructional experience in which the assessment is situated within the context established by the media. Construction paper, modeling dough, and canvas are examples where the assessment is embedded in the media. With interactive video or videodisk, for example, one works through a lesson and generally responds to questions by writing the responses down on paper. With hypermedia or computer-aided-instruction, students may respond to questions or scenarios with responses entered into the system. In some cases, as with intelligent computer-aided instruction (ICAI), the medium responds with reasoning or adjusts the next question or lesson based on the learner response.

**Purpose of assessment.** Determining one's purpose of assessment is the key question one must answer before deciding on using media as a source of assessment. Assessment can be embedded into media if the assessment method is appropriate to the instructional strategy. For example, if the instruction is based on simulations, or approximations to real world events, and if the purpose behind assessment is to measure the problem-solving ability of a learner, then the assessment method should allow the learner to become part of the simulation, to see what he or she can do to solve a problem.

## ☆ SCENARIO

### Consulting Firm: What Is Performance?

Another example of the relevancy of assessment across settings is the use of performance or competencies as *the* key indicator for achieving business or institutional goals. These competency-based assessment tools are seen as a valid measure of worker strengths and weaknesses. As in curriculum settings, key issues include the following items. See how these issues relate to educational settings.

- Appropriate assessment of performance that is trusted by its users and those being measured.

- Whether the tool meets technical standards of the firm for reliability and validity.

- External issues include cost and time to implement.

- Identify and agree upon competencies and communicate some scoring system.

- Tying the system to the firm's overall mission.

Rockford & Associates decided to draw up a performance-based accountability for its staff by first involving those working on the project to submit criteria for performance. The firm's partners reviewed this criteria to ensure that it reflected the principles of the firm. In essence, each project produced different criteria depending on the context of the project and the makeup of the expertise servicing a client.

In many ways firms choosing competency-based assessment systems are also adopting a worker-centered approach where the organization identifies the strengths of individuals, respects cultures and individuality, assumes responsibility for decision-making, and understands that accountability and rewards are based on performance.

> There are several important issues in designing and selecting assessment methods.

# Assessment Issues

There are many, many dimensions to assessment. We can only address a few. This section will describe a procedure to design assessments, ways to improve their validity and reliability, and guidelines to develop them.

**Designing assessments.** Below are listed five steps in designing assessments, based on what we have said so far and tying in with our next chapter on instructional models.

> ### 5 Steps to Design Assessments
>
> 1. Identify the goals and objectives from the Needs Assessment.
> 2. Match the goals and objectives (purposes) with assessment tools.
> 3. Choose the instructional method (Chapter 6).
> 4. Design assessment tasks and scoring methods.
> 5. Think through the implications of your decisions.

**1. Identify the goals and objectives.** Needs assessment tools (Chapter 3) and task analysis (Chapter 4) help to identify what knowledge and skills learners should have at the end of an instructional event, whether it be a unit or a class or a workshop. The needs assessment process, consulting experts, on-site personnel, or your understanding of the problem, can provide you with data describing at what learning level your participants should perform.

**2. Match identified learning purposes with assessment tools.** Knowing what you want learners to be able to know and do and at what learning level gives you the information you need to select your assessment methods. Referring to the learning taxonomies can identify possible activities and words to use in an assessment scoring plan.

**3. Choose the instructional method.** Your assessment framework should also be reflected in your choices of instructional methods, which is why we are discussing assessment before teaching models (the subject of Chapter 6).

**4. Design assessment tasks and scoring methods.** Knowing the assessment methods and instructional approach, you can then design the details to the assessment tasks, such as group projects, presentations, and paper assignments. How these tasks will be scored or evaluated needs to be thought out and the procedures written down. You could start

### Food for Thought

You can begin to sketch out assessment tasks now and revisit these decisions after reading Chapter 6, Instructional Frameworks, and thinking about your instructional strategies.

by adopting the criteria used by others and modify these to suit your needs, or you may need to establish your own criteria or rating scales to best fit the assessment purpose. These criteria and scoring systems will likely take some trial-and-error to work out.

**5. Think about your decisions.** Finally, think about how your participants will react to the assessment and the resultant evaluation. Features may need to be designed that address the changes these assessments will have on the present culture of the learning setting. Think about the differences between the methods used in your instructional setting as compared to methods used by others or that your participants have been used to.

> Here are ways to improve your assessment choices.

**Reliability and validity.** Another set of critical issues in regard to selecting assessment methods is reliability and validity. In addition to identifying your purpose for assessment, it is necessary to select the methods that will support this purpose and generate data in which inferences can be made about learning. One measure of this capability is the validity of the data gathered from assessments. Does the assessment measure what it is designed to measure?

There are several aspects to validity, but the most common is **content validity**—the extent to which an assessment covers the content taught. **Criterion validity**, meanwhile, is the extent to which performance on an assessment predicts a learner's performance on criteria. An example of this is the aptitude test, which tries to predict how well a learner will perform in the future. Student scores on an aptitude test may, for example, predict a student's grade-point average in college. A third aspect is **construct validity**, which focuses on a test score as a

**Key Words**
- Construct validity
- Content validity
- Criterion validity

measure of an educational or psychological construct, such as reading ability.

An important aspect to validity, however, is examining how this validity affects instruction. If an assessment does a good job at measuring performance, then does instruction gravitate to this measure? Is this assessment method adequate to address the learning that is intended and the match between what is instructionally possible and the kind of learning you expect to achieve? The more evidence we have of validity, the higher the confidence we can place on the score-based inferences that are obtained from assessments.

An assessment method should be reliable. Is the assessment stable, or consistent, between successive uses? Is the assessment reliable between and within learners? Does the scoring procedure judge student's performance consistently between all those assessed and does it assess performance within each individual? To improve validity and reliability, check that your testing purpose reflects the learning objectives you have established. Your assessment purpose should be clear and unambiguous.

Many types of high inference assessments require that the task that is the basis for the assessment supports the purpose for assessment and that the task description be fully developed. Scoring criteria and rubrics for task performance also require attention. Scoring criteria identify the factors that determine the adequacy of a learner's performance. They should be learnable and not favor particular individuals (Herman et al., 1992). Validity and reliability can also be improved by careful attention to scoring. Score like-topics or dimensions at the same time and recheck your process periodically.

Finally, there are limits to the degree to which one can make generalizations across some tasks, so to improve the validity of the assessment results, one should provide several performance assessments for each student or provide different tasks (Linn, Baker & Dunbar, 1991).

**Recommendations and guidelines.** Following are some recommendations on the use of assessments:

---

### Assessment Guidelines

1. Start small.
2. Develop clear rubrics.
3. Design a comprehensive assessment plan.
4. Communicate high value to the assessment.
5. Involve students and peers.
6. Don't give up.

Adapted from Rudner, L. M., & Boston, C. (1994). Performance assessment. *ERIC Review*, 3(1), 2-12.

---

**1. Start small.** The first suggestion is simple. Start small. Try out a new assessment task in combination with what you already do. Realize, too, that developing and using these assessments will take time.

**2. Develop clear rubrics.** A **rubric** is a rating scale based on criteria for judging student performances. Decide on the benchmarks for various levels of performances. Share your rubric with others and get their feedback on the choice of criteria, or find someone that will try the method along with you. At the same time, look around for examples. (Rudner & Boston, 1994).

**3. Design a comprehensive assessment plan.** We recommend that you consider the whole range of assessment possibilities. Instructional design provides a systematic process in which to consider assessment in the context of other important issues. An assessment plan should include the purpose of the assessment and the high validity and high reliability methods that measure this purpose.

**Key Words**
- Rubric

**4. Communicate.** Communicate clearly to participants the purpose of the assessment and what you hope to achieve by using it. Also, communicate the value of the experience to help them understand the importance of the task.

**5. Involve.** Consider involving participants in the assessment process by allowing them to suggest criteria and conduct their own self-evaluations on some of the tasks. Involve the suggestions of others, such as peers and experts, when designing assessments and ask them to review what you have designed or the results of implementing them.

**6. Keep going.** Finally, realize that you won't get it right the first time. Make changes in tasks, criteria, and whatever needs adjusting based on your judgment and what the assessments are telling you. This is where **formative evaluation** can be useful. Look for unintended consequences, fairness, adequate coverage of content, meaningfulness of the experience, as well as cost and time spent on developing and using the assessment (Linn et al., 1991).

See Tour 5: The Policeman in "Touring Instructional Design."

The next Design Activity gives you opportunity to summarize your assessment plan.

↓

**Key Words**
• Formative evaluation

# DESIGN ACTIVITY 17

## "Assessment Plan"

### ✍ Task Description

This Design Activity builds on the previous ones in this chapter and gives you a task to adjust your decisions on how to assess your participants.

**1.** Summarize your assessment activities, identifying first the major purposes for assessment in your project.

**2.** List the tools (rubrics) you propose to use that match this purpose.

**3.** Supply reasoning explaining why you chose the tools you did.

| Assessment Purpose | Assessment Tools and Tasks |
|---|---|
| • How is learning assessed? | • Supporting Rationale |
| • What is the context and timeline for these purposes? | • Rubrics |

# Reviewing Design Activities

**Design Activity 15: Your Assessment Purpose(s)**

☐ Identified the purposes for assessment in your project.

**Design Activity 16: Instructional Sequence-Assessment Tools**

☐ Matched your assessment purpose from Activity 15 with appropriated assessment tools.

**Design Activity 17: Assessment Plan**

☐ Summarized your assessment purpose(s).
☐ Provided rationales for the assessment tools chosen.
☐ Identified timelines for when tools will be used.
☐ Matched tools chosen to the original goals.

## ⌂ Summary of Key Ideas

**1.** There are multiple functions and methods for assessment.

2. Match assessment methods to assessment purposes.

3. There are multiple ways to categorize assessment purposes.

**4.** Determine what it is that you are assessing.

**5.** Reliability and validity are important issues in designing and selecting assessment methods.

**Food for Thought**

Eisner (1994) has identified several criteria that should be considered in assessment.

1. Assessment tasks in school need to match world tasks.
- Should include individual and group efforts.
- Should include a big picture view.

2. Problem solving tasks should examine problem solving processes as well as solutions.
- Should consider multiple solutions.

3. Assessment tasks should reflect the value of the learning community that designed them.

4. Assessment tasks should accommodate unintentional learning.

5. Assessment tasks should accommodate learner representations to reveal one's learning.

From THE EDUCATIONAL IMAGINATION by Eisner, E., © 1985. Adapted by pemission of Prentice-Hall, In., Upper Saddle River, NJ.

# √ Your Personal Learning

## Relating Your Beliefs to This Chapter:

You probably have particular beliefs about assessment. Keep in mind the goals established from the needs assessment and examine your beliefs and examine their influence on your selection of assessment methods.

1. How would you define assessment?

2. How would you define evaluation?

3. What is the basis for these definitions?

4. What questions or concerns do you have about assessment?

## Any revisions to your personal ID model?

- Are there provisions for assessment in your design model?

- Have you made any distinctions between assessment and program evaluation?

- What changes need to be made to account for the range of assessment purposes you identified in this chapter?

- Make a few notes now about changes to make it easier to include them in a revised design model later.

## What questions do you have about the information presented in this chapter?

# References

Arter, J., & Spandel, V. (1991). *Using portfolios of student work in instruction and assessment.* Portland, OR: Northwest Regional Educational Laboratory.

Bloom, B. S. (1956). *Taxonomy of educational objectives: The classification of educational goals: Handbook 1: Cognitive domain.* NY: McKay.

Chittenden, E. (1990). Authentic assessment, evaluation, and documentation of student performance. In V. Perrone (Ed.), *Expanding student assessment* (22-31), Alexandria, VA: Association for Supervision and Curriculum Development.

Eisner, E. W. (1994). *The educational imagination* (3rd ed.). NY: Macmillan.

Gronlund, N. E., (1981). *Measurement and evaluation in teaching* (4th ed.). NY: Macmillan.

Gronlund, N. E., (1982). *Constructing achievement tests* (3rd ed.). Englewood Cliffs, NJ: Prentice-Hall.

Gronlund, N. E. & Linn, R. L. (1994). *Measurement and evaluation in teaching* (7th ed.). NY: Macmillan.

Herman, J. L., Aschbacher, P. R., & Winters, L. (1992). *A practical guide to alternative assessment.* Alexandria, VA: Association for Supervision and Curriculum Development.

Linn, R. L., Baker, E. L., & Dunbar, S. B. (1991, November). Complex, performance-based criteria. *Educational Researcher, 20,* 15-21.

Morris, W. (Ed.). (1976). *The American dictionary of the English language.* Boston: Houghton Mifflin.

Murphy, S., & Smith, M. A. (Spring, 1990). Talking about portfolios. *Quarterly of the National Writing Project, 12,* 1-3, 24-27. EJ 429 792.

Norman, D. A. (1993). *Things that make us smart: Defending human attributes in the ages of the machine.* Reading, MA: Addison-Wesley.

Northwest Regional Educational Laboratory. (1991). *Alternative program evaluation ideas for early childhood programs.* Portland, OR.

Popham, W. J. (1995). *Classroom assessment: What teachers need to know.* Boston, MA: Allyn & Bacon.

Rudner, L. M., & Boston, C. (1994). Performance assessment. *ERIC Review, 3*(1), 2-12.

Wiggins, G. (1989, May). A true test: Toward more authentic and equitable assessment. *Phi Delta Kappan,* 703-713.

# For Further Reading

Eisner, E. W. (1994). *The educational imagination* (3rd ed.). NY: Macmillan.

> Eisner offers a contemporary perspective on the design and evaluation of programs that promote flexible understandings and alternative frameworks for learning.

Gronlund, N. E., & Linn, R. L. (1994). *Measurement and evaluation in teaching* (7th ed.). NY: Macmillan.

> A comprehensive text on issues and concepts on the tests and measurements field.

Popham, W. J. (1995). *Classroom assessment: What teachers need to know.* Boston, MA: Allyn & Bacon.

> A practical guide on the understanding, design, and implementation of assessment tools and procedures.

Rudner, L. M., & Boston, C. (1994). Performance assessment. *ERIC Review, 3*(1), 2-12.

> A special issue devoted to performance assessment. Includes a case study of a school's experiment with these assessments, an article on assessments and national standards, performance-based aspects of the National Assessment of Educational Progress (NAEP), along with reading lists and organizations.

# What's Next?

In Chapter 6 we continue our designing by examining instructional models that are appropriate for your goals. During the designing stages it is common to revisit the phases of Instructional Sequence, Assessment, Instructional Framework, Instructional Media, and Prototype (Chapters 4, 5, 6, 7, and 8). For example, decisions made during Assessment may require some changes after thinking about your instructional strategies, the subject of the next chapter.

∞

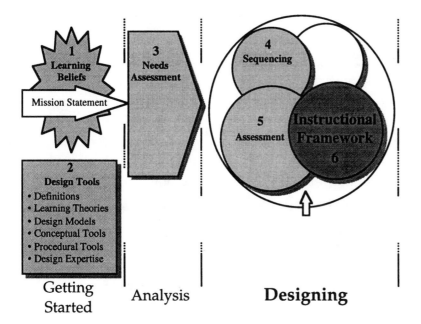

# CHAPTER 6

**H**ow do we put all of this stuff into action?

**T**his chapter examines instructional possibilities—models and strategies—to help you realize your mission and goals within your instructional design.

**Y**ou may find yourself moving back and forth between the designing phases as you make decisions about sequencing, assessment, instructional framework, and instructional media.

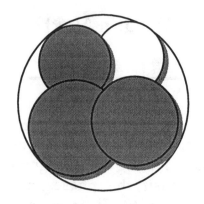

# Instructional Framework

*The most appropriate format depends upon the task, which means that no single format can ever be correct for all purposes.*

(Norman, 1993, p. 60)

---

This chapter summarizes a number of instructional models by describing their major features, benefits, steps, and ways to implement them. This chapter will also suggest ways to enlarge your instructional repertoire.

In this chapter you will:

1. Take stock of how you currently teach, train, or facilitate.

2. Determine an instructional framework and identify appropriate instructional models.

3. Sketch out an action plan to enlarge your instructional repertoire.

# Instruction

**Instruction** is sometimes said to facilitate learning. Ongoing needs assessment—the gathering and analyzing of data about the content—helps to formulate goals about what needs to be learned and how it is to be learned. Instruction is the process that deals with how this is to be accomplished. An **instructional framework** is the structure that supports the details of these methods based on your beliefs and knowledge of teaching-learning processes.

**Instruction influenced by beliefs.** As with assessment, the choice of an instructional framework is highly influenced by one's beliefs and past experiences. It could be said that the way we teach is based to a great degree on how we were taught by other humans, whether in school, at home, or on-the-job. For some, this means that we teach in much the same way these people taught us, modeling the behaviors and methods used by these individuals. For others, their teaching may be based on a desire to shift the role of the instructor to a learner-centered focus.

In addition to prior experiences, our instructional approach may be based on what learning principles we embrace. We may have only a **tacit**, or unspoken, understanding of these principles, as they may be an integral part of the way we teach. Instructional models can help to translate one's tacit learning principles into more effective results. Although models possess systematic steps in which to apply them, they are not recipes or **algorithms** that supply all of the answers to an **instructional problem**. By incorporating models and strategies within an instructional framework, you address the relevant and critical issues of instructional content, context, and learners.

---

**THESAURUS**

**Educate (verb)**

educate, edify (see TEACH)

breed, rear, nurse, nurture, bring up, develop, form, mold, shape, whip into shape

send to school, have taught

tutor, teach, school

ground, train, coach, prime, prep, PREPARE

guide, DIRECT

instruct, INFORM

enlighten, illumine, enlarge the mind, develop the mind, open the mind

sharpen the wits, open the eyes

fill with new ideas, stuff with knowledge, cram with facts, spoonfeed with facts

impress into the memory, drum into the head, inculcate, indoctrinate, imbue, infuse, instill, infix, implant, engraft, sow the seeds of

Roget. (1977). *Roget's Thesaurus of English Words and Phrases*. (Revision by R. L. Chapman). NY: Thomas Crowell, 562.11.

---

**Key Words**
- Algorithms
- Instruction
- Instructional framework
- Instructional problem
- Tacit

First, let's take stock of your prior teaching or learning experiences.

# DESIGN ACTIVITY 18

"How Do You Present Instruction Now?"

 **Task Description**

The purpose of this task is to prompt you to think about and record how you presently teach, train, or facilitate. If you are new to instruction, how would you present instruction if you had the opportunity?

**1.** Describe your teaching, presentation, or facilitation style. How would you title this style?

**2.** What forms the basis for your instructional approach?

**3.** Explain how your learning principles that you identified in an earlier Design Activity influence your instructional approach.

Now, let's continue to examine what we mean by an Instructional Framework!

# Instructional Frameworks

**Instructional frameworks.** An instructional framework is a means to enact and support your instructional goals and objectives. According to Gunter, Estes & Schwab (1995), "an instructional model is a step-by-step procedure that leads to specific learning outcomes" (p. 67).

Instructional models provide a theoretical basis for leveraging learning theories into methods of instruction, based on research about what works in instructional settings. They provide a set of steps to guide a new user or a "jumping-off place" for experienced teachers. In a larger sense, these models also amplify and energize the abilities of teachers to "deliver instruction."

**Families of models.** Joyce and Weil (1996) organize instructional methods in terms of four families "that share orientations toward human beings and how they learn" (p. 5). These orientations include social, information-processing, personal, and behavioral. We have added a fifth family, an integrative family, in which the model combines or blends features of other models. Each of the families possesses a theoretical basis that explains why particular goals may be achieved and a research base that explains how these models work. In the table on the next page we've included examples from the families. Several of these will be examined in the next section of this chapter.

♦ For three references on a more complete account of teaching models and strategies, see Joyce & Weil (1996), Gunter, Estes, & Schwab (1995), and Freiberg & Driscoll (1996) listed in **For Further Reading**

**Key Words**
• Instructional models

### Families of Instructional Models (Joyce & Weil, 1996)

| Family | Model or Strategy | Outcome |
|---|---|---|
| **Behavioral** | Direct instruction | Information recall and skill acquisition |
| | Contingency management | Reinforcement of desired behavior |
| | Training, simulations | Developing skills to an expected level of performance via simplified versions of real-world processes |
| **Social** | Cooperative groups | Learning to work together |
| | Role playing | Learning value systems by adopting and playing out particular roles |
| | Jurisprudential inquiry | Examining social issues through case studies that compare different points of view |
| **Information-processing** | Conceptual attainment | Defining, comprehending, analyzing, and using concepts |
| | Conceptual development | Categorizing, generalizing, and synthesizing information |
| | Inductive learning | Discovery of knowledge, classifying and identifying relationships, and thinking through the implications of these discoveries |
| | Metacognition | Thinking about one's own thinking and making decisions about one's learning |
| | Advance organizers | Structuring information from general to specific and relating this structure to prior learning |
| | Synectics | Creative problem solving by groups identifying analogies to generate new solutions to problems |
| **Personal** | Nondirective | Guiding individual's growth and development |
| | Reflection | Self-assessment of one's learning and using this as a basis for action |
| **Integrative** | Classroom discussion | Formulating questions, developing insights, and fostering critical thinking skills |
| | Cognitive apprenticeships | Learning problem-solving within real-world contexts |

Adapted from Joyce, B.,  & Weil, M. *Models of teaching* , 5/E Copyright© 1996 Boston: Allyn and Bacon. Adapted by permission.

**Behavioral family.** Models in this family have a wide variety of applications but share a common characteristic: learners have the ability to change their behavior based on changes in the environment. Models include direct instruction, which includes interactions between students and teachers, such as modeling, reinforcement, feedback, and guided performance; simulations where behavior is changed based on ongoing reactions to a simplified version of a real-world situation; and contingency management, where "behavior is influenced by the consequences that follow" (Joyce et al., 1992, p. 327-328).

**Social family.** The social family builds on the social processes involved in learning together. Some of these processes include values, self-esteem, social policy, and social development of learners. Instructional models in this family include various forms of cooperative learning (Johnson & Johnson, 1975; Slavin, 1983; Sharan, 1990), group investigation (Thelen, 1960), and role playing (Shaftel & Shaftel, 1982; Chesler & Fox, 1966). Social policy formulation addresses conflicts of values and demands, which can be investigated using a jurisprudential model (Oliver & Shaver, 1966).

**Information processing family.** Models in this family attempt to enhance various kinds of intellectual skills, such as creativity and problem solving (Gordon, 1961), group inquiry (Suchman, 1962), defining concepts (Joyce & Weil, 1996), developing concept understandings (Taba, 1971), and mastering bodies of information (Pressley, Levin & Delaney, 1982). A wide variety of teaching strategies fall under this family, such as advance organizers (Ausubel, 1963), and cognitive maps (Novak & Gowin, 1984), all of which are used to help learners to develop thinking skills as well as content understanding.

**Personal family.** The personal family of models acknowledges the individual person and the development of an integrated self, a person who acknowledges that one has feelings and that change

> **Food for Thought**
>
> Which models reflect what you want to accomplish in your mission and intent statements?

over one's life is inevitable. According to Joyce and Weil (1996) these models help lead an individual toward greater mental and emotional health by improving the concept of self, self-confidence, and the value of feelings between people. These models also accept that learners should have a say in their learning needs and take responsibility for their learning.

**Integrative family.** We have added to Joyce and Weil's original list of families a fifth grouping, an integrative family. Examples of integrative models are the preparation and use of questions in classroom discussion (Gunter et al., 1995); cognitive apprenticeships, mastering complex material in real-world settings (Collins, 1991); and the use of stories (Schank, 1990). Models in this family accommodate features of other models, as well as (1) an integration of instruction and assessment through the use of authentic tasks or activities, and (2) integrative frameworks for tapping what we know about learning.

The integration of instruction and assessment is accomplished through "whole tasks and activities" where the task performance is the basis for assessment (Moll, 1990). A whole activity includes much of the real-world context surrounding it. Activities in which students are given a problem, without an opportunity to establish the goal of the problem-solving activity themselves, lack meaningful student motivation (Newman, Griffin & Cole, 1989).

The integrative family combines features of other models and may adopt a different theoretical framework, such as a **sociocultural** viewpoint, in which the higher intellectual processes are promoted through social interaction and meaning-making activities within a cultural context (Vygotsky, 1978).

**Selection of models.** We believe that there is more than one way to present instruction and that consideration of a range of models opens up many possibilities to address instructional problems. The key is to match your learning goals and objectives and

**Key Words**
- Sociocultural

contextual constraints (realities) with the appropriate models. For example, if your goal is to teach basic skills, facts, and knowledge, the direct instruction model may be the best choice (Gunter et al., 1995). If creative thinking and problem solving are among your goals, the synectics model may be one possibility (Gunter et al., 1995; Joyce & Weil, 1996).

> Time to examine some of these models.
> ⬇

# Instructional Models

In this section we will examine a number of instructional models, which include:

*Cooking well means more than just following recipes.*

(Labensky & Hause, 1995, p. vii)

---

### Instructional Models

- Direct Instruction
- Classroom Discussion
- Cooperative Learning
- Cognitive Apprenticeships
- Contingency Management
- Advance Organizers
- Cognitive Mapping
- Self-concept
- Role Playing
- Synectics

---

**Direct instruction.** Direct instruction is a behavioral model suitable for the teaching of basic skills. Many basic skills need to be taught before moving on to other levels of thinking or learning. Whatever can be taught directly is a candidate for this model. It is characterized by instruction that is broken down into manageable chunks, student practice, and teachers observing behavior and providing feedback until mastery is achieved (Rosenshine, 1983). It is frequently used when time is limited or when a skill needs to be taught in a particular way.

---

### Direct Instruction

1. **Review** what has been learned.
2. **Inform** students what is going to be presented today.
3. **Present** new material.
4. **Provide** guided practice through questions and corrective feedback.
5. **Provide** independent practice in-class and out-of-class.
6. **Review** of practice and **provide** corrective feedback.

Adapted from Joyce, B. R., & Weil, M. *Models of Teaching*, 5/E Copyright © 1996 by Allyn & Bacon. Adapted by permission.

---

The direct instruction model can be incorporated into many other models, particularly at step 3 in the above list (Gunter et al., 1995). This is where the lecture is commonly practiced. Organizers, which will be discussed later, can be used in step 2 to inform students of the day's objectives and step 3 to provide some reference point to the content of a lesson.

Presenting material also involves the organization of content by arranging material into smaller parts, focusing on important points, presenting from general to specific, and taking into consideration ages, styles, and abilities of students. The actual presenting of material can take many forms from lectures to demonstrations, and then observing the reactions and behavior of students to what is being said, presented, shown, or demonstrated.

**Classroom Discussion.** Discussion is an instructional method with a long history and is a major activity for many teachers. Its major feature is a dialogue that generates questions and increases the teacher's ability to engage students in higher level thinking. Durkin's (1978-1979) research suggests that "only rarely do teachers in elementary grades ask questions of students that have any bearing on how to think about text. Goodlad's (1984) observations of secondary classrooms suggest that only one percent of teachers' questions require of students anything but the most superficial thought" (p. 161).

In addition to guiding the planning and selection of questions used in classroom discussions, the model guides the teacher in conducting the classroom interactions during the discussion. Here are the steps:

*When I started teaching at Charles Evans Hughes High School on West 18th Street in New York City, there was one thing that really frightened me: silence.*

(Barell, 1995, p. 91)

---

### Classroom Discussion

1. **Read** the material and prepare questions.

2. **Cluster** basic and follow-up questions.

3. **Introduce** the model and assign the reading.

4. **Conduct** the discussion.

5. **Review** the process and **summarize** students' observations.

Gunter, Estes, & Schwab, *Instruction: A Models Approach* 2/E Copyright © 1995 by Allyn and Bacon. Adapted by permission.

---

*1. Read material.* The first step to this model is to read the material and develop factual, interpretative, and evaluative questions. This is done to help ask more thought-provoking questions in the classroom (Gunter et al., 1995). *Factual* question can be answered by pointing to a section in a book, *interpretive* questions ask what the text means, and *evaluative* questions require students to make value judgments and relate meaning of text to the relevance of the reader. Gunter and colleagues (1995) suggest that good discussion questions be worded precisely so that the intent of the question is clear, narrowed sufficiently to give the discussion direction, and framed in such a manner to reflect doubt, searching, and value.

*2. Cluster questions.* The second step in this model is to compare ideas, reactions, and questions with a co-leader (if possible), and cluster questions by identifying broad, basic questions that raise an issue. Follow-up-questions develop the ideas behind the basic question. Thus, clustering questions focuses discussion and allows students to cover a basic question in depth. The key to this step, however, is to know when to deviate from your prepared questions.

*3. Introduce model.* The third step is to assign the reading, some of which could be done in class. Ask students to prepare questions for discussion and give students adequate time to reread material before discussion.

*4. Conduct the discussion.* Conducting an effective discussion requires a nondirective role, particularly evaluating the weight given to questions that in your view are more correct than others. When students answer questions prompt responses for evidence or elaboration on their meanings. Students are encouraged to offer their opinions on responses, as well as to listen carefully to others' opinions. Constructive discussion accommodates different frameworks of thinking and unique motivations to a subject, and promotes the view that everyone deserves the respect to express their views and to question others.

*5. Review and summarize.* Finally, in step five, students are encouraged to review the main points discussed and summarize what was said in the discussion.

**Cooperative Groups.** Cooperative learning aims to create a positive environment where people learn to work together to achieve their objectives. The model aims to create a positive working environment and to develop cooperation and understanding of others as individuals. The model may be used to supplement other forms of instruction by giving students the opportunity to teach one another, discuss, or put into practice skills or information presented by the instructor (Slavin, 1983). Cooperative groups require time to implement and perhaps several years for instructors to learn.

Although there are numerous structural types of cooperative learning, one approach includes the following major features:

---

### Features of Cooperative Groups

**Interdependence**
*Sink or swim together*

**One-to-one Interaction**
*Students help each other*

**Individual Accountability**
*Individual performance assessed and shared*

**Social Skills**
*Groups need social skills to function*

**Group Processing**
*Group reflects on what and how they are doing*

From Johnson, D. W., Johnson, R. T., & Smith, K. A. (1991). *Active learning: Cooperation in the college classroom.* Reproduced by permission of Interaction Book Company. 7208 Cornelia Dr., Edina, MN 55435.

---

*Interdependence* in a cooperative work group requires a number of features: a clear, mutual goal must be communicated and understood by members of the group, resources must be shared, and tasks must be divided with complementary roles being assigned. The group should be encouraged to establish its own identity and competition with other groups.

*One-to-one interaction* in cooperative groups encourages students to support and help each other, willingly exchange resources so that everyone has access to the information of others, provide feedback, and give opportunities for individuals to challenge each other's conclusions.

*Individual accountability* within the group can be designed into cooperative work groups. One way is to establish small groups and rotate task assignments, such as assigning one member as team leader and another as the recorder, then rotating roles periodically to give everyone in the group shared responsibilities. In essence, individuals teach other members of the group what they learn. Depending on the purpose of the cooperative group, assessment can range from observations, individual tests, or through dialogue.

Groups need *social skills* to function. These skills, however, are not intuitive. Within cooperative groups, students become aware of cooperative skills, such as those listed above. One of the issues that learners have with this model is that individuals pull their weight in the group. This concern becomes acute when the group is graded as a group in addition to or in lieu of assigning individual scores.

**Cognitive apprenticeships**. In this model students develop problem-solving experience by applying content knowledge and learned "tricks of the trade" to learning activities that come as close as possible to real-life situations. Strategies used in this model include demonstrations of the processes used in the world and modeling of the problem-solving performance of experts. The role of the instructor in this model is that of the coach providing students with problem-solving exercises, encouraging them to try different approaches, providing suggestions on performance, while reflecting and justifying their decisions. The elements of this model are summarized on the next page.

## Cognitive Apprenticeships

**1. Content:** Teach tacit, heuristic knowledge as well as textbook knowledge.

**2. Situated learning:** Teach knowledge and skills in contexts that reflect the way the knowledge will be useful in real life.

**3. Modeling and explaining:** Show how a process unfolds and explain why it happens that way.

**4. Coaching:** Observe learners as they try to complete tasks and provide assistance as needed.

**5. Articulation:** Have learners think about their actions and justify their decisions and strategies.

**6. Reflection:** Have learners assess their own performance.

**7. Exploration:** Encourage learners to test out their own strategies.

**8. Sequence:** Present instruction sequenced from simple to complex, with increasing diversity and global knowledge before local knowledge and skills.

From Collins, A. (1991). Cognitive apprenticeship and instructional technology. In L. Idol & B. F. Jones (Eds.), *Educational values and cognitive instruction: Implications for reform*. Reprinted with permission of Lawrence Erlbaum Associates.

**Contingency management.** This model from the behavioral framework analyzes all features of the learning environment and their effects on learner behavior, and ways that features of the environment reinforce the desired behavior. These reinforcers can be social, material, and activity (Joyce et al., 1992). Social reinforcers include smiles, praise, attention, and approval. Material sources of reinforcement can include rewards, such as toys, certificates, money, time-off, and gold stars! Activity reinforcers involve prospects of an enjoyable activity after finishing a task.

Such activities include recess, play, going to the movies, and shopping!

A suggested procedure for contingency management includes the following steps:

---

**Contingency Management**

1. Determine the desired behavior.

2. Determine existing behavior.

3. Decide on features of the environment.

4. Implement the program.

5. Evaluate the behavior.

Adapted from Freiberg & Driscoll, *Universal Teaching Strategies*, 2/E Copyright © 1996 by Allyn & Bacon. Adapted by permission.

---

This model requires that you are clear on what the desired behavior should be and note the differences between what exists and what is desired. The features of the environment—physical, social, and learning activities—are examined and decisions made as to what the appropriate behavior reinforcers should be. In addition, a **reinforcement schedule** is determined for these features.

**Advance organizer.** This is a cognitive tool to help organize ideas and information in ways that are suitable to the learner's degree of present understanding. **Organizers** usually take the form of an outline, but they can also be visual in nature. The most general idea is listed first followed by supporting details relating the idea to what has already been learned. Organizers can be used in other instructional models, such as direct instruction and classroom discussion. It is also used to organize the content of a unit or a complete curriculum and is frequently used to organize the design of instructional materials.

**Key Words**
- Organizer
- Reinforcement schedule

> ## Advance Organizer
>
> 1. Design an organizer.
> 2. Present the organizer.
> 3. Present the new task or new information.
> 4. Connect the organizer to presentation.
>
> Adapted from Joyce, B. R., & Weil, M. *Models of Teaching*, 5/E
> Copyright © 1996 by Allyn & Bacon. Adapted by permission.

The organizer can be used before, during, and after instruction. Organizers can help an instructor to structure a presentation. The organization is presented as a way of reviewing prior instruction, highlighting important points and presenting an agenda for daily instruction. In Step 3 the new information is presented or activities are conducted. Throughout the instruction, new organizers can be used to structure the information, relating it to prior learning or concepts. Step 4 is necessary to strengthen the "cognitive organization" of the learner by review and summary, relating details to the big picture and verbalizing by students. (Ausubel, 1963). After instruction, the organizer can be evaluated in terms of its success and adjustments can be made in its structure for future use.

**Cognitive mapping.** Cognitive maps from the information processing family are attempts to represent what we know by drawing a map. Like physical maps, cognitive maps of our thinking can be inaccurate, approximate, and incomplete (Wandersee, 1990); but they act as records of learning, first as naive representations, later, as more detailed, more accurate, and more useful ones.

The cognitive map type that has been researched heavily is the **concept map** (Novak & Gowin, 1984). Concepts are depicted by circles and organized in a top-down hierarchy from general to specific, with

**Key Words**
- Concept map

concepts and sub-concepts connected by lines that are labeled to describe the relationships between items. Frequent attempts are usually needed to refine a map. This graphic strategy takes time to learn and time to introduce. Wandersee (1990) estimates that it may take a student eight to ten weeks to practice and appreciate the value of the technique.

**Self-concept.** Self-concept is the view that one has of oneself and consists of one's internal beliefs and attitudes (Purkey, 1970). There are many ways to enhance self-concept. It is useful in the context of instructional design to determine the principle self-concept issue, which may consist of one or more of the following areas:

◆  For many examples of self-concept activities, see Canfield & Wells, 1994, listed in **References**

---

### Self-Concept Areas

- Creating self-awareness
- Examining personal strengths
- Examining one's purpose and direction
- Having awareness of body
- Establishing relationships with others

From Canfield, J., & Wells, H. C. *100 ways to enhance self-concept in the classroom* 2/E Copyright © 1994 by Allyn and Bacon. Reprinted by permission.

---

**Role playing.** Role-playing from the social family of models is acting out possible solutions to real problems. Active involvement of participants provides role players and observers with a chance to see, feel, hear, and act out an experience. An advantage of this model is the collective reactions that individuals contribute to everyone's learning.

In this strategy the teacher warms up the group by introducing the problem and explaining the role playing process. Participants are selected for the roles and the line of action is explained. Observers are briefed as to what to look for. In some situations it may be useful to point out particular things to look for. During the role play the action can be halted to review what has happened. The action can resume or individual roles or points of view can shift. At the end of the role play individual experiences and perceptions can be shared with the entire group. General principles of behavior can be constructed and implications for other situations can be discussed.

---

### Role Playing

1. Warm up the group and select the players.
2. Set the stage for players and observers.
3. Enact and discuss; re-enact and discuss.
4. Share experiences.

From Joyce, B., & Weil, M. (1996). *Models of teaching* (5th ed.). Boston: Allyn & Bacon.

---

Role playing can help participants to (1) sensitize themselves to issues and face their feelings about them; (2) acquire new thoughts and behaviors; and (3) improve problem-solving skills, such as openness to other solutions, problem identification, evaluating consequences, and criteria of choices. Participants need to be engaged with an appropriate problem situation and helped to explore the issues and conflicts that might arise.

**Synectics.** This is a problem solving strategy that brings out creative solutions to problems. Synectics taps the creative sum of a group to arrive at metaphorical solutions to tough problems. This strategy uses the power of analogies and the emotional qualities of groups to creatively examine a problem.

Participants are asked to describe something familiar and then identify a problem with this familiar situation or idea. These suggestions are recorded so that all can view them. In Step 2 students are asked for analogies for the problem. In Step 3 students are asked to select a specific analogy for discussion or the instructor may choose to focus on one.

---

### Synectics

1. Teacher provides information on a topic and students supply a product representing their current thinking.

2. Students supply analogies of this product.

3. Students are asked to choose two analogies which are in conflict with each other and discuss the differences.

4. Students are asked to choose one over the other and to create a new list of analogies for this choice.

5. Students choose one of the new items based on some criteria and compare this choice with the original problem.

Adapted from Joyce, B., & Weil, M. *Models of teaching* 5/E Copyright © 1996 by Allyn and Bacon. Adapted by permission.

---

Next, in Step 4, students are asked to imagine how it feels to be like this analogy. Comparisons are then made between two choices that are in conflict with each other. After this discussion students select one over the other. This choice is then matched with a new analogy and another list is made with candidates. Criteria for choosing one can be made by the instructor, such as most valuable, most useful, or most appropriate. The leader encourages students to explore the reasonings for their choice. The group uses what has been developed to help them address the original problem.

To make this strategy work, facilitation skills and familiarity with the synectics process are needed. Joyce and Weil (1996) identify possible uses for synectics as creative writing, exploring social problems, problem solving, creating a design or product, and broadening perspectives of a concept.

# DESIGN ACTIVITY 19

## "Your Instructional Framework"

**1.** Describe the instructional models that are most appropriate for your project and its goals.

**2.** Include a rationale for each model or strategy. If it makes sense to cluster a group of models, organize your description in that way.

**3.** Summarize how your instructional framework serves your instructional goals, supporting objectives, and provides opportunities to meet your assessment purposes.

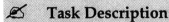 **Task Description**

In this Design Activity, outline the major features of how you will present instruction in ways that reflect your goals and mission.

## ☆ SCENARIO

# Middle School: What Teaching Model Do We Use?

This scenario introduces our third instructional setting: a science program in a middle school. The issue at Roberta W. Morgan Middle School is curriculum change. The science staff, in discussions with the high school, are considering a re-structuring of the science curriculum for the 6th, 7th, and 8th grades. They want to offer an integrated science curriculum for each grade with a half-year of physical science and a half-year of biological sciences. The high school science program used the inquiry approach introduced by the Biological Sciences Curriculum Studies (BSCS), and the two schools have decided that bringing the middle school in-line with this approach would improve middle-school students readiness for high school science.

The middle school is also faced with growing enrollment. Larger classes threatens individual hands-on activities. As a result, the science teachers are looking towards using cooperative learning and group investigation approaches where group problem solving and inquiry can be implemented to reduce individual lab activity requirements. In addition, the staff desires to tap the Internet and multimedia technologies to provide cost-effective science enrichment. Features of this curriculum change include the following:

- Use BSCS texts to support the inquiry approach and develop inquiry activities keyed to identified concepts.

- Develop cooperative learning and group investigation teacher handouts in addition to in-service workshops during the school year.

- Provide Internet access within science labs and increase current Internet access in the Media Center.

- Homework will be replaced with Inquiry Activities conducted in and out of school. These will include research write-ups to reflect the work of scientists.

- The Internet will be used by teachers to gather content materials and by students to conduct background research to support their hands-on activities.

- Students will convert paper write-ups to summaries to be posted to the school's Web site. These links can be used by future classes.

# Instructional Repertoire

Gunter et al. (1995) cite the necessity of sometimes pulling features from different models if this serves instructional purposes. Building one's instructional repertoire can proceed along two levels: personal and peer.

**Building repertoires from within.** Frequently, long-held assumptions drive the choice of instructional strategies. These assumptions need to be examined so that methods match the purposes you have set out for instruction. In addition, evaluation of instructor performance is needed to ensure that instructor actions are appropriate to serve learning needs. As Freiberg and Driscoll (1996) state, "the power of discovering what you are doing and how you can change gives you control of your teaching life" (p. 414).

♦ See Freiberg (1987) in **References** for a self-assessment measure on verbal interaction in the classroom; also Eash & Waxman (1983) for a 40-item questionnaire on teacher effectiveness.

**Building repertoires with others.** Implementing these models requires practice and feedback, which requires assistance from others. "Teachers may have difficulty relating instructional models to appropriate objectives, emphasizing the learning of concepts, rather than activities, and in finding the time to properly learn to use these models in the classroom" (Gunter et al., 1995, p. 69).

Peer assistance can come in the form of small study groups that are interested in putting into practice a particular model. Coaching and peer mentoring can provide the support one needs to persevere in implementation. Choosing a mutual support partner may be just what is needed to provide advice, encouragement, another set of eyes, and shared experiences that teachers need to invigorate their teaching.

See Tour 6: The Schoolhouse in "Touring Instructional Design."

Here are some guidelines for building one's teaching repertoire:

### Enlarging a Teaching Repertoire

1. Examine your view about teaching models.

2. Seek out case studies and research that supports their use.

3. Beginners: start slow. Follow the steps.
   Expert teachers: modify as needed.

4. Implement in appropriate conditions.

5. Seek the advice and support of peers.

6. Seek out the feedback of students.

7. Keep going.

From Gunter, A. A., Estes, T. H., & Schwab, J. H. (1995). *Instruction: A models approach* (2nd ed.). Boston: Allyn & Bacon.

The next Design Activity asks you to think about models and strategies you would like to master.

# DESIGN ACTIVITY 20

## "Your Instructional Repertoire"

✍ **Task Description**

The purpose of this task is to think and record ways to improve how you teach, train, or facilitate.

**1.** In **Design Activity 18** we asked you to reflect on the way you currently present instruction. How would you improve on your methods?

# Reviewing the Design Activities

### Design Activity 18: How Do You Present Instruction Now?

☐ Described instructional style.

☐ Described the basis for this style or approach.

☐ Identified relevant learning principles.

### Design Activity 19: Your Instructional Framework

☐ Described suitable instructional models.

☐ Identified rationale behind choices.

☐ Matched models to goals, learning types, and assessment tools.

### Design Activity 20: Your Instructional Repertoire

☐ Identified models to implement.

☐ Described strategy to implement or improve.

# ⚐ Summary of Important Ideas

**1.** An instructional framework supports instructional models that are appropriate to learners, content, and context.

**2.** Families of instructional models help us to see that these models are based on what we know about learning.

**3.** Selecting an appropriate set of instructional models means identifying our instructional purpose.

**4.** Models have been documented that improve learning. They have a syntax which helps the beginning teacher.

**5.** Designing an instructional framework can help to increase one's instructional repertoire.

---

### Food for Thought

Coldron and Smith (1995) describe teaching as a personal and social achievement consisting of a professional practice that is part this and part that; namely:

- **Teaching as part science.**
The science of teaching looks at why things happen. It consists of a body of scientifically grounded knowledge that helps teachers to make informed judgments as well as scientific procedures to analyze one's own practice.

- **Teaching as part craft.**
Teaching as craft tackles the task of making things work. In this view, teaching can be a "polished and thoughtful performance of expert teachers who continue to extend their craft" (p. 10).

- **Teaching as part art.**
Teaching as art resists analysis because it is "immediately felt or understood and often with considerable emotion" (p. 12).

- **Teaching as part moral activity.**
Because teaching is conducted within a community, it is also a moral activity in which teachers are held accountable to critically evaluate and make decisions about what they are asked to do and what they are not asked to do within the range of options that teachers may have.

# √ Your Personal Learning

### *Relating Your Beliefs to This Chapter:*

An instructional framework provides a structure to connect what you want to do (learning goals) with suitable instructional models. There are many models of instruction, each of which is based on learning theories that explain why it works and situations where it is most appropriate. We urge you to investigate the many instructional models and strategies in the major sources we have cited (Joyce and Weil, 1996; Freiberg & Driscoll, 1996; and Gunter, et al., 1995) to examine the possibilities.

### *Any revisions to your personal ID model?*

**1.** Is your instructional framework represented in your model?

**2.** What is the relationship of instructor to learner?

### *What questions do you have about the information presented in this chapter?*

# References

Ausubel, D. P. (1963*). The psychology of meaningful verbal learning.* NY: Grune & Stratton.

Barell, J. (1995). *Teaching for thoughtfulness: Classroom strategies to enhance intellectual development* (2nd ed.). White Plains NY: Longman.

Canfield, J., & Wells, H. C. (1994). *100 ways to enhance self-concept in the classroom* (2nd ed.). Boston: Allyn & Bacon.

Chesler, M., & Fox, R. (1966). *Role-playing methods in the classroom.* Chicago: Science Research.

Coldron, J., & Smith, R. (1995, April). *Teaching as an amalgam of discourses and the consequent need for appropriate modes of reflection.* Paper presented at the 1995 Annual Meeting of the American Educational Research Association, San Francisco, CA.

Collins, A. (1991). Cognitive apprenticeship and instructional technology. In L. Idol & B. F. Jones (Eds.), *Educational values and cognitive instruction: Implications for reform.* Hillsdale, NJ: Erlbaum.

Durkin, D. (1978-1979). What classroom observations reveal about reading comprehension instruction. *Reading Research Quarterly, 14,* 481-533.

Eash, M. J., & Waxman, H. C. (1983*). Our class and its work user manual.* Chicago: University of Illinois at Chicago, Office of Evaluation Research.

Freiberg, H. J. (1987). Teacher self-evaluation and principle supervision. *NASSP Bulletin,* 71(498), 85-92.

Freiberg, H. J., & Driscoll, A. (1996). *Universal teaching strategies* (2nd ed.). Boston: Allyn & Bacon.

Goodlad, J. (1984). *A place called school: Prospects for the future.* NY: McGraw-Hill.

Gordon, W. J. J. (1961). *Synectics.* NY: Harper & Row.

Gunter, A. A., Estes, T. H., & Schwab, J. H. (1995). *Instruction: A models approach* (2nd ed.). Boston: Allyn & Bacon.

Johnson, D. W., & Johnson, R. T. (1975). *Circles of learning.* Englewood Cliffs, NJ: Prentice-Hall.

Johnson, D. W., Johnson, R. T., & Smith, K. A. (1991). *Active learning: Cooperation in the college classroom.* Edina, MN: Interaction Book.

Joyce, B., & Weil, M. (1996). *Models of teaching* (5th ed.). Boston: Allyn & Bacon.

Joyce, B., Weil, M., & Showers, B. (1992). *Models of teaching* (4th ed.). Englewood Cliffs, NJ: Prentice-Hall.

Labensky, S. R., & Hause, A. M. (1995). *On cooking: Techniques from expert chefs.* Englewood Cliffs, NJ: Prentice Hall.

Moll, L. C. (1990). *Vygotsky and education: Instructional implications and applications of sociohistorical psychology.* Cambridge: Cambridge University Press.

Newman, D., Griffin, P., & Cole, M. (1989). *The construction zone: Working for cognitive change in school.* Cambridge: Cambridge University Press.

Norman, D. A. (1993). *Things that make us smart: Defending human attributes in the ages of the machine.* Reading, MA: Addison-Wesley.

Novak, J. D., & Gowin, D. B. (1984). *Learning how to learn.* NY: Cambridge University Press.

Oliver, D., & Shaver, J. P. (1966). *Teaching public issues in the high school.* Boston: Houghton Mifflin.

Penland. (1994). *Summer catalog.* NC: Penland School of Crafts.

Pressley, M., Levin, J. R., & Delaney, H. D. (1982). The mnemonic keyword method. *Review of Educational Research, 52*(1), 61-91.

Purkey, W. W. (1970). *Self-concept and school achievement.* Englewood Cliffs, NJ: Prentice-Hall.

Roget. (1977). *Roget's International Thesaurus* (4th ed.). Revised by R. L. Chapman. NY: Thomas Crowell.

Rosenshine, B. (1983, March). Teaching functions in instructional programs. *The Elementary School Journal, 83,* 335-350.

Schank, R. C. (1990). *Tell me a story: A new look at real and artificial memory.* NY: Scribner's.

Shaftel, F., & Shaftel, G. (1982). *Role playing in the curriculum.* Englewood Cliffs, NJ: Prentice-Hall.

Sharan, S. (1990). *Cooperative learning: Theory and research:* NY: Praeger.

Slavin, R. E. (1983). *Cooperative learning.* NY: Longman.

Suchman, J. R. (1962). *The elementary school training program in scientific inquiry.* Report to the U.S. Office of Education, Project Title VII. Urbana: University of Illinois Press.

Taba, H. (1971). *Hilda Taba teaching strategies program.* Miami, FL: Institute for Staff Development.

Thelen, H. (1960). *Education and the human quest.* NY: Harper & Row.

Vygotsky, L. S. (1978). *Mind in society: The development of higher psychological processes.* Cambridge, MA: Harvard University Press.

Wandersee, J. H. (1990). Concept mapping and the cartography of cognition. *Journal of Research in Science Teaching, 27*(10), 923-936.

# For Further Reading

Freiberg, H. J., & Driscoll, A. (1996). *Universal teaching strategies* (2nd ed.). Boston: Allyn & Bacon.

> A practical, clearly laid out survey of some common teaching strategies for classroom teachers.

Gunter, A. A., Estes, T. H., & Schwab, J. H. (1995). *Instruction: A models approach.* (2nd ed.). Boston: Allyn & Bacon.

> A practical guide to instructional practice. This text offers examples and exercises that illustrate the nuances of each model.

Joyce, B., & Weil, M. (1996). *Models of teaching* (5th ed.). Boston: Allyn & Bacon.

> A classic synthesis of theory and action in articulating instruction across schooling and training settings.

Tharp, R. G., & Gallimore, R. (1988). *Rousing minds to life: Teaching, learning, and schooling in social context.* Cambridge: Cambridge University Press.

> An important contribution to our understanding of teaching from a truly assistive perspective. Based on Vygotsky's sociocultural perspective, this work epitomizes an integrative approach to daily instruction.

# What's Next?

In Chapter 7, we will examine more closely the possibilities of **instructional media**, another designing phase, in your instructional design and appropriate ways that these materials may enhance learning.

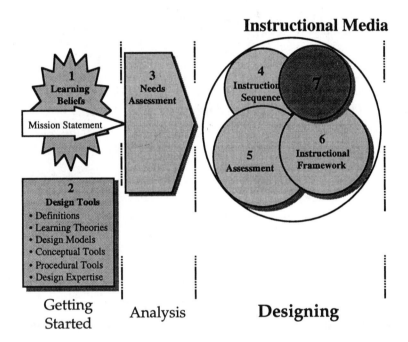

# CHAPTER 7

We hope that you will carefully look at the full range of media materials for instructional use.

We invite you to explore the full range of materials that will enhance learning in your instructional design.

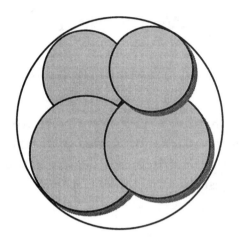

# Instructional Media

*... the present debate about instructional design ideology ... includes questions about the roles in which learners may be cast. The debate should move instructional developers to adopt an ideology that stresses opening up the possibilities of technology to exploit learner strengths.*

(Ullmer, 1989, p. 99)

Instructional media is full of possibilities for instruction. Its use in teaching and learning must be based on the purposes you have worked so hard to determine from earlier phases in the instructional design process. This chapter is not about how to design media materials, but the implications of your media choices for designing instruction.

This chapter will define instructional media and examine the role of technology in these materials. This chapter examines instructional design issues of selecting, modifying, and designing instructional media that are appropriate to your content, the learning context, and learners.

In this chapter you will:

1. Identify media possibilities for your project.

2. Construct a plan for the use of media.

**Media** is the plural of medium, a Latin-derived word meaning "an intervening agency, means, or instrument." The word, media, is generally used as a collective singular, and in our context, is anything that carries information *between* people. Not all media, however, are **instructional media**, only those that are "used to carry messages with an instructional intent" (Heinich, Molenda & Russell & Smaldino, 1996, p. 5).

> What does media mean to you?

# DESIGN ACTIVITY 21

## "Identify Media Possibilities"

1. What types of media do you like to use and/or have used within instruction?

2. What media would be useful in your design project? What kind of "instructional messages" does each of these carry?

 **Task Description**

Think about all of the types of instructional media that might work for you in your project.

**Key Words**
- Instructional media
- Media

## MEDIA EXAMPLES

audio tapes
books
bulletin boards
chalk
computers
construction paper
electronic books
film
filmstrips
games
models
multimedia
notebooks
opaque projection
overhead transparencies
paper
pictures
simulations
slides
software
sports equipment
telecommunications
television
textbooks
video
web pages

# Technology & Learning

Our perceptions of media tend to guide our design decisions, particularly in the choice of instructional media. Frequently, instructional media is viewed as technology-based, because of the influence that products of technology (e. g., pencils, computers, and video) play throughout our lives. These views of technology are not wrong, but they sometimes limit our vision of what technology can mean for learning.

Technology can be viewed as a process that systematically provides answers to problems. However, the common understanding of the term is that technology is a product resulting from the application of scientific and technological principles or processes. In an instructional setting our view of technology is also generally product-based: slides, software, overhead transparencies, or video. People have different views on what they mean by technology and ways that it can be used for learning.

In a general sense designers and end users should view technology as a means to engage learners through a process of solving human problems with tools that possess varying degrees of process or product characteristics. The practical side of people, however, views technology as primarily products, and it is uncommon to view technology for learning in a broader systems perspective.

**Human-centered technology**. It may be helpful to take a fresh look at the role of technology in learning. Technology, according to Norman (1993), is essential for human growth in knowledge and mental capabilities. He advocates a human-centered technology, rather than a machine-centered orientation, which "emphasizes the needs of technology over those of people, thereby forcing people into a supporting role, one for which we are most unsuited" (1993, p. xi).

Norman believes that technology can make us smart. Because our minds are limited in capacity, we need artificial devices—artifacts—to extend our mental capacities. Technology should support people and aid those activities for which humans are cognitively ill suited. Norman cites one characteristic of human intelligence as our ability to construct **cognitive artifacts**. Media, products of technology, help to make us smart by providing a means to communicate in ways that humans cannot manage alone. For example, our minds can imagine a scene, but it cannot remember all of the details in that scene. Film, videotape, videodisk, or software can record the details for us to study at another time. Media can also provide a database of facts, images, experiences, impressions, and notes that we cannot remember. This database could be computer-based, but it could also be a set of note cards, a book, or an electronic book. Norman also cautions that media can make us dumb. Media can be seductive (e.g., television, computer games, and Internet browsing) or frustrating (e.g., programming of VCR's, and software installation and use).

This book is, in fact, a cognitive artifact, a mental tool to help you understand the principles and processes of instructional design. When annotated with your comments, questions, doodles, arrows, and underlining, this book becomes a unique and personal cognitive artifact, an artificial means that extend your mental capacities to learn. The design of cognitive artifacts, tools that aid the mind, are what Norman has in mind for instructional media.

> Next, we will look at some instructional design
> issues in selecting media.

**Key Words**
- Cognitive artifact

# Design Issues with Media

In this section we will examine design issues within the analysis, designing, and program evaluation components of the instructional design process.

**Media issues in analysis.** Needs assessment examines an instructional problem and sharpens its focus with an analysis of the relationships between content, context, and learners. Each of the data sources consulted, whether it be field records, the library, teachers, students, or experts, can shed light on the implications of instructional media for these three issues.

∞

---

**Media Issues in Analysis (Needs Assessment)**

- Matching media and intent.
- Media suitable for instructional content.
- Media appropriate for learners.
- Media achievable within the reality of the setting.

---

Identifying instructional media that are suitable for the content is something that can be discovered by interviewing content and media experts, as well as instructors who have taught the content before. Instructional media that fit the realities of the learning context can be determined partly through a determination of resources and constraints (see **Design Activity 10**). Learners can also supply some information on what media might be interesting and useful to their learning.

Decisions about media can be made based on goals from the Needs Assessment. This is the subject of **Design Activity 22** later in this chapter. With these goals, you can begin to scan the media possibilities for appropriate choices. The information from the needs assessment may have uncovered some justification for media as a major player in design features. You may need to adjust your goals to reflect this shift in intent.

**Media issues in designing.** During the sequencing phase of instructional design you can pencil in how instructional media could affect the structuring of the content. Media may be a supportive element or a central feature in learning activities.

---

### Media Issues in Designing Phases

- In your sequencing plan identify possible uses for media.
- Materials should be appropriate to the content as you have structured it. Does the sequence need changing based on your choices of media?
- Make decisions on acquiring, adapting, or developing media materials.
- Do your materials provide a rich learning experience?

---

The materials should reflect the purposes expressed by your goals and specific learning objectives. The content of the materials should be accurate, relevant, and current. The content needs to be structured in such a way that it maintains attention and is "deep enough" to warrant a learner's attention. Above all, do the materials provide a rich, rewarding experience? Do they take advantage of what cognitive artifacts are designed to do—to extend human capabilities?

**Media issues in program evaluation.** Three main issues regarding media materials should be addressed by program evaluation: (1) do the materials support your intent, (2) is the technical quality of the media

### Food for Thought

Norman (1993) suggests the following checklist for rewarding experiences. Do the materials:

1. Provide a high intensity of interaction and feedback?
2. Have specific goals and established procedures?
3. Motivate?
4. Provide a continual feeling of challenge, one that is neither so difficult as to create a sense of hopelessness and frustration nor so easy as to produce boredom?
5. Provide a sense of direct engagement, producing the feeling of directly experiencing the environment, directly working on the task?
6. Provide appropriate tools that fit the user and task so well that they aid and do not distract?
7. Avoid distractions and disruptions that intervene and destroy the subjective experience?

From Norman, D. A. (1993). *Things that make us smart: Defending human attributes in the age of the machine.* Reading, MA: Addison-Wesley.

adequate, and (3) do the materials help learners learn (Chinien & Hlynka, 1993)?

The answers to the first two questions can be determined from **formative** and **summative evaluations** through the use of experts and learner feedback, while the answer to the third question can be obtained from student assessment data (e. g., feedback, and task performance). Try not to restrict media questions to just a media or a delivery expert, but also include subject matter, language, teaching, and instructional design experts. Otherwise, your questions and responses may miss important issues of content accuracy and adequacy, reading level, a match with objectives, and media design based on learning theories.

---

### Media Issues in Program Evaluation

- How well do media support your instruction? What are your evaluation criteria?
- What is the technical quality of the materials?
- Do the materials aid in learning?

---

The benefits of using experts in the formative evaluation of materials include time savings, cost-effectiveness, enhanced credibility of materials, and feedback on prototypes. However, the downside of experts' opinions involves their subjectivity, inconclusiveness, and difficulty in obtaining them in some fields (Chinien & Hlynka, 1993). Such shortcomings can be improved by extending the range of experts you consult. Those experts include content, language, target, media, format, and delivery-system experts (Thiagarajan, 1978).

Student responses can involve individuals, small groups, or field tests of materials (Dick & Carey, 1996). Criteria should assess their reactions to the materials and their learning performance from using the

**Key Words**
- Formative evaluation
- Summative evaluation

materials. Students selected should be representative of the intended participants and possess the entry-level skills determined from a **learning task analysis**.

---

**Major Issues & Data Sources in Program Evaluation**

<u>Formative:</u>

**Content:** experts
**Technical quality:** experts
**Learnability:** learners

<u>Summative:</u>

**Effectiveness:** external review by experts
**Appeal:** learners
**Efficiency:** designers, teachers, or other users

---

The third question, evaluating media's effectiveness in helping learners learn, can be performed in a summative evaluation, but such evaluation is often ignored, because it is time consuming and there is a lack of criteria to measure its effectiveness. According to Guba and Lincoln (1985), the main aim of summative evaluation "is to critique a completed entity in terms of professional or expert standards so as to be able to certify and warrant" (p. 51) its use. The major issues here include the effectiveness of the materials, their appeal, and their efficiency (see Chapter 9).

Next, instructional design issues of media.

**Key Words**
• Learning task analysis

# Developing Instructional Media

This section addresses the implications of instructional media in your instructional design. Although the issues of media development are beyond the scope of this book, they do impact on the realities surrounding the design and implementation of your instructional design. In particular, the time available to develop, learn, or integrate the materials may severely limit the use of some materials. An instructional designer has three choices to choose from: (1) selecting what's available from existing or outside sources, (2) modifying what you have, or (3) designing your own (Heinich et al., 1996).

**Select what's available.** One option is to choose materials from what is commercially available or what you already have on the shelf. General selection criteria for these instructional media materials include the (1) characteristics of the learner, (2) nature of the objectives, (3) instructional approach, and (4) limitations of the instructional setting. Specific criteria can be applied using media appraisal checklists for specific media formats (Heinich et al., 1996). See "Talking About Media" in Chapter 3 for additional checklists. You may need to modify these checklists to add criteria that fits your media needs.

> One of the new medias are Web pages. The use of these pages for learning have ID issues to address.

# Talking about Media

**ID Issues in Constructing Web Pages**. The World Wide Web is a collection of computer sites (servers) around the world containing "pages" of information. Users select items of interest, which may include text, sound clips, images, animations, or movies. Some items may be "links" to information residing on the same computer site or on a different computer system. Web pages are being constructed by institutions, firms, schools, and individuals that reflect commercial marketing of products and services, public service and informational sites, as well as educational sites. The construction of a Web page involves consideration of the following instructional design issues:

## A Top 9 List of ID Issues for Web Pages

### 1. Personal/institutional beliefs on learning.

Are teaching and learning separate activities? Is your stance on teaching and learning supported by the use of the Web?

### 2. Design tools.

What is the theoretical basis for Web pages? Does this basis support your purposes?

### 3. Needs assessment.

What attributes of your page users/browsers will influence your design of pages? What are the overall goals of your Web pages?

### 4. Sequence of instruction.

What is critical content for your pages? How should this content be structured? What provisions will you need to make to assist the user in navigation?

### 5. Assessment.

How will your Web page help users to learn? How will you determine if any learning is occurring?

### 6. Instructional framework.

What is your orientation towards instruction in your pages? Are you presenting information or links to resources, providing learning activities, or a combination of the two? How much control will you give to users?

### 7. Instructional media.

What media (text, images, sound, animations, movies) should your pages feature?

8 and 9 go together.

**8. Prototype.**

Have you outlined your content and links to information on pages you control?

**9. Program evaluation.**

Have you thought about how to evaluate the effectiveness and appeal of your pages in some fashion? Do the pages, which are "Under Construction," have a means to solicit and retrieve feedback from users?

**Modify what you have.** A second option is to modify existing media to fit your instructional needs. This can be done without any legal problems if the available materials are ones that you have already developed yourself. There are many different ways of using parts of materials or supplementing existing materials in new ways that make them more useful. There are no hard and fast rules here, other than adhering to copyright limitations and making sure that changes serve your instructional purposes.

**Design your own.** A third option is to design your own media materials. This is obviously the best choice for appropriateness of materials, but the time and resources needed are prohibitive to some. However, you may still want to do this for some of your activities. Here are some issues to keep in mind when developing original materials.

---

**Issues to Consider When Designing Your Own Instructional Media Materials**

- Match materials to meet the needs of the instructional objectives.
- Materials need to suit your audience.
- Estimate cost and determine if the budget exists.
- Determine if technical expertise is needed.
- Determine if special equipment is needed.
- Determine if facilities are needed to support media's use.
- Determine the time necessary to learn and use materials.

These concerns should be a part of your constraints and limitations data that you gathered from your Needs Assessment. You can use the criteria from the media appraisal charts to provide a checklist for a particular format. You may also need to update your context analysis as you make more informed decisions on media materials.

Iterative designing represents one of the challenges of not only learning instructional design but also practicing it. Decisions in one phase of designing influences what may need to be revised in other phases. For example, determining the purpose for assessment helps you to select your instructional strategy. Choosing instructional media may also require some changes in other parts of your design. Whenever you make design decisions, examine what effects, what implications, and what issues these choices have on other parts of your design.

## ☆ SCENARIO

### Middle School: Repurposing Media

Our Middle School example of a curriculum-based instructional setting wants to tap the Internet and multimedia as sources of information and activities for their inquiry-focused curriculum. The science staff suggested converting some of their existing instructional media into multimedia for student-produced Web pages. This repurposing of existing materials worried some, who expressed concern about the time involved and the legal issues. Others did not want to produce materials that may not be useful in the future.

A biology specialist in the group suggested that they first think about ways to take advantage of the new media before converting photos or text to multimedia. "Otherwise, we'll just have different buttons to push for the same thing," she said. After some discussion, they decided that they needed to be clear on what they could do.

- The group decided that if they were going to create or move existing materials to new media, it should be because of the need to support the new cooperative-learning/inquiry approach. Thus, the group identified a clear overall purpose to the media.

- Since students would be writing their inquiries and posting the summaries to Web pages, efforts would be made to develop some aids for both teachers and students on the technical issues of adding text and images to Web pages.

- For now, the group decided to keep visuals to still images and stay away from video. A digital camera was requested in the budget to simplify this process, as well as purchasing an image database software product to keep track of all of the images.

- The group decided to make an inventory of multimedia resources in the Media Center and see if the staff there might not consider organizing this collection as a Science Inquiry Workstation.

Finally, the group decided to incorporate other media materials through links to existing Web pages and paper lists of existing materials, so as not to violate copyright laws.

See Tour 7: Bubble, Bubble, Toil and Trouble" in "Touring Instructional Design."

It might help to get a better feel for instructional media by sketching out a media plan. Here is a suggested structure.

↓

# DESIGN ACTIVITY 22

## "Your Instructional Media Plan"

 **Task Description**

Draw up a plan that summarizes how media can be used to enhance learning in your project. Provide a list of possible media materials, connect them with your goals and supporting objectives, and explain why you are using them. In addition, address some of the instructional resources and constraints that come with selecting, designing, and using these materials.

**1. Describe the kinds of media that you intend to use throughout your project.** Referring to your sequencing, instructional models, and resources and constraints, describe the media you plan on using. How do these materials support the goals and objectives you have already established?

| Media Materials | Learning Goals & Objectives |
| --- | --- |
|  |  |

**2. Include a rationale for each media type** you are considering. Also, think about some of the selection, design, and implementation issues for each media material, and update your resources and constraints information, if necessary.

| Media Materials | Rationale | Issues |
| --- | --- | --- |
|  |  |  |

**3. Make a list of lessons or activities** and choose instructional media materials that support the above goals and objectives.

| Lessons or Activities | Rationale | Issues |
| --- | --- | --- |
|  |  |  |

**Food for Thought**

**Learning with instructional media.** Here is a quick summary of what the research says.

- Media comparison studies, due to their faulty research designs, have not proven useful. These studies generally featured one group of learners exposed to an audiovisual presentation while another group received conventional instruction.

- Subsequent research which attempted to control the conditions of the media treatment produced results of higher precision and validity, but failed to resemble normal practices. Thus, it was difficult to generalize from one media program to another. Also the content of these studies was biased in favor of cognitive content over affective and motor skill objectives.

- However, this research points out that the degree to which media is effective depends on how it is integrated into the instructional context, or how it is specified in an instructional design.

For a deeper coverage of how media enhances learning consult in **References:** Wilkinson (1980). *Media in Instruction: 60 Years of Research* ; and Thompson, Simonson & Hargrave. (1992). *Educational Technology: A Review of the Research*, both published by the Association for Educational Communications and Technology (AECT).

# Reviewing the Design Activities

### Design Activity 21: Identify Media Possibilities

☐ Identified media types currently used in instruction.

☐ Identified favorite choices of instructional media.

☐ Described intent of media materials in project.

### Design Activity 22: Your Instructional Media Plan

☐ Described intended media materials and matched them with ID goals and objectives.

☐ Provided a rationale for the use of materials and identified implementation issues.

☐ Listed lessons or activities and selected possible media materials that supported above goals and objectives.

## ꩜ Summary of Important Ideas

**1.** There are many different examples of instructional media and endless ways to use media in instruction.

**2.** Technology, as it applies to instruction, is both a process, a means to devise appropriate solutions to problems, and a product that results from using technological processes. One type of product is a cognitive artifact, a tool to aid the mind.

**3.** The purpose for "instructional" technology is to engage learners in learning.

**4.** Consider the instructional issues, related to content, context, and learners, of media materials during the analysis of learning needs, while designing appropriate responses to those needs, and during evaluation of your instructional design.

**5.** Whether you choose to use what is available, modify existing materials, or develop your own, examine the implications of your media materials and how they support your goals and objectives.

# √ Your Personal Learning

---

### *Relating Your Beliefs to This Chapter:*

Media in education prompts many reactions. To get the most out of this chapter, it will be helpful for you to examine your own beliefs about the use of media for learning.

**1.** How do media help you learn?

**2.** What types of media do you learn best with and why?

**3.** What are your reactions to the increased use of instructional technology in education?

**4.** What about the design and use of media would you like to know more?

### *Any revisions to your personal ID model?*

Where in your instructional design model are instructional media decisions made?

### *What questions do you have about the information presented in this chapter?*

# References

Association for Educational Communications and Technology (1977). *Educational technology: Definition and glossary of terms.* Washington, D. C.

Chinien, C., & Hlynka, D. (1993). Formative evaluation of prototypical products: From expert to connoisseur. *ETTI 30*(1), 60-66.

Dick, W., & Carey, L. (1996). *The systematic design of instruction* (4th ed.). NY: HarperCollins.

Guba, E. G., & Lincoln, Y. S. (1985). *Effective evaluation.* San Francisco: Jossey-Bass.

Heinich, R., Molenda, M., Russell, J. D., & Smaldino, S. E. (1996). *Instructional media and the new technologies of instruction* (5th ed.). Englewood Cliffs, NJ: Prentice-Hall.

Norman, D. A. (1993). *Things that make us smart: Defending human attributes in the age of the machine.* Reading, MA; Addison-Wesley.

Thiagarajan, S. (1978). Instructional product verification and revision: 20 questions and 200 speculations. *Educational Communication and Technology Journal, 26*(2), 133-141.

Thompson, A. D., Simonson, M. R., & Hargrave, C. P. (1992). *Educational technology: A review of the research.* Washington, D.C.: Association for Educational Communications and Technology.

Ullmer, E. J. (1989). High-tech instructional development: It's the thought that counts. *Educational Technology Research & Development, 37*(3), 95-101.

Wilkinson, G. L. (1980). *Media in instruction: 60 years of research.* Washington, D.C.: Association for Educational Communications and Technology.

# For Further Reading ...

Heinich, R., Molenda, M., Russell, J. D., & Smaldino, S. E. (1996). *Instructional media and the new technologies of instruction* (5th ed.). Englewood Cliffs, NJ: Prentice-Hall.

A clear and practical guide to understanding and using a variety of media for instructional purposes.

Norman, D. A. (1993). *Things that make us smart: Defending human attributes in the age of the machine.* Reading, MA; Addison-Wesley.

Norman talks about the possibilities of entertainment and learning and ways that both can occur in the cognitive artifacts (e.g. multimedia) that we construct.

# What's Next?

Chapter 8 is our final designing phase—a chance to confirm in a prototype what fits well together and make decisions about what needs to be adjusted.

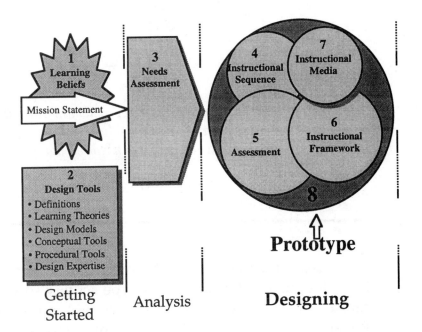

# CHAPTER
# 8

This chapter gives you a chance to see how your design, as constructed so far, will play out in an authentic event.

We borrow heavily from the ideas of Robert Gagné (e.g., 1985, 1992), particularly his ideas on the conditions of learning and the instructional events that support one's internal mental processes.

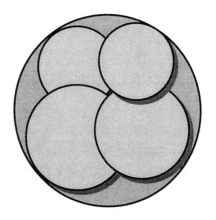

# Prototype

*A teacher need not know how to solve a problem in order to be able ... to help the student search for solutions by imparting ways to sense when progress has been made.*

(Minsky, 1986)

---

This chapter will place the pieces of what you have designed so far into a prototype activity so you can see how they work together. We will introduce Robert Gagné's (1985, 1992) idea of instructional events as a way of addressing the issues in any instructional activity.

In this chapter you will:

**1.** Construct a lesson or activity using instructional events.

**2.** Draw up a sample instructional activity.

**3.** Construct a syllabus or brochure or some means that summarizes and communicates your design project to intended participants.

# Conditions of Learning

In Chapter 2, Design Tools, we discussed how learning theories form the basis of principles useful for designing instruction. In Chapter 6 we presented a variety of instructional models based on learning theories that enlarge the instructional possibilities to meet learning objectives. According to Gagné et al. (1992), what is needed are factors that relate these learning theories and instructional models together, factors he calls the conditions of learning (Gagné, 1985).

According to Gagné, there are two types of conditions of learning. **Internal conditions** involve states of mind that the learner brings to the learning situation, while **external conditions** include stimuli outside of the learner, some of which may include instruction.

**Internal conditions.** Internal conditions include intellectual skills, cognitive strategies, verbal information, attitudes, and motor skills. Humans have different degrees of capability, or internal states, for each of these. Refer back to Chapter 3 for a discussion of Gagné's et al. (1992) learned capabilities taxonomy.

**External conditions.** The question then becomes: how can the internal states of these capabilities be influenced? Instruction is one way. In fact, the definition of instruction in Gagné's et al. definition of instruction is a "deliberately arranged set of external events designed to support internal learning processes" (1992, p. 11). The purpose of these external events is to influence mental (internal) processes, such as attending, learning, remembering, and thinking. These developed processes contribute to one's learned

**Internal Conditions**

- Intellectual skills
- Cognitive strategies
- Verbal information
- Attitudes
- Motor skills

**Key Words**
- External conditions
- Internal conditions

capabilities, which include intellectual skills, cognitive strategies, verbal information, attitudes, and motor skills.

Gagné further elaborated on these external **instructional events,** which are "designed to make it possible for learners to proceed from 'where they are' to achieve a capability expressed in the **target objective**" (1992, p. 189). These events are listed below.

---

---

**Instructional Events** (Gagné, Briggs & Wager, 1992)

1. Gaining attention
2. Informing the learner of the objective
3. Stimulating recall of prerequisite learning
4. Presenting the stimulus material
5. Providing learning guidance
6. Eliciting the performance
7. Providing feedback about performance
8. Assessing the performance
9. Enhancing retention and transfer

From PRINCIPLES OF INSTRUCTIONAL DESIGN, 4/E. by Robert M. Gagné, Leslie J. Briggs, & Walter W. Wager, copyright © 1992 by Holt, Rinehart and Winston, Inc., reproduced by permission of the publisher.

---

Let's take a closer look at instructional events.

---

**Key Words**
- Instructional events
- Target objective

# Instructional Events

These events support our knowledge of how people learn, so the events of instruction can be shown to correspond to specific learning processes (Gagné, et al., 1992).

## Connection of Instructional Events with Learning

| Instructional Events | Learning Process |
|---|---|
| 1. Gaining attention | Reception of stimulus and activating sensory registers. |
| 2. Informing the learner of the objective | Activating executive control. |
| 3. Stimulating recall of prerequisite learning | Retrieval of information to working memory. |
| 4. Presenting the stimulus material | Emphasizing features for selective perception. |
| 5. Providing learning guidance | Semantic encoding; cues for retrieval. |
| 6. Eliciting the performance | Activating response. |
| 7. Providing feedback about performance | Establishing reinforcement. |
| 8. Assessing the performance | Activating retrieval. |
| 9. Enhancing retention and transfer | Providing cues and strategies for retrieval. |

From PRINCIPLES OF INSTRUCTIONAL DESIGN, 4/E. by Robert M. Gagné, Leslie J. Briggs, & Walter W. Wager, copyright © 1992 by Holt, Rinehart and Winston, Inc., reproduced by permission of the publisher.

Instructional events involve a set of activities in roughly the order listed in the margin. Not all instructional activities include all of these events. Some may not be needed or may be emphasized more or less depending on the instructional model selected. Some of these events typically overlap, such as gaining attention and informing the learner of the objective. For example, walking into a classroom and writing on the board the agenda for the days' presentation covers both of these events. We will examine how these events relate to several instructional models later in this chapter.

**1. Gaining attention.** The first three events ready the learner for new instruction. The first event serves to gain the attention of the learner, or in information processing terms, to stimulate one's stimuli receptors to receive patterns of neural impulses. Cognitive theories present learning as a sequence that begins when an individual's brain receives patterns of neural impulses through its eye (receptors), which are changed into a code that is recorded in short-term memory.

**2. Informing the learner of the objective.** A second readying event informs the learner of the objective of the instruction. This prompts one's executive control strategies, which consist of matching estimates of attention, task, and what is at stake with the instructor's statements. These choices also include decisions about which strategies to use and time requirements.

**3. Stimulating recall of prerequisite learning.** The third readying event activates prior knowledge and recalls what was learned previously and relates this to what might be useful in today's instruction. Prior knowledge is stored in long-term memory through a process called semantic encoding in which the codes of this information are connected with what we already know. When the learned information is needed it can be retrieved from long-term memory and transformed into short-term memory once again, sometimes called working memory.

**4. Presenting the stimulus material.** This event begins the presentation of new learning. The exact presentation of new material or new activities depends on the nature of the content and the instructional model employed to "present" new learning opportunities. The stimulus material could consist of case studies, examples, situations, simulations, a lecture, a guest speaker, a hands-on activity, a stimulating key question, or a demonstration. A whole variety of methods exist to present the new material.

**5. Providing learning guidance.** This event serves to assist the learner in various ways from modeling behavior to questioning to reinforcing to the use of organizers.

**6. Eliciting the performance.** This event requires active participation by the learner, demonstrating what one has learned through learning performance, whether it be through recall, synthesis, attitudinal change, physical skill improvement, or some other learning improvement.

**7. Providing feedback.** Upon producing the behavior or performance, it is necessary for the instructor (or fellow learners) to respond to the behavior or performance on a task. This response may take the form of a spoken or written communication of some sort. This event frequently overlaps with the next one.

**8. Assessing performance.** This event determines a level of performance keyed to the objectives of the activity. Will the performance on the task be about the same when faced with the same assessment under different circumstances? Is the performance valid, measuring performance against an objective, and does the performance measure what it is designed to measure? These issues are all critical regardless of the nature of the assessment purpose.

**9. Enhancing retention and transfer.** This event, which is often neglected, attempts to make it possible for the learner to use the new learning in a related situation or to apply what has been learned in different problems. We often need to provide explicit opportunities for learners to make clear bridges between the instructional task and the real-life application of the knowledge/skills inherent in the task.

> How would these instructional events match a key lesson or activity that you are familiar with?

↓

# DESIGN ACTIVITY 23

## "Instructional Events"

 **Task Description**

Pull together what you know and what you have designed so far and construct an activity using Gagné's instructional events to guide you in this task.

**1. Use Gagné's instructional events in your prototype.** Focusing on a key activity, analyze how Gagné's events of instruction fit the tasks and activities you are planning on using. The instructional events help to cover "all the bases," or the instructional opportunities in your activity.

**2.** What events overlap?

**3.** Are there some events that need more attention?

**4.** What strategies could you incorporate?

| Instructional Event | Your Activity | Objective |
| --- | --- | --- |
| 1. Gain attention | | |
| 2. Inform the learner of objective | | |
| 3. Stimulate recall of prior learning | | |
| 4. Present new material | | |
| 5. Provide learning guidance | | |
| 6. Elicit the performance | | |
| 7. Provide feedback | | |
| 8. Assess performance | | |
| 9. Enhance retention and transfer | | |

Next are several instructional models and how they
match up with instructional events.

# Instructional Model
# and Instructional Events

As you might have guessed, each instructional model addresses instructional events in different ways. Following are a number of instructional models and how their steps might relate to these events.

**Direct instruction model.** The steps of the direct instruction model are very similar to the events of instruction (Gunter et al., 1995). Direct instruction is suitable for teaching basic skills, skills that can be taught directly. Note in the model that a review is conducted before communicating the objectives of the new lesson. The order will depend on what works for you. The last instructional event, enhancing instruction, is not specified directly by the model. This points out an important area that may need to be addressed in your instructional design.

Direct instruction provides numerous opportunities for assessment and media use. Assessing the performance, event #8, can include informal as well as formal assessment, such as when grades are needed. Media is typically introduced to present the stimulus material, but some forms of media, such as interactive technologies, may incorporate all of these events.

### Steps of Direct Instruction Model

1. Review previously learned material

2. State objectives for the lesson

3. Present new material

4. Guide practice with corrective feedback

5. Require independent practice with corrective feedback

6. Provide a periodic review with corrective feedback if necessary

(Gunter, Estes & Schwab, 1995)

## Instructional Events and Direct Instruction

| Instructional Event | Possible Instructor Action |
|---|---|
| 1. Gaining attention | Demonstration |
| 2. Informing the learner of the objective | Writing on board, verbal, or handout |
| 3. Stimulating recall of prerequisite learning | Teacher or student summary; questions |
| 4. Presenting the stimulus material | Teacher, student, media |
| 5. Providing learning guidance | Teacher provide examples on board, student attempts examples; teacher walk around |
| 6. Eliciting the performance | Class suggestions; individual prompting |
| 7. Providing feedback about performance correctness | Class examples; lab activities; homework; verbal comments on work |
| 8. Assessing the performance | Comments, grading |
| 9. Enhancing retention | Repeating in subsequent lessons; provide additional diverse examples |

From PRINCIPLES OF INSTRUCTIONAL DESIGN, 4/E. by Robert M. Gagné, Leslie J. Briggs, & Walter W. Wager, copyright © 1992 by Holt, Rinehart and Winston, Inc., reproduced by permission of the publisher.

**Classroom discussion model.** Classroom discussion is an important teaching model because frequently "the quality of those discussions... determines the extent and quality of students' learning" (Gunter et al., 1995, p. 149). The instructor and students read new material in advance, while the instructor prepares questions. The instructor introduces the discussion model in the classroom, conducts the discussion, reviews with students how the discussion fared, and summarizes student responses.

Classroom discussion is a good example of how flexible the events of instruction can be depending on the steps of a particular model. The first two steps, reading the material and constructing the questions, are conducted before the instruction; however, they are key to the success of the model. Although not explicit steps in the model, gaining attention and stimulating recall are two instructional events that can be used by the instructor to supplement the steps of the model. By comparing the steps of the model with the range of instruction provided by "events," one can see how much is involved in Step 4 of the model, conducting the discussion. This step includes the instructional events of providing learning guidance, eliciting performance, providing feedback, and assessing performance.

Issues of assessment and instructional media can be connected into these instructional events. Discussion performance can be observed and recorded by the instructor according to some established criteria. It is essential that the instructor involve the whole class in the discussion and exert care in judging individual responses.

## Instructional Events of Classroom Discussion

| Instructional Event | Possible Instructor Actions |
|---|---|
| 1. Gaining attention | Walking into the classroom and writing on the board. |
| 2. Informing the learner of the objective | Writing on the board "What we are going to do today?" and repeating verbally. |
| 3. Stimulating recall of prerequisite learning | Instructor or student summarizing previous lesson; both asking questions. |
| 4. Presenting the stimulus material | Describing an event or example to begin discussion. |
| 5. Providing learning guidance | Prompting discussion with a key question for the day; writing on the board major topics in a table. |
| 6. Eliciting the performance | Asking penetrating questions. |
| 7. Providing feedback about performance correctness | Including all comments; writing on the board; encouraging all participants; prompting for elaboration, reasoning and source of response. |
| 8. Assessing the performance | Recording participation and responses. |
| 9. Enhancing retention | Periodic guidance on notetaking; providing key ideas; making suggestions for additional work. |

From PRINCIPLES OF INSTRUCTIONAL DESIGN, 4/E. by Robert M. Gagné, Leslie J. Briggs, & Walter W. Wager, copyright © 1992 by Holt, Rinehart and Winston, Inc., reproduced by permission of the publisher.

Instructional media may assume a major role in presenting the stimulus material, another instructional event. A movie may be shown in class to introduce students to new material or relate to prior instruction. Media can also be used to promote learning transfer by asking students to respond to questions about these new media-based examples.

**Simulation model.** The simulation model (Joyce & Weil, 1996) attempts to introduce a close approximation to the real event. The model consists of four phases. The first phase, *orientation*, matches the first two instructional events of gaining attention and informing the participants of the objective of the lesson. The ideas behind simulation are explained and an overview is provided. The first phase could also include a review of previous information or training experiences to supplement the model. Phase Two involves *describing the scenario* of the simulation, assigning roles, and holding brief practice sessions, all of which correspond to the instructional event of presenting the stimulus material.

Phase Three is *conducting the simulation*, obtaining feedback of performance, clarifying misconceptions, and continuing with the simulation. There is some overlap between steps of the model and instructional events, but the requirement of the model is that learners conduct the simulation, receive feedback on their performance, and continue the simulation. A strength of this simulation model lies in the *debriefing*, Phase Four, which summarizes events and perceptions, as well as difficulties and insights gained by the simulation experience. This step also serves to improve the simulation itself by providing the designer or instructor with information in its redesign.

**Steps of Simulation Model**

Phase 1: Orientation

Phase 2: Briefing participants

Phase 3: Running simulation

Phase 4: Debriefing

**Instructional Events and Simulations**

| Instructional Event | Possible Instructor Action |
|---|---|
| 1. Gaining attention | Media as attention |
| 2. Informing the learner of the objective | Verbal tie-in with today's activity |
| 3. Stimulating recall of prerequisite learning | Tie-in with previous lesson |
| 4. Presenting the stimulus material | Instructions as to rules, roles, procedures, scoring |
| 5. Providing learning guidance | Feedback on practice session |
| 6. Eliciting the performance | Establish range of performance |
| 7. Providing feedback about performance correctness | Conduct simulation and evaluate performance; clarify misconceptions |
| 8. Assessing the performance | Feedback and continue simulation |
| 9. Enhancing retention | Summarize what happened, difficulties, relate to course content, then redesign |

From PRINCIPLES OF INSTRUCTIONAL DESIGN, 4/E. by Robert M. Gagné, Leslie J. Briggs, & Walter W. Wager, copyright © 1992 by Holt, Rinehart and Winston, Inc., reproduced by permission of the publisher.

Simulation is an excellent model for assessment and media use. Simulations, by their very nature and requirements, actively employ assessment to improve the learning experience. Media is frequently tapped to provide the simulated environment for learning as well as the technical capability for diagnosing learning and providing recommendations to improve the learning.

**Workshops.** Workshops are frequent choices of new students for instructional design projects. Although workshops may be relatively easy to design because of their fixed boundaries (time, expectations, and audience), actual outcomes are difficult to achieve. For example, the focus of many workshops are attitudinal changes, which take a long time to develop. As a result, workshop goals frequently focus on the tools and methodologies that can be used to effect this change.

**Steps for Workshop Models**

1. Introduction of leader and content
2. Presentations and Demonstrations
3. Participant work
4. Closure and evaluation

Typically, workshops operate under an extreme set of resources and constraints; thus workshops benefit greatly from a context analysis (see **Design Activity 10**), which helps to identify these realities early. One constraint is time limitations. With workshops a great amount of instructional intent is concentrated over a short length of time. Another requirement of workshops is that their focus must be clear to attract participants. The workshop leader(s) may only know general characteristics of participants, although in some institutional settings they may know a great deal.

### Instructional Events and Workshops

| Instructional Event | Workshop Leader or Participant Action |
|---|---|
| 1. Gaining attention | Presentation style, examples |
| 2. Informing the learner of the objective | Visuals, organizers, handouts; materials mailed in advance |
| 3. Stimulating recall of prerequisite learning | Addressing background of participants; review of previous sessions |
| 4. Presenting the stimulus material | Presentation by leader or guest or team; demonstrations, testimonials |
| 5. Providing learning guidance | Discussion, examples |
| 6. Eliciting the performance | Individual activity in a workbook, group activities, volunteer activity; outside assignments |
| 7. Providing feedback about performance | Providing consultation after workshop |
| 8. Assessing the performance | Criteria provided by presentation or in handouts |
| 9. Enhancing retention | Material to take home |

Workshops also require that one design the workshop and address the details of conducting the workshop. Workshops involve attention to logistics and administration, including setting up, establishing the learning climate, agreeing on objectives, directing learning activities, and closing up shop (Davis, 1974). Program evaluation is crucial to the success of workshops, both in their design, through field testing of workshop details, and at the completion of the workshop where learning performance and the appeal of the workshop activities and leader are assessed.

Workshops vary tremendously in their coverage of the nine instructional events, depending on the nature of the workshop, length, participants, and objectives, and content focus (e. g., skill development or attitudinal change).

Here is something similar across all instructional activities.

**Plan Bs.** You might want to place in your instructional design some suggestions about how to modify your instructional activity to match possible problem situations which might arise. These we call Plan Bs, which are alternate courses of action for situations which are likely to occur.

Key moments when Plan Bs are more likely to be needed occur when new or difficult concepts or processes are involved, or the introduction of a new instructional approach. The use of instructional media are common targets for Plan Bs. Workshops are loaded with the need for Plan Bs. Identify critical junctures or points in the workshop schedule where such breakdowns might occur and come up with alternative plans of action. Conducting a workshop with several people can be a wise move, as the group can more easily shift gears to adapt to time pressures or the needs of workshop participants.

# Talking about Media

**Media-based scenarios.** One of the benefits to media is that they can re-create scenes, and settings, and take us to places we have never been before showing us details of the people, things, and culture of those places. Films, movies, videos, videodisks, even filmstrips and slides can tell stories that enhance learning. Software media can also provide environments for learning, in which the learner becomes a participant in the setting. Traditionally, these settings have been ones of fantasy, in which a user becomes a participant acting out a fictional role. Another variation is **scenarios**, learning settings in which users feel they are a part of the learning environment.

Design issues (Keegan, 1995) of scenarios include:

(1) choosing the appropriate scenario for your objectives.

(2) deciding how much interactivity is necessary to provide the illusion that one is within the setting and how much is needed to promote learning via the interaction.

(3) how much challenge to provide different types of learners.

(4) how much feedback the user should receive.

(5) how much information the designer should receive on how the participant uses and interacts with the software.

(6) whether the activity should be linked to other activities and objectives.

(7) how much time is necessary to learn and master the rules of the game, the setting, and the problems posed.

The answers to these and other relevant questions depend on knowing the purpose(s) of the media.

**Key Words**
• Scenarios

# DESIGN ACTIVITY 24

## "Prototype"

**1. Choose a sample instructional event** you would like to feature here.

**2. Outline** it in any way that is appropriate to your choice with sufficient description to communicate your intent to someone else. Identify how your event meets your learning objectives and the overall goals of your design.

**3. Include the instructional model(s) used plus the assessment method(s).** Describe the assessment activity or activities that you will use to determine if your participants achieved either your intent or theirs for this lesson.

**4. Specify instructional materials** and supporting issues that need to be addressed.

**5. Describe alternate plans of action (Plan Bs).**

**6. Review your plan.** Is there anything else you need to know? Make a list of "lessons learned" from this sample lesson, which may require changes made to previous details in your design.

 **Task Description**

Gagné's instructional events were introduced to prompt you to "cover all of the bases" in your learning activities.

## ☆ SCENARIO

### Health Care Setting: Peer and Self-mentoring

The staff at Lakewood Health Systems who will be involved in outreach education and health care will face many new situations, and like workers in other industries, staff development is a major issue. Many of the issues are complex ones and workshop developers have a difficult chore to achieve the outcomes management would like them to achieve. As a result, many staff development efforts inject a dose of "medicine" hoping that the "participants" will be changed for the better.

Whatever programs Lakewood develops to assist their staff in accomplishing quality health care, a great deal of the "learning" will be up to the individual. *Peer mentoring* is sometimes used in curriculum settings where teachers try to find time to assist each other in their daily practice. In many institutional settings work teams have been established to provide, among other things, opportunities for genuine dialogue on the work and their performance.

A new reality entering the workplace is the need to monitor oneself and one's performance on the job in a larger context than ever before; literally, becoming one's own boss in one's own company. The issues facing workers is to become alert to the external influences not only on their job but their firm and industry.

*Self mentoring* is just as challenging to the worker as being aware of one's own learning in school. Schools and institutions have opportunities to integrate "learning how to learn" into the curriculum and staff development programs. Instructional design is a process that can be tapped to analyze and design features that introduce peer and self-mentoring to learners of all ages and settings.

# DESIGN ACTIVITY 25

## "Design a Syllabus or Brochure"

**1. Write a syllabus or brochure copy.**

**OPTION 1: Key components of a syllabus.**

- Name of course and instructor information
- Description of course
- Required and supplementary readings
- Key activities
- Teaching format
- Assessment plan
- Schedule of topics and assignments due

**OPTION 2: Key components of a workshop brochure.**

- Title, dates, and locations
- Sponsor
- Highlights and benefits to participants
- Who should attend
- Agenda and schedule
- Description of leader
- Registration information
- Resources provided

### ✍ Task Description

This Design Activity asks you to step back and look at the big picture of your instructional design, rather than examining only a piece of the design as you did in the Prototype.

The purpose of this Design Activity is to help you think through some of the major features, as well as details, of your design, by designing a key artifact for your project.

- For many classroom projects, drawing up a syllabus will identify key pieces, such as scheduling (sequence) and time limitations, activities, assessment, and media materials.

- Many students choose workshops as their design projects. Sketching out the format and content of a brochure will help you to draw up the major selling points for potential participants, as well as its content and features.

# Tying It All Together

*The objective of the field experience, like the objective of all clinical experience, is to learn to become more reflective under real-time conditions so that effective ad hoc theories of action can be created and tested.*

(Argyris & Schön, 1974, p. 188)

In this book we have asked you to complete quite a few Design Activities. These various activities can be used in designing a prototype learning activity in this chapter. The key activities are listed below:

| | |
|---|---|
| • Mission Statement | • Design Activity 3 |
| • Goals | • Design Activity 11 |
| • Learner Profile | • Design Activity 9 |
| • Context Analysis | • Design Activity 10 |
| • Content Analysis | • Design Activity 13, 14 |
| • Assessment Plan | • Design Activity 17 |
| • Instructional Framework | • Design Activity 19 |
| • Instructional Media | • Design Activity 22 |

**Consistency of design features.** The prototype gives you a chance to incorporate features based on what you have learned from previous phases of the instructional design process. The syllabus or workshop brochure task helps to identify key pieces of your instructional design that need attention. Here are questions to keep in mind as you construct this prototype:

See Tour 8: If We Can't Fit It, It Ain't Broke, in "Touring Instructional Design."

## Consistent Design Activities

**Mission Statement**

- Does your sample lesson or activity resonate with the intent and stance taken in your mission statement?

**Goals**

- Does this lesson, activity, or exercise support your goals and objectives?

**Learner Profile**

- Is this activity appropriate to learner needs? What issues need to be addressed for the range of your participants?

**Content**

- What is the nature of the content to be taught, learned, or presented? If this is a key or critical activity or skill to be taught do you need to analyze it in more detail to better understand how to teach it?

**Context**

- What are the realities of this lesson or activity? Have you thought through the necessary preparation duties, materials, support, physical space needed, and optional Plan Bs that might be needed?

**Assessment**

- How will you assess if your goals and objectives are being achieved? What incidental learning may be taking place?

**Instructional Framework**

- What is the model being used to present this activity? What strategies could improve it or help your learners? Are the assessment tools used within this framework appropriate to the task?

**Instructional Media**

- Are the media materials supportive of your intent and your objectives?

These are some of the detail questions that you may be asking yourself as you construct your instructional design. Seeing how the pieces fit together in the overall big picture requires you to step back and think about the relationships of these pieces to each other.

**Food for Thought**

Here are some suggestions on designing prototypes.

- Evaluate. Be flexible. Try again.

- Try to pilot test key lessons, sessions, or activities. Observe. Jot down notes on how you did after the test or use videotape to record what you did. Obtain feedback from students or peers.

- Listen to what your participants or reviewers say to you.

- Think of changes in the physical environment or logistics that might change: temporary location, lack of materials, or shortened meeting times.

# Reviewing the Design Activities

### Design Activity 23: Instructional Events

☐ Incorporated instructional events in a sample lesson or activity.

☐ Identified events which needed more attention.

### Design Activity 24: Prototype

☐ Outlined a prototype lesson or activity.

☐ Included instructional model plus assessments used.

☐ Specified instructional materials needed and supporting issues (context) to be addressed.

☐ Described alternate plans of action.

### Design Activity 25: Design a Syllabus or Brochure

☐ Designed a syllabus or brochure communicating instructional intent to intended participants.

# Summary of Important Ideas

1. Instructional events influence mental processes, behavior, and learning.

2. Instructional events help instructors provide learners with opportunities to develop capabilities.

3. Instructional models have features that vary but generally address similar or consistent instructional events.

4. The instructional design process generates information to help you design instructional activities in ways that resonate with your mission and goals and are responsive to learners, content, and context.

5. Prototypes give you a chance to iron out inconsistencies and fill in missing pieces.

## √ Your Personal Learning

---

### *Relating Your Beliefs to This Chapter*

You may have opinions about what constitutes a lesson. These beliefs will influence the design of particular lessons. Think first about what the term "lesson" means in the context of the teaching model you have chosen for your design. Then try to list the major features or components that you would need to think about to ensure the lesson was complete.

### *What questions do you have about the information presented in this chapter?*

---

# References

Argyris, C., & Schön, D. A. (1974*). Theory in practice: Increasing professional effectiveness.* San Francisco: Jossey-Bass.

Davis, L. N. (1974). *Planning, conducting, and evaluating workshops.* Austin, TX: Learning Concepts.

Gagné, R. M. (1985). *The conditions of learning* (4th ed.). NY: Holt, Rinehart & Winston.

Gagné, R. M., Briggs, L. J., & Wager, W. W. (1992). *Principles of instructional design* (4th ed.). Fort Worth, TX: Harcourt Brace Jovanovich.

Gunter, A. A., Estes, T. H., & Schwab, J. H. (1995). *Instruction: A models approach* (2nd ed.). Boston: Allyn & Bacon.

Joyce, B., & Weil, M. (1996). *Models of teaching* (5th ed.). Boston: Allyn & Bacon.

Keegan, M. (1995). *Scenario educational software: design and development of discovery learning.* Englewood Cliffs, NJ: Educational Technology.

Minsky, M. (1986). *The society of mind.* NY: Simon & Schuster.

# For Further Reading ...

Minsky, M. (1993). *The children's machine: Rethinking school in the age of the computer.* NY: Basic Books.

A different way of looking at instructional media and the way it is used in learning activities.

Norman, D. A. (1993). *Things that make us smart: Defending human attributes in the ages of the machine.* Reading, MA: Addison-Wesley.

Examines the differences between experiential and reflective learning.

# What's Next?

We wrap up the Instructional Design process with an overview of a critical step, **Program Evaluation**, which helps you to determine whether or not your design helped you to achieve your goals!

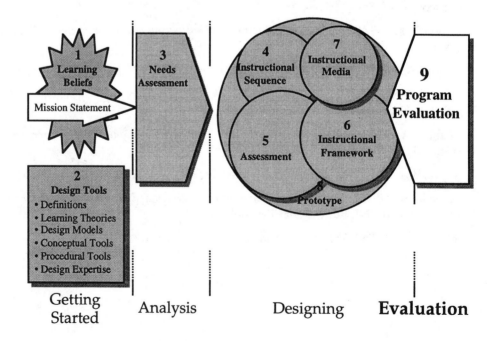

# Evaluation

- **Chapter 9 - Program Evaluation**
- **Chapter 10 - Self Evaluation**

---

YOU ARE NOW AT THE FINAL STAGE OF THE INSTRUCTIONAL DESIGN PROCESS. Chapter 9 looks at ways to help a designer stay focused on the goals established from analysis (Chapter 3, Needs Assessment) during designing and testing of the design, as well as evaluating its responsiveness to these goals after implementation. Chapter 10 helps to assess your own learning and to revise your preliminary instructional design model.

Please remember that based on the nature of a book format we have had to present the instructional design process in a linear fashion. In reality, the nature of the process in practice is iterative, cyclical, and unique to each designer and type of project.

∞

---

"A design is a plan to make something: something that is two dimension or three dimensional, and sometimes in the time dimension. It is always something seen and sometimes something touched and now and then by association, something heard. It is often a single item and just as often a mass-produced product."

(Partners of Pentagram, 1978, p. 7.)

# CHAPTER 9

How will you know if your design works and for whom? This is an important question that program evaluation attempts to answer.

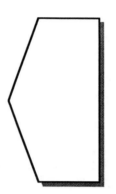

# Program Evaluation

*Make it as simple as possible and no simpler.*

(Einstein in R. S. Root-Bernstein, 1989, p. 418)

Program evaluation is a distinct component of instructional design, quite different in nature and tasks from the previous designing phases of the design process. Within the context of instructional design, program evaluation is a way to step back and systematically determine if your design achieved the results that you intended and how it can be improved.

In this chapter you will:

**1.** Draw up a formative program evaluation plan.

**2.** Draw up a summative program evaluation plan.

# The Value of Program Evaluation

In Chapter 5, Assessment, we provided definitions on assessment, evaluation, and program evaluation. We said that evaluation takes information from assessment and makes judgments and decisions about learners, while **program evaluation** is a set of design tools that appraises the success of a program and to what extent your instructional design contributed to that success. In the context of instructional design and this book, the word "program" means the instructional solution you are submitting in the form of an instructional design plan (i.e., your project).

In some respects program evaluation is complementary to Analysis (Needs Assessment). One aspect of program evaluation, called **formative program evaluation** (Scriven, 1967), is an ongoing analysis of your design during development and implementation, particularly through prototypes and field testing. We introduced formative evaluation back in Chapter 2, so that you could begin to think about ways to evaluate your work while you are designing.

Program evaluation also has a summing-up function called **summative program evaluation** (Scriven, 1967). This process helps to conclude if the instructional design achieved its goals. Should it continue to be implemented? In many cases the information from program evaluation efforts becomes highly valued data to feed into a needs assessment for future designing efforts.

It is important to determine the focus of the program evaluation. One focus is to identify needs and set priorities, select among program approaches, and monitor and adjust programs as they are designed and implemented (Sanders, 1992). Program evaluation also helps to determine whether a program or a design results in the desired goals or outcomes established,

∞

**Key Words**
- Formative program evaluation
- Program evaluation
- Summative program evaluation

such as instructional outcomes, which is focus of this chapter.

**Evaluating instructional outcomes.** Although there are a great many focal points for program evaluation (Worthen & Sanders, 1987), there are several that concern us in the context of evaluating ongoing design efforts and the impact of the finished design on the outcomes of instruction. One such focal point is *needs identification* to help establish program goals and objectives. We are also interested in the *instructional needs* of individual learners and the *instructional outcomes*, to discover the effect of the design on achieving the goals and objectives that we have laid out for them.

---

**Benefits of Evaluating Instructional Outcomes**

**Students:**
- Improve practices that assist learning
- Develop improved and more appropriate learning spaces, materials, and support

**Teachers:**
- Determine effectiveness, appeal, and efficiency
- Choose instructional approaches and materials
- Improve pedagogical practice
- Help set priorities
- Identify needs
- Determine what does and what doesn't work

---

Other areas that your program evaluation plan may focus on include the evaluation of *instructional materials*. Are they helping learners to learn? You may also want to know the effects of your design on assessment of *student progress*, the effectiveness of *instruction*, and to what extent the *learning environment* created from the design has on the learners and instructor.

You can see that this final component of instructional design must address all facets of the design. This comprehensive focus helps us to identify all of the strengths and problems in a design product.

**Communication.**  Before we examine formative and summative program evaluation, Sanders (1992) cites two ideas to remember when it comes to doing program evaluations. The first is that "not everyone will see the program in the same light, and it is important to be informed about how those around you view it" (p. 1). Some will attach goals to the evaluations, while others may approach the evaluation goal-free. In other words, "Let's see what happens." The second idea Sanders suggests is that "one must always consider three aspects of good program evaluation—communication, communication, and communication" (p. 1).

Like all aspects of the design process, program evaluation is a human undertaking. The decisions made from program evaluations have a significant effect on others. They involve people and the programs that are important to them.

> Now, we will examine the two major types of Program Evaluation.

⬇

# Formative Program Evaluation

---

**Purpose of formative program evaluation.** Ongoing, or formative evaluation, helps to determine the effectiveness of lessons, activities, and assessment details while these are in development and can, therefore, be revised (Scriven, 1967). This ongoing evaluation is used to step back and review the design components as they are being constructed. A periodic self-assessment of your design may identify issues that need to be addressed in other areas of the design. You may discover important details have been omitted, or features that are based on incorrect assumptions. Formative evaluation provides information to help you make improved and appropriate design decisions, while a final evaluation—summative evaluation—determines accountability (Stufflebeam, 1967).

Both formative and summative evaluation can be used in both small and large instructional units under study, although smaller ones, such as courses, require decisions on ways to improve their effectiveness, appeal, and efficiency. Larger units, such as programs or curriculums, involve decisions of adoption and continuation (Gagné et al., 1992).

Generally, formative evaluation is conducted internally by the design team, which may include teachers, learners, trainers, and other direct participants. However, there may be some value of obtaining periodic review from external reviewers to give you fresh insights and views on your progress (Worthen & Sanders, 1987).

**Structuring formative program evaluation.** Because program evaluation makes judgments about people and programs, it is necessary that the process be carefully designed, because "the decisions being made can affect many others—perhaps even the well-being of the next generation" (Sanders, 1992, p. 4). To organize your formative evaluation plan, we suggest that you answer the following questions:

---

**Questions to Ask in Formative Program Evaluation**

1. **Who** will be evaluating?
2. **What** criteria and questions will you ask?
3. **How** will you collect and summarize your data?
4. **When** will you evaluate?

---

A measure of effectiveness in the developing design can be examined by studying three major criteria: content, technical quality, and learnability (Chinien & Hlynka, 1993). Judgments regarding content and technical quality will be made by experts, while students provide data on learnability (Nathenson & Henderson, 1980). In addition, Sanders (1992) recommends that you choose an evaluation coordinator that has the time and interest, the expertise and credibility, and the leadership and communication skills necessary to conduct an evaluation. Another source for evaluation comes from the connoisseur, a generalist who possesses a broad background and experiences and can comment on both content and context (Eisner, 1994). Let's examine each of the evaluators in more detail.

**Formative Criteria**

- Content
- Technical quality
- Learnability
- Context

**Experts.** People doing formative evaluations include those who will be making the changes, for example, an instructional design team or an individual teacher. Identifying who has a stake in the design is particularly important in summative evaluation, but the same may hold for formative evaluation. Ask yourself who the important stakeholders are and if they should be a part of the formative evaluation team. In a school setting you might want to include other teachers, department heads, school district personnel, parents, and school board members, while in a commercial setting your stakeholders may include clients, managers, workers, and supervisors.

An internal review of the design can be conducted by designers, the experts closest to the design process. Management tools to gather data can include checklists that are appropriate to each stage of the design process. Observations may be useful if prototypical products are in place for field testing.

**Formative Program Evaluation**

| Who | What | When | How |
|-----|------|------|-----|
| **Experts** | Content Technical Quality | Based on expert | Checklists Panels Interviews |
| **Learners** one-to-one | Learnability | Early phases | Think-aloud Verbal Interviews Questions |
| **Learners** small group | Learnability | Prototypes | Assessments Observations Questions Interviews |
| **Learners** field test | Learnability | End of design | Actual setting Assessments Questions |
| **Connoisseurs** | Context | Throughout | Observations Panels Interviews |

There are several other types of experts you can use, such as subject matter experts (SME), language experts, media, and format experts. The experts use checklists of criteria, panels, individual interviews, and think-alouds. Your formative evaluation plan should specify when these people should be selected. For example, reviews may be useful upon completion of the needs assessment and identification of priorities and goals, the assessment plan, media plan, and sample lesson. Each phase of the design process could easily benefit from identifying an expert in that particular area.

**Learners as evaluators.** Evaluation from learners can come from one-to-one formats, small-groups, and field tests (Dick & Carey, 1996). *One-to-one* evaluations involving individual students with evaluators or subject-matter experts are conducted early in the design to identify problems and obtain students' initial reactions to materials. Data is collected through think-aloud sessions, observations, interviews, tests, and attitude questionnaires (Chinien & Hlynka, 1993).

*Small-group* evaluations are used when the design is nearing its completion. Its purpose is to determine the effect of changes and determine if additional improvements are needed. Data from groups of students or a small number of students using the materials individually can include tests, observations, attitude questionnaires, and interviews.

A *field test* verifies the effectiveness of a product or program in its final form in a simulated or actual setting. The field test helps to identify problems that crop up in real settings and make adjustments before implementing on a larger scale. Students in these settings should represent the target population and possess the necessary prerequisites (Gagné et al., 1992).

**Connoisseurs** are generalists who can scrutinize your content and design within a wider context than that of experts (Eisner, 1994). The traditional view of formative evaluation is to remove error and achieve the best product, while connoisseurship accepts the reality that ambiguities, messiness, complexity, and contradiction are a certainty in educational matters. The connoisseur as formative evaluator accepts the notion that "there is no one best way" (Chinien & Hlynka, 1993, p. 64). Data gathering conducted throughout the design process typically use panel discussions and interviews. Data gathering phases of the design process could also occur during needs assessment and the prototype.

**Questions to ask.** To address the three major issues of content, technical quality, and learnability, a formative program evaluation should specify how you are obtaining the information and the questions you will be asking. In the formative, or growth, stages of your design, evaluators should observe what design components can be witnessed in action, talk with

∞

**Key Words**
- Connoisseur

users of the design, and read relevant documentation (i.e., the design document, checklists, and prepared materials)(Sanders, 1992). For a list of questions to ask, methods of collecting data, types of data to collect, and how to use this data see the table below.

### Questions to Ask during Formative Evaluation

| Data source | Questions to ask |
|---|---|
| **Expert**<br>*Subject matter expert* | Is content adequate, accurate, up-to-date, and relevant? |
| *Language expert* | Is reading level appropriate? |
| *Delivery expert* | Is delivery medium appropriate, cost-effective, meets quality standard? |
| *Pedagogical expert* | Are the objectives and content appropriate? Is the material appropriate for the target population? |
| *Instructional design expert* | Were instructions designed according to a systematic process and on the basis of learning theories? |
| **Learners:** *one-to-one*<br><br>Select learners representative of population. Include learners of high, medium and low ability. | Is the material learnable? What are the most obvious errors, problems and weaknesses within the material? What are the learners' reactions to the material? Are tests appropriate? |
| **Learners:** *small group*<br><br>Select 10 to 20 learners representative of target population. | How effective are changes made during one-to-one evaluation? Are there additional problems and errors in the material? Can learners achieve objectives? Were exercises, tests and feedback appropriate and adequate? |
| **Learners:** *Field Test*<br><br>Select one or more groups representative of target population. | Can learners achieve objectives when using material alone? Are previous revisions effective? Will material be accepted by learners, teachers and administrators? |

Adapted from Chinien, C., & Hlynka, D. (1993). Formative evaluation of prototypical products: From expert to connoisseur. *ETTI, 30*(1), 60-66. Kogan Page, London.

# DESIGN ACTIVITY 26

## "Your Formative Evaluation Plan"

**1. Describe your formative evaluation plan.** Use the table below to specify:

- **Who** will do the ongoing evaluating.
- **What** is being evaluated.
- **When** the evaluation should occur.
- **How** the evaluation will be conducted through the use of design tools.

**2. Describe the criteria** used to evaluate content, technical quality, learnability, and effectiveness.

✍ **Task Description**

Your **formative** plan should outline how you will evaluate your design as it is being constructed, while your **summative** plan should outline and communicate if your design, or your program or product, solved your instructional problem.

| Who | What | When | How |
|---|---|---|---|
| **Experts** | Content<br>Technical Quality<br>Effectiveness | | |
| **Learners**<br>  one-to-one | Learnability | | |
| **Learners**<br>  small group | Learnability | | |
| **Learners**<br>  field test | Learnability | | |
| **Connoisseurs** | Context | | |

[Add your criteria that specifies in more precise terms how the above are evaluated]

# Summative Program Evaluation

**Summative Criteria**

- Effectiveness
- Appeal
- Efficiency

The purpose of a final, or summative program evaluation is to judge the worth or merit of the program (Scriven, 1967). Did your design make a difference? Did it accomplish what you wanted it to do? The big question here is how do you know if those accomplishments can be traced to your design? This is what is meant by summative evaluation's role in accountability.

**Structuring summative program evaluation.** Summative program evaluation is conducted after the program or design has been in place for a complete cycle.

Summative program evaluation is usually conducted by evaluators outside of the design team. As we discussed earlier, it is also important to identify for whom you are evaluating—who are the stakeholders in this design or program? Keeping these various constituencies in mind will help you write a summative evaluation document that clearly communicates to these people.

Criteria in summative evaluation include *effectiveness, appeal,* and *efficiency* (see the chart on the next page for a summary of questions to ask and tools to use to gather data). Determining effectiveness requires asking questions about whether the design accomplishes what it sets out to do. Do learners learn or not? What is it about the design that has an effect on the learners? Is the design coherent within its elements? This achievement information can be gathered through a range of assessments, such as paper tests, products, portfolios, self-evaluation, interviews, and talk-alouds.

Determining a program's appeal means finding out if learners liked the design. More importantly, do they use the information and skills after the instructional event is completed? If the program created from your design does not appeal to learners and teachers, then it's unlikely that it will get used at a later date. Does the design engage learners and teachers? Are the appealing features of the design related to your objectives? Data from these attitudes can be gathered through questionnaires, interviews, student comments, and observations.

## Summative Program Evaluation

| When | Who | What | How |
|---|---|---|---|
| Completed Design | External Sources | **Effectiveness**<br><br>1. Does the design solve the instructional problem?<br>2. What are the criteria?<br>3. Does the design improve on what's currently done?<br>4. Do learners achieve objectives?<br>5. Is instruction implemented as it was designed?<br>6. Does the design allow for unexpected outcomes? | **Achievement**<br><br>Tests<br>Products<br>Portfolios<br>Time measures<br>Self-evaluation<br>Interviews<br>Talk-alouds |
| | | **Appeal**<br><br>1. How do learners feel about instruction?<br>2. What are teacher attitudes and behaviors?<br>3. Will they use the knowledge and skills at a later date? | **Attitudes**<br><br>Questionnaires<br>Interviews<br>Student notes<br>Observations |
| | | **Efficiency**<br><br>1. Is the design cost-effective?<br>2. How much time does it take to implement?<br>3. Is the design doable and realistic?<br>4. Is the design flexible to update? | **Use**<br><br>Questionnaires<br>Interviews<br>Observations |

The third criteria, efficiency, deals with issues of cost effectiveness, practicality, and usefulness. Data providing information on the use of the design can be obtained from questionnaires, interviews, and observations. Summative questions dealing with efficiency could include the following:

---

**Summative Questions for Efficiency**

- Is the design realistic?
- Does it match the teacher's perceptions of the student?
- Is the design achievable?
- Is the design cost-effective?
- Is the design document easy to read and clear to follow?
- Was it written appropriately for those who will read it?
- Is the design complete?
- Is it flexible enough to allow modification to match teacher and learner needs?
- Does it deal with reality, such as the instructor's workload?
- Does the tone of the document respect the limits on the instructor's time?

---

**Goal-directed and goal-free evaluation.** Program evaluation as has been discussed so far has involved determining whether the product, program, course, or workshop accomplished what its goals directed it to do (e.g., Popham, Eisner, Sullivan & Tyler, 1969). However, program evaluation can also be conducted along the lines of goal-free evaluation; that is, a program evaluation that is performed without any regard for program goals or objectives. The evaluation examines the effects of whatever occurs (Scriven, 1974). Obviously, the evaluation can become a complex matter, but it accommodates recording outcomes along a wide range of program evaluation possibilities.

**Key Words**
- Goal-directed evaluation
- Goal-free evaluation

# DESIGN ACTIVITY 27

## "Your Summative Evaluation Plan"

**1. Describe your summative evaluation plan.** We have listed below three measures to evaluate against: effectiveness—did the design or program or product do what it was designed to do and to what extent did the design contribute to the success? Also evaluated is the program's appeal, whether it attracted the attention of teachers and learners, and how the program or product accomplished effectiveness and appeal at what cost in resources (efficiency)?

**2. Describe the criteria** you used to evaluate effectiveness, appeal, and efficiency.

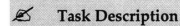 **Task Description**

The chart below can be used to organize the essential features of a summative program evaluation, which is conducted after your design or program is implemented. External sources are traditionally used in summative program evaluation.

| When | Who | What | How |
|---|---|---|---|
| Completed Design | External Sources | Effectiveness | Achievement |
| | | Appeal | Attitudes |
| | | Efficiency | Use |

## Talking about Media

**Evaluating media.** Custom-produced media is frequently evaluated during its development. These versions could be paper prototypes, which give designers a chance to visualize the sequence and impact of its features. A pilot test is a formative evaluation tool to test out the features on users, so that changes can be made. Field trials are ways of evaluating prototypes and supplementary materials and removing the bugs out of initial versions. A summative evaluation can be conducted by using the actual users, bringing in outside experts to observe and make recommendations. Frequently, the stakes are higher if approval or certification is on the line. Media also tends to have an "instructional shelf life," something that you can address in the context analysis of a needs assessment.

Some of the evaluation issues of interactive instructional technologies are their complexity, their embedded data capabilities, and the research tools needed to study their use. Because of their wide range of capabilities, these products deal with a variety of learning issues, such as learner control and learning styles, and their design is equally complex and time-consuming to develop, test, and evaluate. Interactive authoring packages provide the capability to retrieve data on how learners use them. Finally, tools exist, borrowed from anthropology and sociology, to analyze the effects of these technologies on people (Savenye, 1992).

Much of the qualitative nature of what happens when instructional programs are implemented in human settings can be captured through a design tool called "critical incidents."

## ☆ SCENARIO

### Middle School: Critical Incidents

One way to learn more about how a program is faring is the sharing of "critical incidents," those events which capture the essence of the project, program, or prototype. Critical incidents could be viewed as mini case studies, but typically they address issues from the viewpoint of an individual. Critical incidents can be key informing documents to support a program evaluation, particularly with the introduction of new programs.

The critical incidents we select say a lot about our take on the significance of the choice. These incidents can be ones we feel good or unhappy about. They can be shared with others or used as a tool to self assess.

David Tripp, an educator specializing in teacher education and professional development, recommends that a system is necessary to document each incident and be useful in the long run (Tripp, 1993).

The science faculty in this scenario decided that each of them would begin such a file and share it among the group, so as to model the cooperative learning and group inquiry instructional approaches they were implementing. They decided upon a beginning list of categories to organize their entries. This would structure their comments in a useful format rather than diary entries—although their files might begin in this fashion.

The categories in each critical incident file depends on the nature of the events in the setting. The group realized that over the school year their categories would likely change. In reality, a critical incident file contains entries that may be rewritten many times to retrieve the most meaning from the original entries.

Their initial categories were:

- Course Topics
- Student Activities
- Class Observations
- Student Profiles
- Reflection on Efforts
- Learning & Using New Media

From what is written by each teacher and from the group discussions, themes may emerge. The group acknowledged that this was the first time they had been involved in an activity where "teacher thinking" was being shared. They even discussed the possibility of writing up their experiences, if they could find the time and energy.

Critical incident files can be very useful in program evaluation efforts, particularly ongoing evaluation of an innovation. On a personal level they can be structured in ways to reflect on instructional experiences or on one's professional learning. Such files can also be valuable needs assessment data from key participants.

# Reviewing the Design Activities

**Food for Thought**

Program evaluation is a phase of the ID process that we tend to avoid for a number of reasons:

1. We're afraid to face the facts.
2. We don't make the time.
3. We don't have the energy.
4. We don't have the institutional support for such an effort.

**Design Activity 26: Your Formative Evaluation Plan**

☐ Constructed a Formative Evaluation plan.

☐ Described the criteria for evaluation.

**Design Activity 27: Your Summative Evaluation Plan**

☐ Constructed a Summative Evaluation plan.

☐ Described the criteria for evaluation.

# 📖 Summary of Important Ideas

**1.** Program evaluation is a systematic process that determines the effect of your instructional design on educational "programs."

**2.** There are numerous functions and purposes for Program Evaluation, one of which is the evaluation of instructional outcomes.

**3.** Formative program evaluation scrutinizes (who, what, how, when) your design during its growth stages.

**4.** Summative program evaluation, in the context of instructional design, answers the question: did the design accomplish its goals?

📖 See Tour 8: Off With Her Head, in "Touring Instructional Design."

# √ Your Personal Learning

*Relating Your Beliefs to This Chapter:*

Record your responses to the following questions on program evaluation to begin to understand the scope of program evaluation.

**1.** How have you evaluated the success of any new program, product, or other change in your experiences in learning settings?

**2.** What do you think are the benefits and disadvantages of program evaluation?

**3.** How do you feel about the prospects of your instructional design being evaluated?

*What questions do you have about the information presented in this chapter?*

# References

Chinien, C., & Hlynka, D. (1993). Formative evaluation of prototypical products: From expert to connoisseur. *ETTI 30*(1), 60-66.

Dick, W., & Carey, L. (1996). *The systematic design of instruction* (4th ed.). NY: HarperCollins.

Gagné, R. M., Briggs, L. J., & Wager, W. W. (1992). *Principles of instructional design* (4th ed.). Fort Worth, TX: Harcourt Brace Jovanovich.

Eisner, E. (1994). *The educational imagination* (3rd ed.). NY: Macmillan.

Nathenson, M. B., & Henderson, E. S. (1980). *Using student feedback to improve learning materials.* London: Croom Helm.

Pentagram Design Group. (1978). *Living by design.* NY: Whitney Library of Design.

Popham, W. J., Eisner, E. W., Sullivan, H. J., & Tyler, L. L. (1969). *Instructional objectives.* American Educational Research Association Monograph Series in Curriculum Evaluation, No. 1. Chicago: Rand McNally.

Root-Bernstein, R. S. (1989). *Discovering.* Cambridge: Harvard University.

Sanders, J. R. (1992). *Evaluating school programs: An educator's guide.* Newbury Park, CA: Corwin Press.

Savenye, W. C. (February, 1992). *Alternate methods for conducting formative evaluations of interactive instructional technologies.* Paper presented at the National Conference of the Association for Educational Communications and Technology, Washington, D. C.

Scriven, M. (1974). Evaluation perspectives and procedures. In W. J. Popham (Ed.), *Evaluation in education.* Berkeley, CA: McCutchan.

Scriven, M. (1967). The methodology of evaluation. In R. E. Stake (Ed.), *Curriculum evaluation.* American Educational Research Association Monograph Series on Evaluation, No. 1. Chicago: Rand McNally.

Stufflebeam, D. M. (1967). *Evaluation as a basis for decision making.* Paper presented to the American Educational Research Association, Chicago, Illinois.

Tripp, D. (1993). *Critical incidents in teaching: Developing professional judgment.* NY: Routledge.

Worthen, B. R., & Sanders, J. R. (1987). *Educational evaluation: Alternative approaches and practical guidelines.* White Plains, NY: Longman.

# For Further Reading ...

Sanders, J. R. (1992). *Evaluating school programs: An educator's guide.* Newbury Park, CA: Corwin Press.

> A clear, concise guide to the evaluation of school programs. An excellent primer for the novice program evaluator.

Eisner, E. (1994). *The educational imagination* (3rd ed.). NY: Macmillan.

> A comprehensive examination of the evaluation of school programs.

Worthen, B. R., & Sanders, J. R. (1987). *Educational evaluation: Alternative approaches and practical guidelines.* White Plains, NY: Longman.

> A classic comprehensive guide to educational evaluation. The process and tools for evaluation are clearly explained and illustrated.

# The Big Picture

OK, here we are. Back to the big picture! Here are all the pieces of the instructional design process as we have presented them in this book. What an adventure! Does it all come together for you at this point? The next chapter will examine your learning of this process.

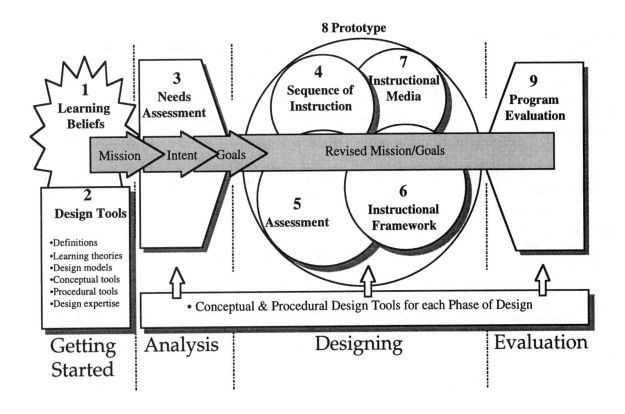

## CHAPTER 10

In many ways we are back to where we began in Chapter 1: You!

This is a short chapter reviewing your learning of the important principles and processes of instructional design.

We hope you have enjoyed this book and found it helpful in your learning. Good luck in your future designing efforts!

# Self Evaluation

*The journey does matter.*

Madeleine L'Engle

Welcome to the last chapter, a chance to review where you have been and what you have learned. Self Evaluation is an important piece of Program Evaluation, because as a designer it is valuable to take stock of your designing efforts. This chapter is designed to help you to self assess what you have learned and how this book helped you.

In this chapter you will:

1. Revise your preliminary instructional design model.
2. Examine what you have learned from this book.
3. Please provide us with feedback!

# Where Were You?

*Sure, there's a lot of nuts and bolts in here, but that's not really my focus. This is more of a design/build book. That's why you should read this book first. We will start with what you already know the most about—yourself. It's the only book that will show you how to think about design and construction—as design/build. After you have read this, you will have a unified overview. You will then be able to read any of the hundreds of other "how-to" books and know where the specific information fits into the big picture. But it isn't a step-by-step sort of thing. It's more reiterative. You will find yourself coming back to this book many times to get your bearings. It asks the big questions first.*

(Connell, 1993, p. 1-3)

How have you been using this space?
⇩
Did this space work for you?
How could it be improved?

---

The instructional design process, as we have presented it in this book, has been structured around the classic major aspects of the systems approach: analysis, design, evaluation. The systems approach is a means to comprehensively address an instructional problem—learners, content, and learning context.

Like other fields of design, instructional design is essentially a problem-solving process, one that attempts to arrive at the best possible solution considering the available information, realities, and expertise of the designer and other supporting players.

Having been introduced to the important design components in the previous nine chapters, you are now ready to revise your preliminary instructional design model from **Design Activity 5**. In this revision you can incorporate your views of how instructional design should proceed, considering your expertise, personal views and beliefs, and particular design context.

> Revise your preliminary ID model in the next Design Activity.

⬇

# DESIGN ACTIVITY 28

## "Your Revised Instructional Design Model"

1. Review your preliminary instructional design model from **Design Activity 5**. Would you represent the important processes of instructional design (e.g., needs, goals, assessment, media, etc.) any differently? How would you make any revisions on your visual model?

2. Provide a written description of the model to accompany the visual, as if you had mailed your model to someone and could not be there in person to explain its features.

3. What are the major attributes of your model that set it apart from others? What would you title it?

Now, let's examine your project.

↓

# Learning from a Project

*Initially, the student does not and cannot understand what designing means.... They do not at first understand the essential things.... They can be grasped only through the experience of actual designing.*

(Schön, 1987, p. 82)

Learning instructional design through a design project is necessary, because it is difficult to comprehend the whole instructional design process without actually designing. The project provides a base understanding of the component parts and the relationships of the parts to each other.

The project is, as we discussed in the chapter on Assessment, both a process and a product representation of your learning. The project document can form the basis of an actual implementation or as a reference for future ID opportunities. You can review what you designed and make the necessary changes that will be necessary to completely address your instructional opportunity.

Instructional design in practice may vary considerably from this learning experience, but we have found that after becoming aware of critical issues in each of the ID components, students are more informed in their future designing.

Let's critically examine what you have learned.

# DESIGN ACTIVITY 29

## "Self Assessment of Your Learning"

✍ **Task Description**

The purpose for this activity is to examine through writing what you learned about the ID process.

1. What instructional design processes were the most valuable to you?

2. What did you learn about the ID process from doing a design project?

3. What do you need to learn more about or have more experience with?

4. During the learning of ID principles and processes, what did you learn about yourself?

5 How might you use this process in future instructional designing work?

📖 If you wrote a set of fictional stories about instructional design, what adventures would your characters encounter?

# Mastering the Possibilities

*I can tell you that there is something you need to know, and
with my help you may be able to learn it. But I cannot tell
you what it is in a way you can now understand. I can only
arrange for you to have the right sorts of experiences for
yourself. You must be willing, therefore, to have these
experiences. Then you will be able to make an informed
choice about whether you wish to continue. If you are
unwilling to step into this new experience without knowing
ahead of time what it will be like, I cannot help you. You
must trust me.*

(Schön, 1987, p. 93)

---

We hope that you enjoyed the adventure in learning instructional design. The adventure does not end here; as in practice ID can take you down many different roads. We believe instructional design is a powerful process, both in its potential to systematically address important learning issues, and in its flexibility to accommodate the complexity of designing for human instructional needs.

Designing requires making choices and decisions. It implies taking the time to discover what you can about the challenge in front of you and designing features that are appropriate to the instructional issues. You are now in a better position to responsively design than ever before, and to do so reflecting, not only on your learning experiences here, but on every design experience from now on. Good luck to your future design endeavors! We would like to hear from you.

# DESIGN ACTIVITY 30

## "Feedback to Us"

✍ **Task Description**

We would appreciate any feedback you could give us. We would like to hear from you, particularly, your responses to the following questions and rating scales on the next page. You can contact us at the following addresses:

R. Neal Shambaugh
201 Media Bldg.
Blacksburg, VA 24061-0133
neals@vt.edu

Dr. Susan G. Magliaro
313 War Memorial Hall
Virginia Tech
Blacksburg, VA 24061-0313
sumags@vt.edu

1. How did this book help you to learn instructional design?

2. What could we do to improve it?

3. How could the book be better structured to support your learning?

4. What topics or chapters need more work?

5. What did you find engaging or appealing in this book?

6. How was this book used in your course?

7. What other materials (e.g., textbook) were used?

8. Is there anything else you would like to tell us?

Please complete the rating questions on the next page.

Please rate the effectiveness of the following
features:

---

| Design Activities | Poor 1 2 3 4 5 Excellent |
| Supporting Text | Poor 1 2 3 4 5 Excellent |
| Scenarios | Poor 1 2 3 4 5 Excellent |
| Talking about Media | Poor 1 2 3 4 5 Excellent |
| Design Tools | Poor 1 2 3 4 5 Excellent |
| Touring ID (Stories) | Poor 1 2 3 4 5 Excellent |
| "Food for Thought" | Poor 1 2 3 4 5 Excellent |
| Self Assessment | Poor 1 2 3 4 5 Excellent |
| Reading Lists | Poor 1 2 3 4 5 Excellent |
| Glossary | Poor 1 2 3 4 5 Excellent |

---

Use the space below for any comments on how
we can improve the above features.

# References

Connell, J. (1993). *Homing instinct: Using your lifestyle to design and build your home..* NY: Warner Books.

L'Engle, M. C. (1995). *Creativity: Touching the divine.* Television documentary.

Schön, D. A. (1987). *Educating the reflective practitioner.* San Francisco: Jossey-Bass.

# For further reading . . .

Norman, D. A. (1993). *What makes people smart: Defending human attributes in the age of the machine.* Reading, MA: Addison-Wesley.

A book about human-centered technology and the design of cognitive artifacts to extend our learning potential.

Schön, D. A. (1987). *Educating the reflective practitioner.* San Francisco: Jossey-Bass.

Schön, D. A. (1983). *The reflective practitioner: How professionals think and act.* New York: Basic Books.

Schön, D. A. (1991). *The reflective turn: Case studies in and on educational practice* (Ed.). NY: Teachers College.

A trio of books related to the learning environments created by a joint dialogue between teacher and learner.

# TOURING INSTRUCTIONAL DESIGN

*Explanations settle issues, showing that matters must end as they have. Narratives raise issues, showing that matters do not end as they must but as they do. Explanation sets the need for further inquiry aside; narrative invites us to rethink what we thought we knew.*

James P. Carse (1986). *Finite and Infinite Games.*

Illustrations by George V. Wills

## Tour 1
### *The Starting Point*

"I wonder what this class is going to be about?" asked Leslie who was walking alongside Michael, a fellow graduate student.

"Who knows?" sighed Michael. "You know the routine. We'll get a syllabus. We'll leave early and by tomorrow, we will have settled in to school as usual. We're really rather good at it, you know."

"Good at it? Good at what?" asked Leslie.

Michael chuckled. "Student mode. You know. Lectures. Busy work. Tests. Maybe do a paper. Probably have to get up and talk about something. Student mode. Kick back. Take it all in. Same old, same old."

"Michael, you're *so* cynical. You sound like an undergrad'. You're a grad student, for heaven's sake!"

"And three months from having to teach a seventh grade history class," remarked Michael.

*"Same old. same old."*

"Oh, boy. . ." laughed Leslie.

"Oh, boy is right," added Michael. Both laughed and continued to walk down the sidewalk past the dorms. Michael thought to himself, *Yeah, right, but what am I gonna do?*

*

Michael and Leslie stopped in front of a campus building and as Michael opened the front door, he asked, "What's the room number to this class, anyway?"

Leslie opened her backpack and found her class schedule. "Ah, 400. I didn't know this building had a fourth floor!"

"C'mon Michael, don't be a wimp. Let's try the stairs!"

"Well, it wouldn't surprise me if the computer goofed again," piped Michael. "Hey, where's the elevator?"

"C'mon Michael, don't be a wimp. Let's try the stairs!"

The two trudged up the first flight of stairs passing the entrance to the second floor, then up the third floor where a small sign was taped to the wall: "400 This Way." An arrow pointed up.

"Sorry Michael, no computer foul up this time," as the two climbed the final flight of stairs. "We're gonna be late." Leslie pulled the door to Room 400. It didn't open.

"Pull a little harder. Might be stuck. Look at all these boxes stacked up here! Try again," urged Michael. The pair dropped their backpacks and together gave the door a good tug. Both of them shot back across the stair landing and found themselves buried in old cardboard boxes much like collapsing in a bean bag chair. They laughed and helped each other up, slapping off the dust from their back sides.

"Look!" yelled Leslie. "The door's open. I guess we go in."

"We must be the first ones here," said Michael who fumbled for the light switch inside the door, found it and flipped it.

"Wow, get a load of this place," said Leslie. The room was filled with school desks, the kind with lids that hinged up and places for pencils on top. At the front of the room was a green chalk board above which was the alphabet in printed and script letters in both upper and lower case. There were hundreds of books in book cases lining one side of the wall. The other side of the room was covered with construction paper and artwork of various types. A row of lockers lined the back of the room.

"You know," said Leslie, "I haven't seen a locker like that since. . ."

"GRADE SCHOOL?"

The voice had come from the far corner of the classroom. A very small man sat hunched over a pile of papers, his fingers covered in chalk dust, and seemingly engrossed over scribblings on the blackboard behind him. The man looked up and as he leaned back his wooden chair squeaked, which cued a change in his expression from concentration to an ear-to-ear smile. "I'll bet you weren't expecting to see the likes of me. I teach this class."

*"I'll bet you weren't expecting to see the likes of me."*

"You're the teacher?" asked Michael.

"I teach in this room, but I'm not your teacher," replied the man who grasped the arms of the chair to help push himself up.

"That doesn't make a lot of sense. Is this Instructional Design?" asked Leslie.

"It's whatever class you want it to be," said the man who walked out to greet the pair. "You know, not many people make it up to this floor. So, I'm guessin' that your being here means, well, that you're ready for what this class of yours has to offer."

"And what would that be?" asked Michael a bit annoyed. "So, what's this classroom for, anyway?"

"Why, my boy. . ." The man laughed. "For both of you, you're at The Starting Point!"

"Starting point!" yelled Michael.

The man paused for a moment to gather his thoughts, "You can't expect to start an adventure unless you find the Starting Point. Do you know where your Starting Point is?"

Michael turned to Leslie, "What is this man talking about?"

The man looked down at his feet and pointed to the pair. "It's one of those chicken and egg things, when people don't know where they are, they can't start anywhere. And if you can't start, well, you can't get anywhere."

"This is just a class. Is this the place or not?" asked Michael pulling tighter on the strap of his backpack.

"Well, *you* see and *I* can see that you *don't* see that *not* seeing is part of the problem." The teacher a moment. "You see that line on the floor? You're standing on it."

The pair looked down, took a step in different directions and ran into each other.

"That's the Show-and-Tell Line. It's kind of a starting point. On Fridays the kids will start here demonstrating what they've brought from home. And whatever they do from that point on will take them away from here. You see it's just a starting point." The man looked at the two matter of factly, reassured that his explanation was adequate, but still waiting to see if it made any sense to the two. It didn't.

Michael and Leslie looked at each other.

The man motioned to them. "You're here to learn, aren't you? Well, you need a starting point. And because you don't have one, I guess I'll have to show you one." The man turned around to them and looked hard in their eyes. "Now mind you, I can get you close, but you'll have to discover your own. I'm just the teacher."

"So, where is this place, this Starting Point?" queried Leslie.

The man replied, "Well, it's a room sort of like this one, but, come see for yourself. This way."

The two stared at each other and shrugged, but the man had disappeared behind the door to the classroom.

"It's on the fifth floor!" The two could hear the man's voice quickly decreasing.

"Let's go," said Leslie. "Hurry. We might as well follow this guy."

"But there's no fifth floor, Leslie. Leslie?"

*

"Ah! Here we are," said the man searching for the right key to open the door to a room on the fifth floor. The pair were out of breath as they reached the top of the stairs.

"Didn't know there was a fifth floor?" said Leslie.

The man responded, "Most people don't need to know. It would be useless information, unless they were ready."

"Ready for what?" asked Michael.

The man inserted a key into the keyhole of the door and pulled it open. "You are very fortunate. I envy you."

"Aren't you coming in?" asked Leslie.

"No, this is your adventure. I know where my starting point is. It is not here. But yours will begin somewhere in there. Please, you can begin now." The man backed quietly away from the pair.

"I don't like this one bit," said Michael. "We're late for class now for sure."

The man stopped and asked, "This is your class. What did you call it?"

"Instructional Design," answered Leslie.

"Yes, well, what you call it is fine. This is your doorway. Once you find your starting point, you will know where you will be going. It will be wonderful," smiled the man.

"C'mon, Michael, let's go. Might be fun. I know this sounds weird, but let's give it a go," encouraged Leslie who nudged Michael with her backpack. "Thanks for showing us, ah, where to begin."

"My pleasure," said the man. "It's my job, after all. I am the teacher."

The two stared at each for a moment. The teacher turned to walk away but turned around and said, "You'll need a weapon."

"What for?" asked Leslie.

"There will be moments when you will come to a crossroads. There you will meet your enemy. You will have to make a decision," said the teacher. "You see, you need a weapon."

"We have none," said Leslie.

"Then take these." The teacher handed Leslie a canning jar and inside were. . .

"Tongue depressors?" squealed Leslie. "Tongue depressors! These are tongue depressors. Geez, some weapon."

"Please take them," insisted the teacher.

So Leslie, with the canning jar of tongue depressors, thanked the man as he was closing the door. Her last sight of him was that eerie smile, eerie in the sense that it was so sincere and so well-meaning. She wasn't used to it.

"Wow, look at this place," yelled Michael. A room they had thought would be just another classroom had turned into a small café off a side street. There were many small tables with two or three chairs around each table. Fans rotated overhead. There was a large counter that could have been a bar, but no bottles were lined up against the wall.

"Look at all of these mirrors," beamed Leslie. "I've never seen such a place as this." The light from the windows reflected against glass and mirror. It was hard to take in the total effect of the room.

"We're not open yet."

Leslie and Michael turned to locate the source of the voice. They ventured slowly to the counter or bar or whatever. Behind was a mirror that seemed to have no beginning or end. It was just there. It wrapped around the perimeter of the room. As they approached the counter the surface of the mirror focused. A figure also took shape. Leslie looked for a smile, but it was not forthcoming. In fact, this fellow did not seem happy to see them at all.

# Tour 2:
## *The Learning Café*

---

"I said we're closed, can't you read the sign?" said the man.

The two looked around.

"We didn't see any sign. We'll come back later. Leslie, let's go," said Michael.

"Wait a minute," said Leslie. "Isn't this Instructional Design, you know, the class?"

The man behind the counter replied, "I don't know anything 'bout no Design class. Yeah, come back tomorrow!"

Leslie walked up to the counter and dropped her backpack in front of the man. "Look, the guy downstairs, the teacher? He said we could find our Starting Point here. Geez, now I'm talking like that man."

"Yeah, yeah. Ya' don't have to yell."

"So where is this Starting Point we're supposed to find?" asked Michael.

"Ha! You're standing on it!" laughed the man. "You don't get it, do you? I gotta explain this to everybody who shows up. I gotta do all the work."

"What do you mean this is the Starting Point? It's just a bar. This is a bar, isn't it?" asked Leslie.

"Call it whatever you want," said the man. "The only thing is that if you don't know what you want, how are you going to order anything?"

"What we want?" asked Michael.

"Yeah, what do you mean by that? asked Leslie. "We just want to take a class and be done with it." Even Leslie was growing a little impatient with matters. "What does this place have to do with Instructional Design or school or learning?"

The man leaned over to Leslie and whispered to her face. "Now you're figuring it out. Look behind you on the sign above the door. See, this is the Learning Café. So, whatcha' be ordering today?"

\*

Michael and Leslie looked at each other. *Learning Café?*

"I don't see any food or beverages to order. I don't see any menu!" yelled Michael.

"If this is a learning café, and we can order anything we want," said Leslie. "And if this is supposed to be. . .OK, I want to learn about instructional design."

"Yeah, an order of instructional design," laughed Michael.

"No problem," said the man behind the counter, "Here's your quarter."

"What's this for?" asked Michael.

"You'll need it for the jukebox over there in the corner. Drop it in and press B-3," said the man.

Leslie and Michael picked up their backpacks from the counter and walked together across the room to the jukebox.

*"What's this for?"*

"Hey, there are no selections here! Just buttons with letters and numbers!" exclaimed Michael.

"Go on, put in the quarter," urged Leslie.

Michael inserted the quarter into the slot and found the buttons B and 3 and pushed them. Immediately, the jukebox began to hum and lit up revealing the innards of the machine. The machine sluggishly retrieved one of the 45's from its slot. Sound came out of the jukebox but it was all wrong. Words came first in the form of a chorus. The chorus stopped, then the music began. It was all very odd.

Believe this, believe that
This is what I learned today:
That Columbus sailed in 1492
And questions have answers
When written in a certain way.
Believe this, believe that
That is what I wonder about
Could it be OK to doubt?

The words stopped. They weren't so much as sung as exclaimed. Leslie thought, *This must be what William Blake poems sound like if one had the courage to sing them.* Then the music started up. There was no rhythm, just a blaring of sounds. Then the chorus started again.

Believe this, believe that
This is what I learned, you see:
That a bluebird is almost always blue
And things are never
What they appear to be.
Believe this, believe that
Why can't I feel this way
When I feel I have something to say?

Believe this, believe that
This is what I learned today:
That pictures can be painted where the
    rabbit sat
And turtles say hello
When they pass my way

Believe this, believe that
Please don't tell me it's true
When I can look up and know the sky is
    blue.

Believe this, believe that
This is what I learned, you see:
That hearing what you have to say
And sharing what I have to think
Are ways that help make sense for me
Believe this, believe that
My day is a deeper hue
When I spend exploring it with you.

The music and voices stopped and the record returned to its place in the jukebox. The whirring of the mechanism ceased and the rainbow of lights turned off. The pair turned to see if the man behind the counter was still there. He was gone.

"This is very odd, indeed," said Leslie.

"This whole day is pretty weird, if you ask me," said Michael. "This is what I get for missing orientation."

"Yikes, where are we now?" asked Michael wide-eyed. The mirrors and the counter and the Café had disappeared. Leslie and Michael found themselves in a forest of orchids.

\*

"So, where do we go from here?" mumbled Michael.

"IT ALL DEPENDS."

"*THERE'S NO DEPENDING TO IT!*"

"Who said that?" asked Leslie. "Do you mind showing yourself? We have had quite a day."

"QUITE ASSUREDLY," said the first voice.

*"I KNOW EXACTLY HOW YOU FEEL,"* added the second voice.

There was a rustling behind the vermilliads. A row or two behind the path parted a bit to reveal, well, something quite indescribable.

The first voice looked like Michael. The other looked like Leslie, but both were not exact replicas of the two, but caricatures of them, definitely. Michael's version approximated the Tin Man from Oz, while Leslie's double had bits and pieces of several nice features, a composite body that borrowed its niceties from different arms, noses, and waists.

Leslie turned up her nose and frowned.

"So, who are you two?" asked Michael, "and why do you look like us, kind of?"

"That does not look like me," snorted Leslie, "You can speak for yourself, but that is not me!"

"HOW DO YOU KNOW THAT? HAVE YOU LOOKED AT YOURSELF LATELY?" said the Leslie look-alike.

"I've looked at myself plenty, but I have never dreamed that I could look as cockeyed as you. You should look at yourself," said Leslie.

"A GOOD IDEA!" said the Leslie Look-a-Like.

Leslie and the Leslie Look-a-Like looked at each other for quite awhile. Leslie did not look like a very happy graduate student. The Leslie Look-a-Like looked at Leslie with a rather empty stare, blinking her eyes once or twice.

*"That does not look like me,"*

Michael laughed.

"All I see is YOU!" exclaimed Leslie.

"EXACTLY. VERY GOOD. I KNEW SHE WAS SHARP. DIDN'T I TELL YOU?" remarked the Leslie Look-a-Like.

*"IT DOESN'T TAKE MUCH OF A WIT TO SEE THE OBVIOUS,"* said the Michael Look-a-Like.

"He may not look just like you, but he talks a lot like you," laughed Leslie.

"Where are we, anyway?" asked Michael.

*"WHERE WOULD YOU LIKE TO BE?"* replied the Michael Look-a-Like.

"Well. We're here! That's all I know," said Leslie.

"AN EXCELLENT OBSERVATION," said the Leslie Look-a-Like, "YOU ARE HERE."

*"THAT WE CAN AGREE ON, YES WE CAN,"* said the Michael Look-a-Like.

"I don't believe any of this!" said Michael.

*"THEN YOU MUST START OVER,"* said the Michael Look-a-Like, *"THAT'S ALL THERE IS TO IT."*

"Start over!" yelled Michael.

*"YES, START OVER FROM THE BEGINNING,"* said the Michael Look-a-Like.

*"WHAT IS IT THAT YOU BELIEVE IN?"* insisted the Leslie Look-a-Like who had remained very still during this questioning.

"Me?" asked Leslie, "What do I believe? Believe about what?"

*"BELIEVE ABOUT LEARNING, OF COURSE,"* said the Leslie Look-a-Like, *"THAT IS THE BUTTON YOU PUSHED? B-3? IT'S ALL VERY CLEAR."*

*"YES, INDEED. IT'S ALL IN THE BOOK. YOU DO CARRY THE BOOK WITH YOU?"* the Michael Look-a-Like wanted to know.

Michael looked at Leslie.

"What book?" asked the pair in unison.

The Look-a-Like's looked at each other.

*"THE BOOK OF BELIEFS, OF COURSE,"* replied the pair of Look-a-Likes.

"I don't carry such a book," said Michael.

*"BALDERDAH, WHAT THINKING!"* replied the Michael Look-a-Like. *"I CAN'T BELIEVE YOU ARE HERE! HUTZPAH. RIBBLEDECK, JITTERDA."* The Michael Look-a-Like was clearly having problems with Michael's response.

*"WAFFLEDING. INCREDIBLE. RATTLEWICK..."* exclaimed the Michael Look-a-Like.

*"I AM AFRAID THAT MY COMPANION IS OF NO FURTHER USE HERE. WITH NO BELIEFS, HE CANNOT FUNCTION CORRECTLY. YOU WILL HAVE TO WATCH HIM. HE COULD HURT HIMSELF,"* said the Leslie Look-a-Like.

*Oh dear,* thought Leslie, *I will have to try and be more careful.*

*"VISSERWALL. KOOKOOTCHIEKOO."*

"I have beliefs," muttered Leslie. The Leslie Look-a-Like stared sternly at Leslie. The orchids surrounding her bristled as if a wind was blowing. "My beliefs about learning..."

The Leslie Look-a-Like slowly smiled, "YES?"

The orchids stilled their shivering.

"I believe that learning is the responsibility of each of us and..."

*"WRITE IT DOWN. WRITE IT DOWN."* urged the Leslie Look-a-Like.

Leslie set down her backpack and found a notepad. "Michael, give me a pen."

"Yeah, here," said Michael who was was quite busy keeping his Look-a-Like from rotating himself through the orchid forest and taking all the plants with him.

*"GO ON,"* insisted the Leslie Look-a-Like.

"Ah, learning is an individual thing," continued Leslie, "and learning is.."

"WHY IS THAT?" asked the Leslie Look-a-Like.

*Why?* wondered Leslie.

"WHY INDEED?" asked the Look-a-Like.

"Because each of us bring different experiences and we're interested in different things, " said Leslie.

"YES." The Leslie Look-a-Like seemed to want to hear more.

"Each of us might learn best in different ways," Leslie added feeling pressed.

"HOW SO?"

"Because each of us is different?" replied Leslie.

"IN WHAT WAYS?"

"I know I like to learn with other people," said Leslie. "Michael here doesn't like group projects. He thinks that people don't pull their weight in a group, right Michael?" Michael was nowhere to be seen.

Leslie picked up her backpack, "Sorry, I have to find Michael."

"IT IS TIME TO MOVE ON," said the Leslie Look-a-Like.

"Hey, you know, you kinda look like me." *I swear this wasn't the case when I first saw her,* thought Leslie walking away.

"THAT IS BECAUSE YOU SEE YOURSELF BETTER NOW," remarked the Look-a-Like.

Leslie stopped and turned around. Her Look-a-Like was gone. She turned around again. *Now where was Michael?*

# Tour 3:
# *The Gatekeeper*

Leslie set off through the orchid forest looking for Michael.

"Michael, Michael, are you out there?" yelled Leslie.

Leslie tried to peer over the *Odontoglossum grande,* but they were over her head. She would have liked a stick or something to help cut her way through the *Dactylorhizas* and the *Cymbidiums,* but the *Pleurothallis* in particular were much too beautiful, so she made her way through the forest by twisting her arms and back.

"Michael? It's Leslie!"

"Why must you yell so?" a voice asked.

"Oh, no, not another one," mumbled Leslie. She stopped and looked around and saw nothing. "OK, who's there?"

"Please. No shouting. You will never find your way by shouting. Stop and look up," advised the voice.

Above the orchid canopy Leslie saw mounted at the end of an orchid stem, a head that rotated a third of the way around, paused, then rotated in the other direction. This back and forth rotation continued, the head taking no notice of Leslie whatsoever.

"Who are you?" asked Leslie.

"I am a Milepost. Certainly, that is obvious."

"What milepost are you then?" asked Leslie.

"Wherever you are in your search, of course. I'm not the only one you know. There are others, many others," answered the Milepost.

"I'm looking for my friend? He was running behind his, ah, his Look-a-Like," said Leslie.

"A likely story. I have heard it before. What does that have to do with your search?" inquired the Milepost.

"As I said," continued Leslie, "I'm looking for my friend. Have you seen him?"

*"I am a Milepost. Certainly, that is obvious."*

"Yes, yes, but that search is only a minor matter. It will last you only a moment and for that you do not need

me. Where are you? That is the problem," said the Milepost, who looked up, rotated halfway around then returned to its original position. The head on the end of the orchid stem looked about for a moment before peering down at Leslie once again.

"Problem?" said Leslie. "I don't have any problem, other than trying to find Michael, trying to figure out where I am and how to get us out of here. Other than that, I can see no problem here," said Leslie quite sternly.

"Well, now," said the Milepost, "that is the question, is it not?"

"What is the question?" asked Leslie.

"What is your problem?" asked the Milepost.

"I don't understand any of this," sighed Leslie.

"Well, when you do not understand, you must check the Book," said the Milepost rather matter-of-factly.

"You mean the Book of Beliefs?" said Leslie.

"Yes, that is a very fine book, but you must consult the Book of Needs Justified," said the Milepost.

"Well, I'm sorry, but I don't have such a book, and frankly I don't care much at this point," said Leslie who was growing tired and feeling a bit hungry.

"I am sorry, too, but without such a Book you cannot move on. It is not possible," said the Milepost. "So please. Check your Book and move on or you will have to begin one. You can choose to sing it, or dance it. Most people choose to write out their Book of Needs Justified."

"How 'bout if I just dream mine?" asked Leslie.

"Sorry. No dreaming or imagining allowed here. These things must be evidenced," responded the Milepost.

"But, couldn't we start such a book by thinking it?" asked Leslie.

"Yes, yes," said the Milepost, "But you need a Book you can consult. How then can you prove that you have any Needs?"

"When you are ready I will be here watching. I am a Milepost. This is my job, you know." The Milepost continue to whirl about scanning the orchid forest for whatever or whomever needed guidance.

Leslie sat down on her backpack and put her head in her hands. *How am I to write such a book if this is what I must do to move on?* wondered Leslie. *What does this have to do with instructional design, anyway, and where is Michael? Problems? Ha! I got problems!*

"How is it that you know you have a problem?" asked the Milepost.

"I just said so or I thought it, isn't that enough?" replied Leslie. "Hey! I didn't say that out loud!"

"Not quite enough. No, I am afraid this will not do." said the Milepost who rotated to take in another view, then returned to look at Leslie. "This problem of yours," said the Milepost who opened its eyes further still. "Is it a real problem?"

"You could say this is a most unreal problem," sighed Leslie.

"Real or unreal, makes no difference," said the Milepost, "Either way, your problem must be justified."

"OK, so how do I justify my problem?" *This sounds silly*, thought Leslie.

"Well, that all depends if you have a problem," said the Milepost. "You may discover that you do not have a problem at all."

Orchids began to rustle. The sound grew louder.

"Oh oh, looks like a *new* problem heading my way." Leslie stood up and gripped her backpack not exactly sure what she was going to meet.

Orchid stems parted. There stood Michael a bit out of breath and looking like he had just emerged from the jungle, which was, in fact, what he had just done.

"Leslie." This was all that Michael could manage as he collapsed beside her.

"Where have you been?" asked Leslie.

Michael turned and stared up at Leslie. "I have met the Gatekeeper. We'll have to go back." Michael was still out of breath.

Leslie bent down and placed her hands on her hips, "I've been trying to get a fix on how to get out of here, while you've been..."

"No, no! We gotta go back and face the Gatekeeper," insisted Michael.

"Boy, what has happened to you? I thought you were all fired up to find our class and be done with this nonsense," said Leslie.

"Leslie, *this* is the class. This is instructional design. Don't ask me how, but this is the real thing. You have to trust me," urged Michael.

"You can't be serious?" said Leslie.

Michael managed to stand. "Look, I don't know how I know, but I was trying to keep track of my Look-a-Like and the more I thought about this place, the more it seemed like, well, this place *is* the class. Everything we've seen and experienced. The Cafe', the Look-a-Like's, this forest. This is our classroom!" Michael opened his arms and twirled around. His backpack fell to the ground. "And I remember stopping. I looked around and my Look-a-Like was gone but somehow I knew that I was on the right track. And at that moment I was face to face with The Gatekeeper!"

*Somebody has put something in Michael's tea*, thought Leslie.

*

"So, who is this gatekeeper?" Leslie asked with a bit of contempt in her voice.

"Big time, Leslie. Looks like a major player in whatever place this is," said Michael.

Leslie thought, *Opscanland*. She laughed.

"Leslie, are you listening? We've got to go back!"

"Yeah, OK, we'll go back." Leslie patted Michael on the shoulder. "I'm gettin' kind of tired of this party anyway." Leslie looked around for some new character which might object to her attitude, but the only possible objector was the Milepost which ignored their presence altogether.

"Don't you see, Leslie? Now that we've figured out that we don't need a classroom in the classical sense, we don't have to wait for class to start. We don't even need a teacher."

"You don't even know what you're saying," snapped Leslie. "I wouldn't know where to start, and that's not going to help you graduate, you know. No teacher, no credits, no piece of paper. What are you here for anyway?"

"Ah, but Leslie, here the teacher will find us!"

"Tell me, Michael, what's the source of this enlightenment?"

"Oh, glad you asked." Michael picked up his backpack and pulled out what looked like a green banana with a broccoli head on one end.

"What...is...that?" asked Leslie.

"It's called a bananoli."

"A what? Sorry, I don't eat green food," said Leslie.

"A banan..oli. Provides all the benefits of a banana plus the iron of broccoli," answered Michael.

"Looks like Bette Midler."

Michael was not amused. "Here, all I know is that when I ate one of these, my head cleared. I could think straight for once and I could see the possibilities."

"Possibilities?" asked Leslie. "You mean, like getting out of here?"

"Well, no. I was thinking more of the learning possibilities," said Michael.

*Hmm, strong tea*, thought Leslie. "I could lean against a tree and read all day. Is that what you mean?"

"Oh Leslie, more than that. It's like thinking of the infinite ways that you can help make learning happen! For you. For me. For everyone! That's what this place is for—to help us see the possibilities!"

Leslie began to peel off the green skin of the bananoli. "You say these taste good?" Leslie took a bite out of Bette Midler's neck. "Uggh!"

"I didn't say they tasted good..." said Michael who stepped back from Leslie. "You'll get used to it. The more I ate the better it tasted. That's what the Gatekeeper told me would happen."

"Echhh. I guess we should meet this Gatekeeper fellow," said Leslie. "How far do we have to go?"

"Not far," said Michael who was already disappearing back into the Orchid Forest.

Leslie caught up to Michael who had stopped and was looking around.

"OK, are we there yet?" quipped Leslie.

"Well, I thought this was the way."

"Great. Next semester, let's make sure we don't take the same class," said Leslie.

"I know," exclaimed Michael. "This might be a good time to try one of those tongue depressors." Michael motioned to Jane's backpack.

"What are we going to do with a tongue depressor?" yelled Leslie looking at Michael.

"Go on, get one out."

Leslie reached into her backpack and pulled out the quart canning jar. "Michael, this is the weirdest thing..."

Michael grabbed the jar and unscrewed the lid. "Here, try one." Michael handed the jar to Leslie who pulled out a stick.

"Now, what am I going to do with this?" said Leslie.

"What does one usually do with a tongue depressor? C'mon, Leslie. You're the one who's always egging me on. Go ahead. Say, aghh." urged Michael.

"Michael, this is really dumb."

"C'mon Leslie, just go with it."

Leslie looked at the stick then placed it in her mouth. She looked at Michael and pulled the tongue depressor out of her mouth. "I don't feel any different."

"Any thoughts?" asked Michael. "Any ideas?"

"No, Michael, no thoughts, no ideas."

"Hey look!" Michael pointed to the tongue depressor that Leslie was holding. "There's writing on it!"

\*

Leslie brought the tongue depressor closer so she could read what had appeared on its surface.

"What does it say?" asked Michael. "C'mon, read what it says."

LEARNING IS NOT A DESTINATION. IT IS A PATHWAY THAT ONLY THE LEARNER CAN TRAVEL, AND GOALS OPEN GATES TO THESE PATHWAYS.

Michael and Leslie looked at each other. Leslie stared at the writing on the stick.

"TICKETS! I MUST HAVE YOUR TICKETS!"

Michael squealed. "We found him. The Gatekeeper!"

Leslie and Michael picked up their backpacks and began making their way through the orchid forest to the source of the voice. After walking what seemed like a great distance, which in fact was only about twenty feet, the pair found themselves at the edge of the orchid forest but facing a stone wall that was at least ten feet high.

"TICKETS, PLEASE."

Emerging from the stone wall itself was a uniformed man, whose clothing fit him rather tightly.

"Ah, we have no ticket, sorry," said Leslie.

"THAT IS QUITE OBVIOUS. I CANNOT OPEN THE GATE."

"Leslie show him the tongue depressor. Maybe that will help," suggested Michael.

The Gatekeeper bent over as far as he could, which was not far. The stone uniform did not have much give to it.

"YOU ARE JUST NOW READING THIS?" asked the Gatekeeper. "YOU SHOULD HAVE CONSULTED YOUR WEAPON MUCH EARLIER. IT IS NO WONDER THAT YOU HAVE NO TICKETS. BUT WITHOUT TICKETS YOU CANNOT PASS."

"Why should we want to pass through your gate, anyway," replied Leslie. "There are many more gates we can try."

"TICKETS, PLEASE."

The Gatekeeper moved toward Leslie. "THIS IS TRUE, BUT ANY OTHER GATE WOULD BE THE WRONG GATE. WHY WOULD YOU WANT TO ENTER SOMEONE ELSE'S GATE?"

"So how do we get tickets then?" said Leslie.

The Gatekeeper sighed. "YOU MUST BE NEW HERE. YOU HAVE GOALS, DON'T YOU?"

Michael and Leslie looked once again at each other. Both shrugged.

"YOU CANNOT BUY TICKETS! YOU MAKE THEM YOURSELF. BUT YOU HAVE TO HAVE GOALS."

"If you can't buy them, then how..." Leslie blurted out.

"YOU WILL HAVE YOUR TICKETS WHEN YOU KNOW YOUR GOALS. USE YOUR WEAPONS. DON'T JUST

CARRY THEM AROUND WITH YOU. USE THEM."

Leslie was exasperated. "How do I use a tongue depressor as a weapon? How do I use this to discover what my goals are?"

"*YOUR* GOALS?"

"Well, we're gonna be the teachers," said Michael.

"I AM SORRY. I AM NOT QUALIFIED TO ANSWER THESE QUESTIONS. I JUST OPEN DOORS." The Gatekeeper started to return his keys to his belt. "*YOU* HAVE TO ANSWER THESE QUESTIONS. WHO ELSE CAN ANSWER THEM?"

Leslie yelled out, "Hey, all we want to do is learn how to design. Can that be so much to ask?"

The Gatekeeper turned its head. "THAT IS A GREAT DEAL TO ASK, MY DEAR." Reaching for its keys, the Gatekeeper added, "YOU SHOULD HAVE SAID THAT IN THE FIRST PLACE. THESE MATTERS ARE SO MUCH EASIER WHEN YOU HAVE A TICKET. PEOPLE ARE ALWAYS TRYING TO PASS THROUGH HERE WITHOUT ONE."

Michael grabbed both his and Leslie's backpacks. "C'mon, Leslie, let's go! The gate! It's open!"

Leslie looked a bit dumbfounded. "Why didn't you just tell us..."

"IT'S NOT WHAT I WANT." The key turned in the lock. The sound of the mechanism clunked. The Gatekeeper pulled open the gate with great effort. "IT'S ALL A MATTER OF WHAT *YOU* WANT."

The Gatekeeper motioned the pair through the gate. "HERE, EAT ONE OF THESE. YOUR HEAD WILL CLEAR." The Gatekeeper handed them a bunch of bananolies.

"Hey, before we go through, Michael, why don't you try one of those sticks. We may need a weapon."

The Gatekeeper bowed ever so slightly.

Michael pulled out a tongue depressor from the quart canning jar in Leslie's backpack. He inserted it into his mouth.

"Hey, big boy, not feeling well?" laughed Leslie.

"Funny, Leslie, funny," the depressor still resting under Michael's tongue.

"What does it say?"

YOUR BELIEFS WILL TAKE YOU WHERE YOU WANT TO GO. ALL YOU HAVE TO DO IS LET THEM GO AND FOLLOW THEM.

The pair looked at each other, shrugged and hoisted their backpacks.

"Well, let's go then," said Michael. "Let go a belief, Leslie."

"I believe in restrooms."

"Ah, good point, but I don't think that's gonna buy us much here," said Michael.

The Gatekeeper motioned them through again and bowed once again slightly, the stone uniform crunched and its stone parts produced a grinding noise.

Michael and Leslie left the orchid forest and walked through the Gate of the stone wall.

# Tour 4:
## *The Director*

---

Michael and Leslie took one step through the Gate and were greeted by an eyeful of dust as a carriage pulled madly by two horses nearly ran them over.

"You there! Stand aside!" yelled the coachman who turned his attention back to controlling his horses. The pair could hear him bellow as he quickly disappeared, "There's a road here. It's not for people."

Having managed their way through the Gate, the pair held their chests trying to catch their breaths.

"Well, that was hardly a break in our day," muttered Leslie.

"Where do you think we are now?" asked Michael.

They set down their backpacks bulging with the bunch of bananolis and a quart canning jar of tongue depressors.

"Can't see for all of this dust," replied Leslie. The two waved back and forth through the dense layers. They could barely see each other. "Do something," said Leslie.

Michael batted at the dust and managed to create a hole the size of a pie plate. Through the hole, one could hear sounds, sounds of people.

"Here, make this hole bigger," said Michael.

*Dust as thick and smelly as cigar smoke in a pool hall*, thought Leslie.

The two created a hole big enough to step through. Michael handed Leslie the backpacks, while he held the dust hole open. Then Leslie switched places as dust holder allowing Michael to step through. The hole closed up.

Leslie and Michael turned around. In front of them were indeed people, people walking between shops and crossing the street. They all seemed quite busy and none of them paid the pair any mind at all. However, another carriage turned the corner about a block up ahead. The pair jumped to the boardwalk closest to the street.

\*

"Now there, what's your business?" The pair turned around to find a man leaning on a broom.

*"Let me see your list."*

"We have no business," Leslie fired back.

"Well then, what good are you then?" said the man who resumed his sweeping the boardwalk in front of his shop. "Move your foot!"

"Hey," said Michael, "good has nothing to do with it."

"Good? I'm talking about business."

"What is your business?" asked Leslie.

"Can't you read the sign? The sign!"

The two looked up, but could not find the sign. The sun was too bright. They stepped back and stumbled off the boardwalk.

"The MERCANTILE. OK, so what's inside?" asked Michael.

"The storekeeper straightened up. "What EVER you need. Let me see your list." The storekeeper rested the broom handle in one hand and reached out his other hand.

"List?" said Leslie.

"You do know what you want? If you are here, then you must have goals, so you would be needing what I have. Now, step inside. Brush off the dust first."

The store inside was cooler than out on the town street. The air felt a little musty combined with wonderful smells. Wooden buckets were stacked on the floors, clothing that hadn't sold, barrels of wooden blocks, baskets of fruit, bins that smelled of herbs. There were toys stacked in the corner and great numbers of small drawers lined an entire wall. There were maps and tools.

"I can see why you need a list," admitted Leslie.

"Yes, a list is most helpful," said the storekeeper. "Without one people just grab as much as they can carry and discover when they are way down the road that they have bought way too much of the wrong goods. Well, just look around." The storekeeper handed the pair a pencil and a piece of paper, the turned around and walked off. The pair looked at each other then looked at the storekeeper. The man laughed.

"OK, so we need stuff. I don't know, Leslie, what do we need?"

"I'm hungry. Those banana what-evers weren't enough for me."

"If you'd be needing food, then there's a store down the street for that business. Besides, young folks, these goods. . . well they're not for you. They're for your learners!" The man continued his chuckling, occasionally a laugh burst out like a belch that couldn't be stopped. "Over here is fruit, all types. Them learners eat this and Shatsa! There's knowledge in their hands. You can smell these, touch them, but they spoil easily, so choose only what you'll be able to use. I also have leather-bound books on all subjects, and parchment paper for writing."

"Look at these gadgets," exclaimed Michael.

"Ah, those are the toys, measuring devices, and various contraptions for your curious types. See these prisms and lenses?" said the storekeeper who handed Michael a kaleidoscope to look through.

"I like these smells," said Leslie who had her nose buried in a bin of dried herbs. "Strong."

"Yes, those make fine attitudes, don't you think?"said the storekeeper. "They add wonderful seasoning and variety and flavor to the learning. Fill a sack of what you need. They are quite inexpensive and they go a long way if used."

The storekeeper handed Leslie some brown paper bags. As she was deciding on what to put in those bags, Michael climbed a stairway to a loft.

"Up there are the moving tools," said the storekeeper, "I have instructions on how to use them."

"Moving tools?" said Michael.

"Walking tools, running tools. Devices to help one be more flexible is my understanding. I don't claim to be an expert at these," replied the storekeeper.

Michael continued to paw through the mechanical gadgets and implements not really knowing what he was looking for.

"Michael?" Leslie yelled up the stairs. "I've made up my list of the things I think we'll need. Hope you don't mind. The storekeeper says they'll be ready for us when we need them."

Michael descended the stairs reluctantly a little perturbed that he could find nothing that he just had to have. "What's this stuff going to cost us anyhow?"

"Your credit's good here. You have goals."

"Right. Love them goals," said Michael. Leslie laughed.

"Besides, you'll have to pay up soon enough," said the storekeeper. "Everyone pays up in this store. Just business."

The pair frowned.

"Well, thanks, I guess," said Michael.

"Where do you suggest we go now?" said Leslie thinking that maybe they should be asking directions from now on rather than bumping into any more situations.

The storekeeper looked up to the ceiling. "I would think that The Playhouse would be right for you. There's a new play starting soon."

The two left the store and looked up and down the street.

"She's right over there," said the storekeeper pointing up the street away from the road that circled the town. "At night she's all lit up. Everyone goes. I guess not as much as they used to. Kids love to go there on Saturdays. I see the marquee hasn't been changed yet. I suspect you'll have a say in that."

"What? I don't follow," said Michael.

"C'mon, time to go," said Leslie.

The two tightened their backpacks around their shoulders and set off down the street for The Playhouse.

"They'll be back," grinned the storekeeper, "but, no matter, I have everything they'll ever need right here."

\*

The Playhouse was dark and empty when they entered. They walked down one of the aisles and slowly explored their way through the darkness to the only light in the building. It was one of the stage lights.

"Excellent! Please, up here! There are stairs to the left or right of the stage," yelled a voice from somewhere on the stage. Walking into the light was a shadow of a boisterous woman with clipboard in hand. The shadow unwound a scarf and placed it on a chair on the stage. The woman moved closer and into the light.

*Holy...*thought Michael, *looks my 6th grade teacher, Mrs., ahh, what was her name?*

"I am your play director. Did you bring the scripts?"

"I'm sorry, but we were sent by the storekeeper," said Leslie.

"That man is always sending me novices. When will I ever get professionals?" bellowed the woman.

"I'm sorry again, but we are not actors. We're only students," said Leslie.

"My sweet, innocent novice," replied the Director who placed her clipboard on the floor, "We are all students. Oh, I was so hoping you would have brought scripts. Without a script, do you know what you don't have?"

"No idea," said Michael. *No job,* he thought.

"No script, no TITLE. Nothing for the marquee out front," said the Director. "We can't let the public in on our little secret without a suitable billboard."

*"Did you bring the scripts?"*

"How about *Work in Progress,*" suggested Leslie.

"Not suitable."

"*We'll get back to you*?" chuckled Michael.

"Not in the least!"

"How about *Closed for the Season*?" said Leslie.

"NO!"

"What's so important about..."

"A script? No script, no title, no excitement, no lines outside scrambling for tickets, no playbills, NO PLAY!" The Director's voice reverberated throughout the Playhouse.

Leslie and Michael started to laugh.

"No laughing. I'M THE DIRECTOR! I should be commanding respect, especially from novices."

"Why?" asked Leslie.

"Why indeed!" snorted the Director. "I know the order of things. I know how one should act out the beginning. I know where the middle should be. I know when the audience should laugh, when they should cry. They don't cry until I say so. I know the outcome of this play and I know what should be in their minds."

"What about their hearts?" snorted Leslie back.

"Every season. It's all the same. They send me novices with no scripts."

"Maybe we're supposed to write our own scripts," said Leslie.

"Well, I won't be responsible for the results," barked the Director.

"Hey, we're responsible!" yelled Michael.

"It doesn't sound like a plan to me. How will you know where to begin? How will you know when to end it? How will the audience know when the play is over?" said the Director.

"It's not supposed to be over," blurted Michael.

"Well, aren't we the wise one," said the Director. "But you forget one thing. See that clock?"

Michael and Leslie turned around to see a dimly lit ornate clock hanging from the side wall.

"When it's nine o'clock the play is scheduled to begin. You haven't much time, my novice designers. Without a script you haven't a goose of a chance."

*Goose?* Wondered Leslie.

"And it's obvious you don't need me. Make it up as you go along. They'll want their money back. They'll throw fruit at you. They'll throw their shiny shoes at you. And they'll attack you in the papers. Good luck to you!" And with that the Director left the stage howling. "You'll be chased from town. They'll ask for your resignation."

"Well, what do we do now? We didn't learn much from Madame Director," said Michael.

"Oh, I don't know," remarked Leslie, "I think we learned a lot."

# Tour 5:
## *The Policeman*

---

Michael and Leslie left the Playhouse and once again found themselves on the main street. People passed them by without taking any notice.

"Well, what now?" asked Michael.

"I could try a tongue depressor," suggested Leslie.

"Sure, why not. It's the only thing that seems to work around here," said Michael.

Leslie sat down her backpack and pulled out the quart canning jar.

"Here," she said, "Your choice."

"Hey, it's your turn."

"OK, here goes. Cheers!" Leslie inserted the stick in her mouth. Her face twisted up like she had just placed a bar of soap in her mouth.

"Well?"

Leslie removed the depressor from her mouth. "Hey, nothing. There's nothing here. This is one is a dud."

"Maybe these only work out there in the Orchid Garden," suggested Michael.

"I'M SORRY BUT YOU TWO WILL HAVE TO COME WITH ME!"

Michael felt something touch his shoulder. His eyes ran along the curve of a nightstick up to the sternful gaze of a policeman.

"Come along now. Both of you," urged the policeman who was motioning with his nightstick.

"Why? What for?" asked Leslie.

"It is against the law here to carry a weapon," replied the policeman.

"But we haven't used it on anybody," said Michael.

"That is not the issue, ma'm. Those things there. You don't use on others. You use them on you and THAT is against the law."

"What law?" said Leslie.

The policeman sighed. "Section 2, paragraph 5, line item 4:  No weapons shall be displayed in a public place."

"Well, we'll just put it away, for heaven's sake. No harm done," said Leslie.

"Harm? You've brandished a weapon in a public street!" The policeman pulled out a metal pad and opened it.

Leslie broke out laughing.

"AND, you've laughed at a public servant. A very serious offense, I'm sure you know."

"I'm sure we don't know," said Michael. Leslie had fallen to the ground laughing.

"AND, creating a public nuisance. Three strikes, you're out. Isn't that the popular expression?" said the policeman.

Leslie laughed louder.

"Now," said Michael, "You're not going to haul us to jail for publicly displaying a tongue depressor and for laughing in the street. Well, sitting in the street, I can see, but..."

"Young man." The policeman stiffened his back and pushed down on his gunbelt. "Jail is not the punishment here. I am afraid that you two will have to take a, a TEST!"

Michael and Leslie looked at each other and both burst out laughing louder than ever.

"Oh, no! Not a test!" slobbered Leslie.

"Yes, a multiple choice test," said the policeman who pulled out a packet of papers from his metal folder case. "Now here are your Number 2 pencils, an answer form and a test sheet. Now sit down and be still and remember to read the directions completely before you begin. Remember to fill in the circles completely. See, there's a sample question. If you change your answer, you will have to erase it completely. And, there is a fifteen minute time limit. When I say STOP, you will put your pencils down! If you finish early you will remain quiet until time is up. Do you understand?"

*"I'm afraid that you two will have to take a, a test."*

Leslie held her mouth with both hands. She was ready to bust at any moment.

"Ready, now begin! You have fifteen minutes."

The pair opened up their test booklets on cue. There were three questions. The first went like this:

QUESTION 1:

IN THE 1840'S THE AMERICAN ECONOMY ENTERED ANOTHER PHASE OF ECONOMIC DECLINE. THE RESULTS HAD PREDICTABLE EFFECTS ON THE COUNTRY'S FARMERS AND CONSUMERS, BUT THE INDUSTRIAL SECTOR FARED QUITE DIFFERENTLY. CHOOSE THE ANSWER BELOW THAT MOST NEARLY

APPROXIMATES THE TRUE SITUATION AT THAT TIME.

A) Companies were formed at a rapid rate.
B) Many large firms were begun during this period.
C) Exports increased dramatically.
D) Most of the above are true.
E) None of the above are true.

"Who can answer this?" Leslie had stopped her snickering.

"No talking!" barked the policeman. "You have ten minutes."

QUESTION 2:

THIS STATEMENT IS FALSE.

A) True
B) False

"Well, this is quite impossible," said Michael.

QUESTION 3:

AN EXECUTIVE DECIDED TO TAKE THE TRAIN TO WORK, RATHER THAN DRIVE. HOWEVER, THE EXECUTIVE HAD TO CHOOSE BETWEEN TWO DIFFERENT ROUTES. WHICH OF THESE WILL RESULT IN THE SHORTEST TIME?

ROUTE 1 BEGINS AT STATION A AND TAKES 10 MINUTES BEFORE REACHING STATION B. A PASSENGER MUST TRANSFER AND PROCEED ALONG THE BLUE LINE FOR 5 STOPS, WHICH THEORETICALLY TAKES 25 MINUTES, BUT CAN TAKE UP TO 38 MINUTES.

ROUTE 2 REQUIRES TAKING A BUS TO THE TRANSFER STOP. HOWEVER, THE WAITING CAN TAKE UP TO 8 MINUTES IF PASSENGERS LEAVE THEIR HOMES 10 MINUTES BEFORE THE HOUR. IF THE EXECUTIVE WALKS AT AN AVERAGE OF 6 MPH, THE EXECUTIVE WILL ARRIVE AT THE BUS STOP 2 MINUTES BEFORE

THE BUS WILL THEORETICALLY ARRIVE. THE BUS TRANSFER LASTS 12 MINUTES. THE TRAIN FROM THE TRANSFER POINT TAKES ONLY 32 MINUTES TO REACH THE DESIRED DESTINATION.

A) Route 1 is fastest.
B) Route 2 is fastest.

"Please keep all scratch work on the back of the scoring sheet. Do not write on the test form. You have five minutes," said the test police.

"I give up," said Leslie. "I've never been a math person."

*What good is this anyway,* wondered Michael.

"Alright, put your pencils down. Time is up. Please hand in your test forms first, then pass in your scoring sheets."

Michael and Leslie handed the policeman their test papers.

"Thank you, thank you. You can stop by the station in five business days. The scores will be posted."

Leslie and Michael stood up and stretched and brushed the dust off their clothes.

"Boy, I could use a TONGUE DEPRESSOR RIGHT NOW!" yelled Michael under his breath.

"Shhhh, not here. That's what got us into trouble in the first place," said Leslie.

"Move along now," urged the policeman swinging his nightstick back and forth.

BONG BONG

Leslie pointed to the town clock up the street.

BONG BONG BONG

"Five o'clock."

"Four hours left," said Michael

"There's never enough time for designing," muttered Leslie.

*Bark, Bark*

The pair looked down. It was a dog.

"Hey, look at the mutt!" said Michael.

*"Begging your pardon?"* asked the dog.

"Yow! A talking dog at that," said Leslie.

*"Am I only a mutt?"*

"Who are you anyway?"

*"Am I not what one calls a companion animal? What would you like to call me?"*

"Socrates, I would think from what we've heard," said Leslie.

*"Socrates?"*

"It seems to me like an awful waste of a dog who can talk but can't answer," said Michael.

*"Should not one live with what cards are dealt one?"* asked the philosopher dog who sat down on his hind legs and began to lick its left forepaw.

"We should be going. We haven't much time," said Leslie.

*"Ah, you're on deadline then?"* asked the dog.

"I guess you could say we are. We have to be done and out of this place by nine o'clock tonight," said Michael.

*"You're designing then?"* asked the dog.

*"Am I only a mutt?"*

"Yeah, I guess we are," said Michael who turned and grinned at Leslie.

*"Should I not ask the questions?"* asked the dog.

"Well, why not," said Leslie, "Ask away but I don't see where asking questions is going to get us anywhere."

*"What do you believe then?"* asked the dog.

"Haven't we crossed this bridge already?" said Michael.

*"Are not your beliefs to be constantly met and crossed?"* asked the dog.

"I've never met such a strange dog," said Leslie.

*"Are you not as unique? Why do you carry your beliefs around with you? Why do you not allow your beliefs to lead you?"* asked the dog.

"I think it's time we should be going," said Leslie.

*"Where would you like to go?"* asked the dog.

"You tell us," said Michael. "Oh, that's right, you can only ask questions. I think Socrates is your name. But I still don't see where questions will lead us."

*"Are you not always a learner?"* asked the dog.

"Let's walk, then," suggested Leslie. "Maybe as long as we're moving we'll get somewhere."

"But we only have four hours left," said Michael.

*"Should we not walk faster then?"* asked the dog.

# Tour 6:
## *The Schoolhouse*

*"Is that my name then?"* asked Socrates.

"Do you like it?" asked Michael in return.

*"Why shouldn't I like it?"*

"Would you like a different name?" asked Michael with a smile.

*"How should a different name help?"* asked Socrates.

"I guess any name is as good as another," said Michael.

*"How so?"* said Socrates.

"Oh, stop it, you two. We're not getting anywhere with this," said Leslie.

*"Are we not in a different place than before?"* asked Socrates.

"I guess everyone has to be *somewhere,"* said Leslie.

*"Is that a rhetorical question?"* asked Socrates.

"Look, we've walked past a candy store, a dress-maker, a butcher shop. Which one do we choose? Which one do we need?" asked Michael.

*"Which one do we need?"* asked Socrates.

"The one that will give us the most help!" said Leslie.

*"How about this one?"* Socrates stopped and sat down on the sidewalk facing a two-story brick building with very large windows and a very large front door and porch.

"What is this place?" asked Michael.

"Let's go inside and see." Leslie thought the building looked friendly. Maybe someone could help them. "C'mon, this feels right to me."

"Are you coming Socrates," asked Michael.

*"Are dogs allowed?"*

The pair walked up the brick building  leaving the dog sitting on the sidewalk.

*I don't think so,* thought Socrates.

\*

Michael and Leslie opened the big doors and found themselves faced with a hallway that extended a great distance. Doors lined both sides of the hallway.

"Hello, there." A short voice entered the room. "I am your Tour Guide to the Schoolhouse."

"Ah, so this is a school," said Leslie.

"What you see is the Schoolhouse, but the school is inside each of these rooms," said the Tour Guide.

"There's a difference?" asked Michael.

"Yes," replied the Tour Guide.

"Well, we're looking for some ideas for our design," said Leslie.

"There are many possibilities in The Schoolhouse. Where would you like to begin?" asked the Tour Guide.

"How about this door?" suggested Michael.

"Follow me."

"We'll be quiet," promised Leslie.

"That is not necessary. No one will know you are present," said the Tour Guide opening the door.

"Wow, look at the size of this place," exclaimed Michael.

"Yes, it is a very large lecture hall," said  the Tour Guide.

*How could anyone learn in here?* wondered Leslie.

The Tour Guide turned to Leslie and said, "Watch and learn."

The class was full. Every seat was taken. The instructor walked down the aisle, said hello to several students, and walked up to the stage from one of the side stairs.

"Good afternoon, everybody. Thank you for coming." The instructor wrapped a microphone around his neck. "We'll try to do right by you today. It's nice to see you. Again, I apologize for the size of this room. We treat you so shabbily. You deserve better. I will try to make this course interesting."

Michael and Leslie leaned against the back wall of the auditorium. "He's got a lot of energy," said Michael.

"I like how he's jumping around. I don't think he *needs* a microphone," said Leslie. They turned their attention to the lecture.

"Now try to think instead of what would be the consequences if you had imperfect information. Would this be bad? Consider the case, the rare case, if you had perfect information, then your decision might be obvious, but would it? It all depends on what the firm's goals are or what the real goals of the moment are. Hold that thought. So, if you had imperfect information you would have to make a decision. Consider the idea that imperfect information leads to controlled risk taking and that such risk taking leads you out of mediocrity."

The instructor paused to let this thought sink in. "Risk-taking moves you forward because of imperfect information. So consider the possibility that you should know your information gathering goals, whether it should be a computerized information system, or just someone walking around. Perhaps the goal of such activities should be to gather enough of the right kind of

information that prompts action. You can't get results unless you act, and you cannot act without decisions."

*"Good afternoon, everybody. Thank you for coming."*

The instructor climbed onto the table at the corner of the stage. "You cannot act without decisions. No decisions without information. Now this information..." The instructor jumped to the floor and sat on the edge of the stage. This information might be gut instinct!"

"I like listening to this guy, makes me think," said Michael.

"We need to go," said Leslie.

"You go on, I'll stay," said Michael.

"No, Michael, c'mon." Leslie grabbed Michael and pushed him to the door. The Tour Guide quietly followed.

"Say, that lecture hall was bigger than the building. Is it underground?" asked Michael.

The Tour Guide smiled, "Where would you like to go next?"

"How about the Tour?" said Leslie.

"That will take some time and I understand that you don't have much time," said the Tour Guide.

"Yes, we're designers," sighed Leslie. "There's never enough time."

"Maybe this room might interest you," said the Tour Guide who opened another door. The three ventured inside tentatively. The room was dark, but they could hear giggles and over the giggles they could hear an older voice.

"OK, now reach into the box as it is passed around to you and pull out an object."

There were more giggles, a few "ooh's."

"Does everyone have an object?" said the older voice. "Now I want you to hold the object with both hands. What you have in your hands are math shapes. Now feel and think about these shapes and what these shapes might be used for. Or how you might use them."

There were more giggles.

"Now here is another box being passed around. Each of you take out a paper bag and place your object inside the bag. Then fold the top of the bag. You can take it out later. When all of you have your object in your bag, we will turn on the lights."

In a few minutes, after everyone had placed their math shape in a paper bag, the lights were turned on. There was a general squealing as eyes adjusted to the light.

"Now I want you to return to your desks. Get out a piece of notebook paper and write a short paragraph about your math object. Write about its shape and what you think it is used for and how you might use it."

"Wow, math shapes!" said Michael. "Who would have thought you could touch math?"

"Why not?" said the Tour Guide, "Anything is possible when you close your eyes and imagine things. You can learn a lot with your imagination."

"And what is that exactly?" asked Leslie.

"You learn that all things are possible," said the Tour Guide. "Come, follow me. There's a new room we've just added. You are some of the first to visit this room."

The Tour Guide motioned them to the end of the hall. Michael and Leslie wondered what was behind the doors of those that they walked by.

"In here," said the Tour Guide. "Please watch your step."

The pair walked through the doorway into another dark room. "I can't see a thing," said Leslie.

"Stand still for a moment while I close the door," said the Tour Guide.

Lights flashed. The floor seemed to give way.

"Whoa! What's going on," yelled Leslie.

Michael and Leslie reached for something to hang onto, but could only find each other. Above them the ceiling faded away to an early morning sky.

"What is this place," asked Michael.

"This is the Virtual Classroom," said the Tour Guide.

"Virtual classroom?" asked Leslie.

"Anything is possible here. Any setting you'd like. Any place," said the Tour Guide.

"What makes this room run anyhow?" said Michael.

"Your wishes," replied the Tour Guide.

"So if I want to go to a baseball game, this room will take me there?" asked Michael.

"If your wish is a learning wish, yes," said the Tour Guide.

"And who decides that?" asked Leslie.

"The learner does," responded the Tour Guide.

"We should wish something then," said Michael.

"What is your learning wish then?" asked the Tour Guide.

Leslie thought she could hear Socrates in that question. "Well, we're supposed to be learning how to design."

The Tour Guide turned away from them and looked out into the room.

"Look!" said Michael pointed to an image that was forming a few yards from them.

"What is it?" asked Leslie.

The room filled with trees and blue sky. A high pitched set of notes was heard through a light breeze that managed to sway only the tops of the trees. In front of these trees was a tall post with a bird house mounted on top. More notes. These were cautionary tones. Peering out from the small hole of the bird house was the head of a bluebird who in short order stepped out on a short perch and looked around.

# Tour 7:
# *Bubble, Bubble,*
# *Toil & Trouble*

---

"What do you think the bluebird means?" asked Michael.

"Must have something to do with learning instructional design or why were we shown that scene?" said Leslie.

"We should ask Socrates. Hey, where is that dog?" said Michael.

BONG BONG

The pair turned to look down the street they had just walked.

BONG BONG

"How many is that?" asked Leslie.

"Wait," urged Michael.

BONG BONG BONG

"Seven o'clock," said Michael.

"Two hours, Michael! We haven't designed a thing!" said Leslie.

"Designing is like that. . . sometimes."

The voice came from across the street.

"Sometimes." The voice grew closer. Pushing a cart towards them was an old woman.

"Great. Now what?" said Michael.

"Who are you?" asked Leslie.

"Your ally, I think," replied the old woman who leaned on the cart as she stepped onto the sidewalk. "I am a witch."

"A witch as an ally?" said Leslie, "You can help us then?"

"Most certainly, if you desire it?" replied the pushcart witch. "Desire it, yes, most definitely."

"How can you help us?" asked Michael.

"I will test you," said the pushcart witch.

"Oh, oh, another test," said Leslie.

"Test you, yes, I will."

Michael fumbled in his backpack for a pencil.

"First, you must want my help," said the pushcart witch.

"How do we do that?" asked Leslie.

"Show me," replied the pushcart witch. "Give me something of yourself."

"We have these tongue depressors," said Michael.

"All we have is ourselves. We will eagerly listen to what you have to say and try to act on your advice," said Leslie.

*"I will test you."*

"You have passed the first test. You give of yourself. You give willingness to learn," said the witch.

"First test?" asked Michael.

"Next you must demonstrate your willingness to do the designing," said the pushcart witch.

"How do we design if we don't know how to design?" asked Leslie.

"Ahh, you will need a special potion, if I can but find it," said the witch. "Such a potion works miracles, but, hmm..."

"Oh great, finally, a short-cut, but now she can't find it," said Michael.

"Ah, here it is! No, this is not it either, but this! This you might find useful."

"What is that?" asked Michael.

"You talk into it, then you use it to hear yourself at the other end with the answer. Here, try it out."

Leslie took the box from the old woman. She put it up to her mouth and spoke into it. "What do bluebirds have to do with learning?" she asked.

The pushcart witch pointed to the box. "Now turn the box around and place it near your ear and listen to your answer."

Leslie rotated the box and slowly brought it close to her ear. The box spoke. *Bluebirds already know how to learn.*

"I'm not sure I understand," said Leslie lowering and looking at the box, then turning to the old woman.

"Now, your third test," said the witch.

"Another one," asked Leslie.

"You must want to reflect on your doing," said the witch.

"Exactly how do we do that?" asked Michael.

"By sitting down," replied the witch.

"Sitting down?" said Leslie.

"Yes, you listen better when you sit down."

Michael and Leslie gladly sat down cross-legged on the sidewalk with the witch and her pushcart in front of them.

"You don't mind if I set up, do you?" The witch began unloading her cart. The witch unpacked small bowls and various utensils from her cart. Without looking up she asked, "What have you got for me?"

"What have we got?" asked Leslie.

"Well, your design ingredients, of course," replied the witch who walked around to the back of the cart. "Can you get me some firewood?" asked the witch. She tugged at a black kettle and turned it on its side. She rolled it carefully out of the cart trying to shoulder its fall to the ground. Michael stepped over to help ease it from the cart.

THUD.

The witch looked around and pointed to various locations around the cart. "Yes, you know, your goals, your assessments, your teaching models. If you could fetch me some water, we could throw them all in the pot!"

Michael and Leslie looked at each other.

"What about media?" asked Michael shrugging to Leslie.

"Sure throw that in, too," said the witch.

"Why should we?" asked Leslie. "What's the point?"

"Look," said the witch, "How are you going to know if your recipes have any chance of working if you don't throw the ingredients together, mix 'em up, and see how they taste?"

"Well, I just don't get any of this," said Michael.

The witch returned to the cart to retrieve more pots and spoons. "So, what are your instructions? How much of this and how much of that do you want in the pot? And what order do you want me to dump in your ingredients? This makes a difference, you know."

Leslie and Michael looked at each other again.

"How are your learners going to react? You need to try the recipe out first," said the witch.

"We're not really sure what to put in," said Michael.

"Well," said the witch, "It's your decision. You are the designers."

"Yes, we've heard that," said Leslie.

"There is an easier way," said the witch. The pair inched forward from their seats on the ground. "Yes, I am bound to warn you that this way may not be the best way."

"Let's hear it then," urged Michael.

"Why not see for yourself?" said the witch who threw some powders in the pot. Yellow smoke billowed quickly from the pot. Coughing quickly followed.

"Jeez, what have you done?" yelled Leslie.

"Ask the professor," replied the witch.

"Professor?" asked Michael.

*

A man emerged out of the smoke stopping to brush debris off his thick wool suit. The air was filled with yellow pieces of paper that had pealed off the man's suit. The man tried to retrieve the slips of paper, but he could not owing to the rolled up tubes he

clutched tightly with both arms. Many more remained behind, stuffed into the pockets of the man's vest, coat, and trousers.

"I am Professor Tucumcari. I have plans for all contingencies, all problems, and all Plan Bs. What plan would you like to see? What is your instructional problem?"

Michael and Leslie looked at each other, then to the witch who was quite busy arranging her cooking gear.

Leslie spoke up, "Well, I guess we want to run a summer workshop for kids about science—about bluebirds, actually."

"Hmmm?" The Professor searched his body looking through several notes stuck to his waistcoat. "Bluebirds. That sounds clever." The searching continued systematically through more notes from the man's trousers and jacket. "What you need is a list of science goals. These should work fine." The Professor handed Michael the list, which unfolded like a collection of credit cards or pictures of nieces and nephews.

"This is quite the list of goals," commented Michael.

"Yeah, but how do we know that these goals fit our situation?" asked Leslie.

Professor Tucumcari frowned, then cleared his throat. "Those goals, my dear, have been carefully thought out. They have worked for many, many designs."

"Yes, but do they work on people?" asked Leslie.

"We can pick and choose from this list?" asked Michael.

"Absolutely," replied the Professor who started to smile.

"Which of these fit our situation?" asked Michael.

"Hey," yelled Leslie, "Why should we be limited to the goals on this list?"

"Because I have detailed plans for all contingencies, all problems, and all Plan Bs." The Professor set his plans on the ground and began to unroll them out on the sidewalk. "See, examine this one."

The plan was detailed indeed, filled with a complex set of boxes and circles, arrows and dotted lines. A work of art looking at it from a distance. Color-coded sections referenced even more details inset into the corners of the plan.

"This is something," said Michael.

"It is beautiful. I can't take my eyes off it," marveled Leslie.

The Professor smiled and moved his hand over the plan. "Yes, note that all major contingencies, problems, and all Plan Bs are covered by this Plan. And I have others, too." Professor Tucumcari continued rolling out other plans anchoring each corner with the closest rock or stick.

"You don't have a bluebird plan, then?" asked Leslie.

"Of course not, I have not had such a need before," replied the Professor.

"You do now!" exclaimed Leslie. "And that's what *we* need!"

The Professor stood up and blinked several times before responding. "I have plans for all contingencies, problems, and Plan Bs."

"Except he has no bluebirds," whispered Leslie to Michael.

The Professor continued, "Note the intricate and detailed finishing on this Plan. It is quite elegant, don't you think?"

"We don't need elegance," squealed Leslie. "We need relevance!"

"These plans are very easy to use," remarked the Professor. "You can fill in each box. Then follow these lines until you reach the end of the Plan. Which one would you like? I have plans for all contingencies, problems, and Plan B's."

"I think we'll pass," replied Leslie.

"Looks like more trouble than it's worth," said Michael.

"We could modify one of these Plans to fit our needs," said Leslie.

"Yes, but it looks like we might as well design our own," commented Michael.

Laughter. It came from the witch. The Professor once again knelt down to survey his various Plans of Contingencies, Problems, and Plan Bs.

The witch spoke, "I told you this might not be the best recipe for my pot."

"I'd hate to be limited by these, but they are pretty," said Leslie.

"We'd spend more time filling in the blanks than deciding what we really need to do," said Michael.

The witch laughed again. So did Michael and Leslie.

"So, when you decide on what you need," said the witch, "Just ask for me and I will be glad to mix up some learnin' brew for you two." The witch dug out a card from her person. "Here's my business card. Call me anytime, except Mondays. I don't work on Mondays."

"What do we do now?" asked Michael.

"You could pick up one of those plans," suggested the witch. "They would tell you what to do next."

"No, thanks," said Leslie.

"I can tell you two more things, though," said the witch.

"Yes?" said Leslie.

"Check back up the street there," said the witch. "The fix-it store. You should check into your media needs."

"OK," said Michael, "And the second thing?"

BONG    BONG

The witch pointed to the pair, "You are running out of time."

BONG    BONG    BONG

# Tour 8: *If We Can't Fix It, It Ain't Broke*

BONG BONG BONG

"Eight o'clock," said Michael.

"Only one hour to go! What are we going to do?" said Leslie.

"What do we do now?" asked Michael.

"We need some major league help. We're running out of time!" said Leslie.

The pair began walking up the street back into the village.

"Wow, look at this place!" said Michael. The two had stopped in front of a hi-fi store. The window was stacked with televisions and old radios, and signs in the window. A big one read:

### IF WE CAN'T FIX IT,

### IT AIN'T BROKE

Michael opened the door. A musty smell greeted him. And snow. TV snow. TV sets lined the shelves along one wall. Some were on. All displayed different programs. There were shelves of radios, phonograph players, tape recorders, old microphones. Along a wall in the back was a bench with hundreds of plastic bins and electronic parts all over the bench. Vacuum tubes and wire and TV sets torn apart.

"What can I do for you, two? Said a voice from the back. "Suppose, you need something fixed?" A man wandered out from a back room.

"You must be the owner of this place?" asked Michael.

"Yeah, actually, it was left to me. I've been stuck here doling out technology," said the man. "Didn't want to, you understand. It's just that you get pegged, you know. Show a little interest, and WHAM, you're tagged with being an expert."

"The witch down the street told us you might be able to help us with our media needs," said Leslie.

"Yeah, she's always sending folks over here," said the fixer. Everybody wants media. And I'm the guy who gets stuck with fixin' things. Always the last minute. See, people just want to stick media in. What happens? WHAM. It all comes back here to live on these shelves." The man sighed. Began walking to one of the shelves. The media fixer rummaged through some boxes. "But people forget about things like this."

"Chalk?" said Leslie.

"And this."

"Crayons?" said Michael.

"And this."

"What's that?" asked Michael pointing to a large dull green metal box with a sloping front.

"Don't get much requests for this anymore," said the media man. He blew off the dust. "There is a wide slot at the top. You read the question up here, and you write your answer in this smaller slot down here. Then you turn the knob to see if you were right or wrong and turn this knob here to move on. This box, as I remember, teaches spelling."

*

"Hey, I remember these!" exclaimed Leslie.

The store owner handed Leslie a plastic 3D viewer.

"I loved looking through one of these." Leslie rested the viewer on her nose. "Oh, pooh, no reels!"

The man rummaged through a box and removed an old, must paper slipcase. Inside were three reels. "Look before you leap!" warned the man.

Leslie carefully inserted one of the reels into the viewer and clicked the lever.

"What do you see?" asked Michael.

"Ooooo, nice," replied Leslie.

Leslie advanced the reel to the next image.

"C'mon, what are you seeing?" insisted Michael.

*Media possibilities (from the narrator)*

*"Ooooo, nice."*

"Neat," said Leslie. "Geez, I forgot how wonderful these things are."

"Let me look, then" said Michael. Leslie handed Michael the viewer. What glorious 3-D color! Michael saw a village scene in one image, then the inside of a workshop in another, a workshop full of artisans mulling about with a sense of urgency. There were acts of design, construction, somber testing on the part of these characters. Michael advanced the reel. Close-ups of facial features and their reactions to works in progress. Michael advanced again. He could hear cheers of 'Yay!' from the gatherings of workers.

"This is just one of many types of media," said the fix-it store owner. "There are many others. Just look around you. Eventually everyone brings their favorite into my shop to have it fixed."

"So, why don't you fix them?" asked Michael. "I mean they're still here!"

"Well, young man. It's like this," said the man who walked out from behind the counter. "People bring in their media to get them fixed, but what they are really wanting is to just to have a place to bring it. You see, what they bring in is probably out of date, doesn't work, doesn't work like they figured, or they can't figure out how to get any darn good use out of it. So it ends up here. Media is like that, I guess."

The man continued his tour of the shop. "This is pretty much stuff that people bought into when they bought into the latest fad, 'cause someone said it would revolutionize learning. People forget that they don't need this stuff to revolutionize anything. It don't come down to revolutionizing, just doin' what needs to be done. And maybe this stuff will help."

"So why should we look at any of this stuff?" asked Leslie.

"Cause it's full of possibilities, I would think," replied the fix-it man. "Yes, many possibilities, but people close down their thinkin' to gadgets and gizmos without thinkin' of all the possibilities."

"What do you mean, exactly," asked Michael.

"Well, you can create the media you need," replied the fix-it media man.

"Yes, but who's got the time?" said Leslie.

"Well, all I know is that you two haven't got the time!" *Well, not in this story*, thought the fix-it media possibilities man.

"You're saying the creating media is one choice. There are others?" asked Michael.

"Here, try another reel." The store owner handed Michael another viewer reel. Michael carefully removed the first reel and handed it to Leslie. Michael inserted the new one and returned the viewer to his eyes. He grinned.

"Alright, what do you see?" asked Leslie.

"Well, I see children with modeling clay. They are making elephants with oversized trunks. Some have fashioned people with round noses." Michael clicked the lever. "I see houses made up of rolled clay logs!"

"So, this is our second option?" said Leslie to the media man. "To use clay?"

"You have the option to adapt existing media to suit your needs and the needs of your learners," replied the media man. "As long as you know what your needs are." The fix-it media man smiled and walked behind the counter again.

"I think we've heard that line before," said Michael.

"So what is our third option?" asked Leslie.

The media man motioned to the reels. Michael removed the second reel and inserted a third reel into the viewer. He began advancing the reel.

"I see more village workshops and people and. . . I see the closeup of a store. There are people talking outside . . . Ah, people buying things. A merchant is loading a package onto a wagon." Michael removed the viewer from his eyes. "So what does it mean?" he asked. "This is our third choice?"

"Yes," replied the media man, "You can make media. You can adapt media, and you can also buy it, like these people did with all of this stuff you see around here."

"Well, that would be the easiest, but who would want any of this old stuff?" said Leslie.

"No," said the media man, "but you could order it. Here's a catalog." The catalog was very thick. "How do you think I make a living anyway?"

"Well, why don't you warn people that what they buy may not be what they need?" asked Leslie.

The man leaned over to Leslie. "Because they wouldn't listen. Because it's easier to spend money than it is to stop and think about exactly what they need. Thinking of the possibilities takes effort. People don't do it because they don't have the time, but I think

it's because they forgot that such possibilities exist. You see, that's what this store is for. To remind you that there are possibilities, but you have to look for them."

"But this viewer is a great possibility," said Leslie. "How come teachers don't use them?"

The media man shrugged. "Maybe because we think it's a toy and somehow we get the idea that toys can't teach."

"Well, that's a silly notion," said Leslie.

"And because it requires thinking about how to use media with your goals. Takes more than just doing things. You gotta have a reason for doing things. Funny though."

"What's funny?" asked Michael.

"Well, things like that viewer you're holdin'," said the media storage man. "You see kids bringin' in stuff like that for Show and Tell. And sometimes teachers don't get it that kids are tellin' them somethin' like maybe this viewer has possibilities. Go ahead, take it with you. Remind you of what I've been sayin'."

"Neat!" replied Leslie.

BONG    BONG

"Oh, Oh," chimed Michael. "We're in trouble now."

BONG    BONG

"What do we do now?" shrieked Michael.

Leslie was looking through the viewer again.

BONG    BONG

"Leslie, I think we better be going now. Leslie!"

"Yeah, yeah, you're right. OK, well thanks Mister," said Leslie.

Michael urged Leslie onward with both hands carrying backpacks on each shoulder.

"Sure, glad to help." *I wonder if they understood anything that I said,* thought the media man.

# Tour 9:
## *"Off with Her Head"*

---

"Back to The Playhouse!" yelled Leslie. Michael ran behind juggling backpacks.

"Why The Playhouse?" yelled back Michael.

"That's where the Play is! I guess!"

"OK, I'm right behind you! I think!"

The pair ran as hard as they could with Leslie clutching her 3D viewer and three media "possibility" reels with Michael not far behind lugging backpacks containing what was left of the bananoli's and a quart jar of tongue depressors. When they reached the Playhouse they stopped suddenly as if they were horses refusing to jump a stream.

"Yikes! Will you look at that?" Michael pointed to the marquee, which was all lit up as light bulbs

flashed on and off around its perimeter.

## THE BLUEBIRD LEARNING PROJECT

"We are in trouble now," mumbled Leslie. "C'mon, we might as well pay the piper."

The pair breathed deeply and looked at each other for what they thought would be the last time. They entered the Playhouse, which was filled with people. Yelling filled the building. *This is not good,* thought Leslie.

"Scripts! Scripts!" yelled a person walking briskly toward them. It was the Director.

"Oh, goody," mumbled Michael.

"Revisions! Where are your revisions?" demanded the Director. "Your changes. These scripts of yours. Well, they are very fine, but your changes. The actors. You understand actors are very temperamental. They are demanding to see the writers. So here you are. Please come with me. Please, this way."

The Director escorted the pair down the aisles and noted the pair's backward glances at the audience.

"Don't worry about them. They are your practice audience. They are used to this sort of things, but we must hurry. Your actors. Well, they are not happy at all. You stand here. I'll be right back."

Approaching the stage Michael and Leslie surveyed the actors. There were two people sitting at the end of a long table yelling at everyone else. "It

7

cannot be this way," said one. "That's not how it is done," said the other.

Milling about the table, some sitting, some standing were lesser figures who more or less talked with each other; however, they generally stayed clear of the bombastity from the pair at the table. A boy and girl sat at the other end of the table away from everyone. Their hands folded together and their heads bent downward. They giggled when Leslie came up to them.

"What is going on here?" Leslie inquired.

The pair giggled again. "They are fighting among themselves," responded the girl.

"What are they fighting about?" asked Michael.

"Your design, of course," said the boy.

"But mostly they are arguing for the sake of arguing. That's what adults do best," added the girl.

"What are they finding wrong with it?" asked Leslie.

"Everything," said the boy.

"I don't understand," said Michael.

"Those two at the other end of the table," said the boy. "Those are the experts."

"Meaning they don't agree on anything," added the girl. "And because they are in the same room, they can't appear to agree to anything."

"Who are all of those other people?" asked Michael.

"Those people are like you -- designers, teachers," said the boy.

"What do they think of our design?" asked Michael.

"Most like it, I think," replied the girl. "Some don't know how to use it. Some think they can use parts of it. A few have said that it will take a lot of time to use. Things like that."

"What do you think of our design?" asked Leslie.

"No one's ever asked that of us before," said the boy.

"We're the learners," said the girl. "We like it but no one seems interested in hearing what we think."

"You could have asked us in the beginning," said the boy.

"At the middle, too," added the girl.

"I guess we didn't think of the obvious. We're sorry," said Leslie.

"That's OK," said the girl. "We think your design will be fun to do."

"Yes, when can we start using it?" asked the boy.

"Whenever you want, I guess," said Michael.

"Neat," said the girl.

"Thanks," added the boy.

The boy and girl excused themselves from the table and hurried off the stage.

"Wow, those are the first people I think we actually pleased in this whole strange place," observed Michael.

"Well, they're the ones who count," remarked Leslie.

"BUT, IT'S NOT POSSIBLE!" The booming voice came from the other end of the table. Leslie fell back into a chair.

"What's not possible?" whispered Leslie to Michael.

"It's those two so-called Experts. I think they want to talk to us. They're looking straight at us," replied Michael.

"Well, shoo, then!" The Director had returned. "Go! Go! The actors are waiting. They need your rewrites!"

"I think we better talk to your Experts first," said Michael.

"Yes, of course. Hurry up then," replied the Director. "I just want to know what I can tell the actors."

"Tell them, ah..." Leslie thought for a second. "Ah, tell them to start without us!"

"You mean with your original scripts?" The Director stared dumbfounded at the two.

"Well, yeah. Isn't that what's usually done?" Leslie stood up from the chair.

"Well, yes, all the time," said the Director. "But no one's ever told us to start. We usually just sit in our dressing room waiting to go on!"

"Yes, yes, by all means, start, go!" said Leslie.

"You will watch us then?"

"Of course!"

"Can the audience watch, too?"

"Absolutely!"

The Director started to exit stage left.

"IT'S JUST NOT THE WAY," said another booming voice.

The Director lightly pushed Leslie and Michael forward. "Go ahead, hear what they have to say. They're in your script," said the Director.

"So, here you are," said Expert A.

The second Expert leaned forward, "We must tell you that we are in complete agreement on what you have designed," said Expert B.

"Yes, we agree that your approach is crazy and crackpot," said Expert A.

"But," interjected Expert B, "We're unsure as to whether it is crazy enough to be correct."

"We think your design might be possible because we cannot understand it," said Expert A.

"After all," said Expert B, "The best papers are the ones no reviewer can understand."

The two Experts looked at each other. Expert A asked the two, "Do you understand completely what you have designed?"

"No, not really," replied Michael.

"You see, it's a work-in-progress," said Leslie.

"That excuse won't always work. I have heard this before," said Expert B.

"Well, it's a mystery to us, so there must be something to it," added Expert A.

"Yes, it does look crazy to us, so we have concluded that there is indeed some hope for it," said Expert B.

"However, before you take leave of us, we must stress that your craziness does not mean that you can be sloppy or hazy about your thinking," added Expert A.

"You must hurry," urged the Director.

"Why is that?" asked Leslie.

"Yes, what do you mean?" asked Michael.

"Quickly, go now," said the Director who nudged the pair to a Playhouse exit. As the Director pushed the pair out the door she yelled, "Remember, the Play's the thing!"

Michael and Leslie looked around. Not only were they outside The Playhouse, but they were back on campus again.

*

"Well, here we are, back where we started," said Leslie.

"Was all that real?" asked Michael.

"Check your backpack," urged Michael, "See if you got any more of those strange fruits. They did clear one's head, but they sure tasted awful."

"I like to think they were thinking fruits." Leslie looked into her backpack. "Well, whatever was left is now a gooey mess. Yuck. Time for a new backpack anyway. Hey! But look!" Leslie pulled out the quart canning jar, but there was only one tongue depressor left. Leslie pulled it out.

"What's this one say?" asked Michael.

**ENJOY BEING A NOVICE.**

"Well, this *has* been different," admitted Leslie.

"So, what do you think this was all about anyhow?" said Michael.

"I think we learned a lot about designing because we didn't know anything about designing," said Leslie.

"Yes, but we didn't do any designing, did we? I mean it was all done when..."

Leslie interrupted. "See, that's because of the place. I think we did do the designing in the manner fitting that wonderful, strange place we were in. Now we're in this place. Reality, again. So we've got to do it differently, but in the same spirit. Get what I'm sayin'?"

"Hmm. Maybe we were in the Big Picture somehow and we got to see the whole process. What do you think?" asked Michael.

"Maybe that's what the class was supposed to be about," suggested Leslie.

"Hey, look there," yelled Michael. "It's Socrates. Long time, no see. How did you get here?"

The dog responded by wagging its tail.

"Cat got your tongue?" laughed Leslie.

The dog inched closer, than sat down and began to pant.

"He's smiling. He must be Socrates," said Michael.

"Yeah, but he can't talk," remarked Leslie.

"Well, we might as well get moving. What's the other class you're taking?" asked Michael.

"Statistics," replied Leslie.

"Me, too!" yelled Michael.

"Oh great," they yelled in unison. They both laughed.

So Michael and Leslie picked up their backpacks and started to walk down the sidewalk.

"You coming, Socrates?" asked Leslie.

The dog stood up on all fours and began to walk alongside the pair.

*Sure, lead on,* thought the dog. *Might be fun.*

*"Sure, lead on. Might be fun."*

# Design Glossary

**Dictionary,** *n. A malevolent literary device for cramping the growth of a language and making it hard and inelastic. This dictionary, however, is a most useful work.*

Ambrose Bierce

The entries in this glossary have been compiled from **bold** entries in the text. The definitions are based on the context established by each chapter.

---

**Achievement tests.** An assessment method that attempts to measure the best performance in one or more content areas.

**Affective domain.** A learning dimension that differentiates the complexities of emotional and attitudinal states.

**Algorithms.** Procedures that when performed as specified will guarantee the correct answer.

**Analysis.** A systematic process or set of processes that helps humans to understand human needs by breaking a phenomenon down into its component parts. In instructional design, analysis identifies the learning needs of humans.

**Aptitude test.** An assessment method that attempts to measure one's learning ability or potential.

**Assessment.** A process that determines if learning is occurring.

**Assessment plan.** A written plan that outlines an assessment strategy.

**Attitudes.** Opinions or feelings; a component of the *affective domain.*

**Authentic activities.** Learning activities that attempt to model or duplicate actual events in real life so the learner masters knowledge or a skill over time in the setting in which it is practiced.

**Authentic contexts.** Learning settings which attempt to incorporate as much of the realities of a real life situation.

**Behaviorism.** A theory of learning which emphasizes environmental influences and responses to those influences.

**Beliefs.** Personal understandings that contribute to thinking, feeling, and doing.

**Classroom discussion.** An instructional model in which an instructor uses interactions among participants to engage learners in higher level thinking.

**Cognition.** Mental processes.

**Cognitive.** Involving thinking or mental processes.

**Cognitive apprenticeships.** A model of instruction where learners learn from experts and gradually master target tasks and skills.

**Cognitive artifacts.** Human-created products that extend mental capacities.

**Cognitive domain.** A learning dimension, which deals with all aspects of thinking processes.

**Cognitive skills.** A range of thinking abilities, including that of recall, inferring, generalizing, planning, and deciding, among many others.

**Cognitive strategies.** Personalized mental skills used to monitor and control thinking processes.

**Communities of learners.** Learning is developed through a joint involvement and shared vision of individuals, such as learners, teachers, institutions, cultures, and language.

**Concept map.** A visual representation of one's understanding of a concept and the relationships of its component parts.

**Conceptual attainment.** An instructional model in which the initial learning of concepts is achieved by defining a concept and determining its attributes.

**Conceptual design tool.** A means to help one make sense of an idea or concept.

**Conditions of learning.** The factors, *internal* and *external*, which relate learning theories, principles, and instructional models.

**Connoisseurs.** In the context of program evaluation, generalists who can use their knowledge and expertise to evaluate the details of an instructional design, program, or product, and point out issues that would be missed by experts or participants.

**Construct validity.** The extent to which an assessment method measures a theoretical, educational, or psychological construct, such as reading ability.

**Constructed response assessment.** Assessment methods that require learners to supply or construct their own answers. Examples include short answer, completion (fill-in-the-blank), and essay.

**Constructivism.** A view that knowledge is developed by the individual.

**Content validity.** The extent to which an assessment method accurately measures the content taught.

**Context.** The *physical*, emotional, and *use* (including political) factors that make up the instructional setting.

**Context analysis.** A *procedural design tool* that examines the instructional environment and identifies the resources and constraints that affect learning.

**Contingency management.** A behavioral strategy that leverages ways that the learning environment can influence desired learner behavior.

**Cooperative learning.** A group of instructional models that aims to facilitate individual learning through a positive environment in which individuals work together in small groups to achieve mutual goals.

**Criterion-referenced assessment.** An assessment that measures learning performance according to a pre-determined task competence level.

**Criterion validity.** The extent to which an assessment method measures a learner's performance based on established or otherwise standardized criteria.

**Definitions.** A design tool that presents concise verbal representations of topics.

**Design.** A process that helps humans construct solutions to human problems. Instructional design is a systematic means to specify features that address instructional problems in ways that are appropriate to learners, content, and context.

**Design thinking.** The capability to think in ways that facilitate the construction of *instructional design plans*, such as tool selection and use, decision-making, and handling multiple priorities and issues; seeing the big picture, but managing details.

**Design tools.** Aids to help designers analyze, construct, and evaluate design components, including *models, conceptual* and *procedural tools,* and *expertise.*

**Direct instruction.** A behavioral *instructional model* suitable for the teaching of basic skills; characterized by instruction that is broken down into manageable chunks, student practice, and instructor observation and feedback.

**Discriminations.** In the hierarchy of *intellectual skills,* the simplest level that enables one to make decisions on the differences between items.

**Entry level.** Learning competencies that learners need to have in order to begin mastering *performance objectives.*

**Essays.** A constructed response assessment method that consists of students writing a response to a question. Essays consist of multiple sentences or paragraphs and are useful in determining how a learner organizes a response and communicates it to an audience.

**Essential prerequisites.** Skills that must be mastered before one can learn new skills.

**Evaluation.** Making judgments and decisions from assessment information.

**Expertise.** One's collected understandings of a skill or field, developed over time.

**External conditions.** Environmental stimuli outside of the learner which influences the learner.

**Flexible understandings.** The idea that individuals have unique representations to knowledge that may differ from those of others, but nevertheless, represent to the individual an accurate and useful view of the knowledge.

**Formative program evaluation.** An in-progress determination of whether the features of an instructional design are internally consistent and contribute to the realization of design goals.

**Goal-directed program evaluation.** Evaluation of a program, product, or design based on the goals that were established for it from a needs assessment and other criteria specified in a *program evaluation plan*.

**Goal-free program evaluation.** *Evaluation* of a program, product, or design based on what happens without any reference to goals or criteria.

**Group investigation.** A socially-oriented instructional model which combines inquiry with social interaction. This model emphasizes a democratic inquiry where the outcomes cannot be totally predicted.

**Heuristic.** A personalized manner of investigation. From the Greek "to find out."

**Higher order rules.** Within the hierarchy of *intellectual skills*, a level of *rules* that apply to a wide variety of applications.

**Hypermedia.** Information-embedded entities linked together through computer software that allows the user to select choices among these entities in a non-linear fashion.

**Ideal.** Within the context of learning instructional design, a statement that summarizes what you have discovered in a *needs assessment* of the optimum response to an *instructional problem*.

**Instruction.** A structured means to assist learners in learning. Definition may vary, according to one's beliefs.

**Instructional analysis.** A method to determine the requirements of learning content or skill.

**Instructional content.** The subject matter to be taught or learned.

**Instructional design.** An intellectual process which provides systematic features to assist designers in their construction of structured possibilities to address the needs of learners, and are responsive to the nature of the content to be taught, and the realities of the instructional setting.

**Instructional design model.** A written and visual depiction of a designer's framework for addressing instructional issues and for constructing *instructional design plans*.

**Instructional design plan.** A written document that describes and communicates the details of an instructional design to address an *instructional problem*.

**Instructional event.** Phases of instruction, based on Gagné's theory that relates these phases to stages of information processing.

**Instructional framework.** An overall structure for instruction, incorporating instructional models and strategies appropriate to learners, content, and context of the instructional problem.

**Instructional level.** A class or level within a hierarchy of instructional activities, which commonly include course, topic, unit, and lesson.

**Instructional lifespan.** The length of time that an activity or program is relevant to the needs of learners or institution.

**Instructional media.** Media materials with instructional intent.

**Instructional method.** Sometimes viewed as synonymous with *instructional strategy* or *teaching model*, but generally a specific teaching procedure.

**Instructional model.** A *model* that depicts structured ways to present instruction.

**Instructional problem.** An opportunity to address an educational need.

**Intellectual skills.** A range of competencies to deal with the environment, composed of *higher-order rules*, *skills*, *concepts*, and *discriminations*.

**Intent statement.** A written description of what one would like to accomplish in an *instructional design* describing learners, purpose, intended changes or effects, duration of treatment, and readers of the plan.

**Instructional strategy.** An overall teaching approach or plan derived from goals. Can include various instructional models, methods, or strategies.

**Internal conditions.** States of mind or *learned capabilities* that the learner brings to the learning.

**Interviews.** Within the context of ID, (1) *needs assessment* activities useful in analyzing learner needs and uncovering the realities and context of an *instructional problem* or setting; (2) an *assessment* method used to profile learners, question depth of understanding, clarify performance, and determine learning difficulties; and (3) within *program evaluation* to determine the effectiveness and reactions to an instructional product.

**Iterative.** Characterizing a method in which successive attempts address previous efforts.

**Learned capabilities.** Internal human states, according to Gagné, consisting of *intellectual skills*, *cognitive strategies*, *verbal information*, *psychomotor skills*, and *attitudes*.

**Learner profile.** A *procedural design tool* used to examine the major characteristics of individual learners and provide a picture of the range of learner needs within an instructional setting.

**Learning.** The process of acquiring knowledge and skills; a definition is heavily dependent on one's beliefs.

**Learning beliefs.** A set of convictions about what learning is, how it occurs, and ways to promote it in humans.

**Learning objectives.** Operational statements that communicate what performance a learner needs to attain. According to Mager (see Chapter 4), the learning objectives specify the level of performance, the conditions of that performance, and what level of performance (criteria) is acceptable.

**Learning prerequisites.** Requirements that something must be learned before a *target objective* can be learned.

**Learning principle.** A written statement that describes a relationship between concepts.

**Learning requirements.** What learners need to know or be able to do in order to accomplish *performance objectives*.

**Learning task analysis.** A procedural design tool to help determine the component skills of a task (*task analysis*) and identify what one needs to learn in order to master these skills (*instructional analysis*).

**Learning theories.** Research-supported explanations on how humans learn. Within ID learning theories provide foundations from which to design, particularly through the use of *learning principles*.

**Lesson.** An example of a planned arrangement of activities to assist learners.

**Level of inference.** The amount of judgment or variance inherent in an assessment method. A low-inference method requires the user to make a low amount of inference about a learner's performance, while a high level inference method requires a greater need to draw conclusions about the extent to which a learner is achieving the desired learning performance.

**Media.** Transformation and storage of meanings or understandings in a form that can be communicated.

**Media appraisal checklists.** Lists of criteria used to determine the suitability of different forms and modes of media for learning.

**Mental models.** *Models* that are created in the mind, which depict how one views an aspect of the world and guides one's reasoning on an idea or task.

**Metacognition.** Knowledge about and awareness of one's mental activity.

**Mission Statement.** A written statement that communicates personal or institutional *learning beliefs* in the context of an *instructional problem* that will be addressed by an *instructional design plan*. This document helps the designer to see if these beliefs are consistent, appropriate, and adequately communicated at the beginning of an instructional design plan. The mission statement can also be used as a means to evaluate whether a plan is meeting the goals set out in the *needs assessment*.

**Model.** A human construction that depicts or simulates reality, communicates meanings, and reveals our hidden understanding of the world.

**Motor skills.** The ability to conduct physical movements in ways that complete a task.

**Needs assessment.** A set of *analysis* tools, which in *instructional design* aims to determine the nature of an *instructional problem*, establish learning priorities, understand the realities of learners, determine the nature of the content to be learned, and the reality of the instructional setting, from which teaching and learning goals can be drawn up.

**Norm-referenced assessment.** An assessment method which measures learning performance according to a relative position in a group.

**Observations.** A means to (1) make ongoing adjustments in instruction or (2) note learning performance. Can be both informal or formal, depending on how systematic the observations are recorded and used.

**Organizers.** Written, spoken, and visual means that represent topics as related to prior topics and structured to match the developmental and content level of the learner.

**Pedagogy.** The functions and work of teaching.

**Performance.** The extent to which a learner fulfills, renders, enacts, or executes an action or process; the basis for an *assessment*.

**Performance objective.** A statement that describes what a learner needs to be able to know or do.

**Physical factors.** Concrete factors that create and support an instructional setting. Characterized by Tessmer, (see Chapter 3) they include facilities, equipment, and instructional lifespan.

**Plan Bs.** Alternate plans for an instructional activity, based on the probable failure of some features of that activity.

**Portfolio.** A learning activity and assessment method that documents learning over time through the collection and presentation of one's production and performance. Portfolios are both *product* and *process* forms of *assessment*.

**Procedural design tool.** A means to organize data gathering, analysis, and presentation.

**Procedures.** In the hierarchy of *intellectual skills*, multiple *higher order rules*.

**Process approach.** An integrative instructional method that is based on assisting learners to construct personalized meanings through authentic, meaningful tasks.

**Process assessment.** An assessment method which measures learning performance over time.

**Product assessment.** An assessment method which measures learning performance on the basis of a tangible product that summarizes the learning, such as a *project*, report, *essay*, or *constructed response test*.

**Program evaluation.** A systematic feedback component and *design tool* of instructional design that provides information to the designer and other interested parties as to whether the goals of the design have been met.

**Program evaluation plan.** A document that specifies how program evaluation will be conducted and communicated.

**Projects.** A combined *process* and *product* form of assessment that provides a comprehensive demonstration of a learner's skills and knowledge.

**Protocol analysis.** A *procedural design tool* that analyzes verbal reports (records of what individuals say about what they are thinking) by coding verbal responses based on criteria. These codings represent a state of knowledge or cognitive processes used when the verbalization was made.

**Prototype.** An early version or image of a product that models essential features of an instructional event or activity, and is useful for ongoing, or *formative evaluation*.

**Prototyping.** A process of developing an initial version of a product and having typical users test out its features.

**Psychomotor domain.** An aspect of learning differentiated so as to examine the complexities of learning physical abilities.

**Radical constructivism.** A *constructivist* point of view where reality is perceived and learning occurs solely within the individual.

**Reality.** Within the context of learning *instructional design*, a statement that summarizes what you have discovered in a *needs assessment* on what is possible to address an *instructional problem*, usually in terms of learners, content, and context.

**Reciprocal teaching.** A method of instruction where students model the activities of the teacher, slowly assuming more responsibility for the teaching.

**Reflection-in-action.** Reflecting on what one is doing in the present so as to influence subsequent actions.

**Reinforcement schedule.** A plan that prescribes periodic stimuli to strengthen or weaken selected behavior.

**Reliability.** The extent or consistency to which an assessment can be trusted over repeated uses, or the scoring procedure is consistent across individuals.

**Role playing.** An instructional model or strategy in which participants act out human situations and discuss the results.

**Rubric.** An overall plan, including criteria, used to score assessments.

**Rules.** Within the hierarchy of *intellectual skills*, statements of regularity.

**Scenarios.** Simulated settings composed of people, things, and cultures, in which the learner becomes a participant.

**Selected response assessments.** Assessment methods, such as multiple choice, matching, and true-false tests, which require that students select responses from given alternatives.

**Self assessment.** An assessment method in which learners examine and make judgments about their own learning.

**Self-concept.** Perceptions about ourselves that enable us to think, act, and feel with a sense of confidence.

**Sequencing.** A phase of *instructional design* which identifies how content should be ordered. Influenced by learning principles, instructional framework, and type of learning desired (see *taxonomy*).

**Simulation.** The act or process of representing something through the functioning of another entity.

**Situated learning.** The idea that learning is facilitated by careful consideration of settings, purposes, tools, and tasks that are authentic (i.e., those that take place in real settings).

**Social constructivism.** A philosophical stance in which learning is seen to be constructed individually through language and group interaction.

**Sociocultural.** An orientation in which learning is viewed as a mix of mental functioning and development within social and cultural contexts; consequently, instruction consists of assisting the learner in ways that take this mix into account.

**Stakeholders.** Those individuals or groups who have a vested interest in an instructional design.

**Stories.** Literary and mental models of understandings and meanings.

**Strategies.** Plans of action with specific intended outcomes in mind.

**Summative program evaluation.** A *procedural design tool* that determines whether the goals of a design were achieved and whether the *instructional lifespan* has been exceeded.

**Supporting prerequisites.** Skills that are not required, but are helpful in learning new skills.

**Synectics.** A problem-solving technique which uses the collective creativity of individuals in groups through the use of analogies to make metaphor connections between problems and possible solutions.

**Systems approach.** A structured process that determines and characterizes essential features and relationships of physical or symbolic entities and uses these entities or systems to address human needs.

**Tacit.** Inherent understandings that are not expressed openly, but are integral to our understanding.

**Target objective.** A statement that identifies what learners need to know or do after an instructional activity.

**Task analysis.** A *procedural design tool* that breaks down a task into its component subskills. Frequently coupled with *instructional analysis*.

**Taxonomy.** A *conceptual design tool* that differentiates the complexity of a particular concern. In the context of instructional design, a learning taxonomy is a classification system that examines the components of learning along a particular dimension (e. g., *cognitive, affective,* and *psychomotor*) and arranges this differentiation into classes or levels, so as to depict the makeup, characteristics, and relationships of learning along that dimension.

**Teaching models.** Structured systems to implement instruction, usually based on a set of related learning principles.

**Teaching repertoire.** The stock of teaching methods and *models* that one can effectively employ in instruction.

**Technology.** A human means or process to improve the human condition. A means of thinking and the resultant products of that thinking.

**Think alouds.** A method that records verbal comments from individuals.

**Use factors.** Factors discovered in a *context analysis* that reveal how teachers and students use the instructional environment.

**Validity.** The degree or extent to which an assessment method measures what it is intended to measure.

**Verbal information.** Declarative knowledge expressed in spoken or written form.

# Index

# Sexy Love

# Also From Carly Phillips

### The Sexy Series
Book 1: More Than Sexy
Book 2: Twice As Sexy
Book 3: Better Than Sexy
Novella: Sexy Love

### The Knight Brothers
Take Me Again
Take the Bride
Take Me Down
Dare Me Tonight

### Rosewood Bay
Fearless
Breathe
Freed
Dream

### Bodyguard Bad Boys
Rock Me
Tempt Me
His to Protect

### Dare to Love Series
Dare to Love
Dare to Desire
Dare to Touch
Dare to Hold
Dare to Rock
Dare to Take

### Dare NY Series (NY Dare Cousins)
Dare to Surrender
Dare to Submit
Dare to Seduce

**Billionaire Bad Boys**
Going Down Easy
Going Down Hard
Going Down Fast
Going In Deep

**Hot Zone Series**
Hot Stuff
Hot Number
Hot Item
Hot Property

**Lucky Series**
Lucky Charm
Lucky Streak
Lucky Break

# Sexy Love

A Sexy Series Novella

## By Carly Phillips

1001 DARK NIGHTS
PRESS

Sexy Love
A Sexy Series Novella
By Carly Phillips

1001 Dark Nights
Copyright 2020 Carly Phillips
ISBN: 978-1-970077-65-0

Foreword: Copyright 2014 M. J. Rose

Published by 1001 Dark Nights Press, an imprint of Evil Eye Concepts,
Incorporated

Sign up for the 1001 Dark Nights Newsletter
and be entered to win a Tiffany Key necklace.

There's a contest every month!

Go to www.1001DarkNights.com to subscribe.

**As a bonus, all subscribers can download
FIVE FREE exclusive books!**

# One Thousand and One Dark Nights

Once upon a time, in the future…

I was a student fascinated with stories and learning.
I studied philosophy, poetry, history, the occult, and
the art and science of love and magic. I had a vast
library at my father's home and collected thousands
of volumes of fantastic tales.

I learned all about ancient races and bygone
times. About myths and legends and dreams of all
people through the millennium. And the more I read
the stronger my imagination grew until I discovered
that I was able to travel into the stories … to actually
become part of them.

I wish I could say that I listened to my teacher
and respected my gift, as I ought to have. If I had, I
would not be telling you this tale now.
But I was foolhardy and confused, showing off
with bravery.

One afternoon, curious about the myth of the
Arabian Nights, I traveled back to ancient Persia to
see for myself if it was true that every day Shahryar
(Persian: شهریار, "king,") married a new virgin, and then
sent yesterday's wife to be beheaded. It was written
and I had read, that by the time he met Scheherazade,
the vizier's daughter, he'd killed one thousand
women.

Something went wrong with my efforts. I arrived in the midst of the story and somehow exchanged places with Scheherazade — a phenomena that had never occurred before and that still to this day, I cannot explain.

Now I am trapped in that ancient past. I have taken on Scheherazade's life and the only way I can protect myself and stay alive is to do what she did to protect herself and stay alive.

Every night the King calls for me and listens as I spin tales. And when the evening ends and dawn breaks, I stop at a point that leaves him breathless and yearning for more. And so the King spares my life for one more day, so that he might hear the rest of my dark tale.

As soon as I finish a story... I begin a new one... like the one that you, dear reader, have before you now.

# Chapter One

Amber Davis inserted the key into the lock and opened the door to her new home, a simple one-story ranch that represented a whole new life in a brand-new state.

"Surprise!"

She jerked back, startled, as she realized the most important people in her life were there to greet her.

"Uncle Landon!" Her ten-year-old son, L.J., dashed past her and ran into his uncle's arms. Landon's twin, Levi, who'd passed away before she'd known she was pregnant, was L.J.'s father.

Standing beside Landon were Tanner Grayson and Jason Dare, her son's other godparents, the men who'd made it possible for her to purchase this house with their generosity. When she looked at these three men, who she'd known for the last ten years, she saw three handsome, accomplished guys who'd worked hard to get where they were in life. Who'd overcome pain and hardship and stuck together through it all, including her in their long-term, deep friendship. They were like brothers to her and uncles to her son. With their brown hair in varying shades and muscular forms, at a glance they could be brothers, although on inspection, each had their own distinctive look. They'd only recently found their own happily ever afters and she was so thrilled for them all.

"Welcome home," Jason said, pulling her into a hug, then passing her to Tanner and then to Landon, who still had his arm around his nephew.

"Can I go check out the rest of the house?" L.J. asked.

Amber nodded, looking around the still-empty space. The movers would be here later this afternoon. "Go for it."

He dashed off, the echo of his footsteps and shrieks of excitement bouncing off the walls and making her smile.

"What are you guys doing here? You're supposed to be in Manhattan." And in a little while, Landon's parents, L.J.'s grandparents, were due to arrive and take him to the city for his summer adventure, leaving her ready to start one of her own.

"We decided to surprise you. Help you unpack and move in," Landon said with a grin. He'd always been easygoing, even after the tragedy that had befallen all of them.

They never failed to do right by her and she smiled. "You didn't have to drop everything for me. You already helped enough, lending me the money to buy this place." Something she felt guilty about already.

"*Giving* you the money," they all said at the same time.

She shot them a glare. They all knew how important it was for her to be independent just like she understood why they felt obligated to help her. Not just because Levi had been Landon's twin but because all three men had been there the night he died in a tragic college hazing incident when the guys were freshmen, and Amber a sophomore, and they felt guilty for not being able to prevent his death.

She'd discovered she was pregnant while she'd been grieving, but the guys had always been there for her. As had Landon's mom and dad, Carrie and Samuel Bennett, as well as her own parents, Lydia and John, in Florida. When she'd quit college, packed up, and moved home, they'd stepped in to help her raise her son.

"Mom, look at the size of my room!" L.J. called to her.

Laughing, she shot the guys a warning look and headed toward the hallway leading to the two bedrooms in the house, hearing their footsteps behind her.

"Do you like it?" she asked from the doorway of the room across from her own.

"It's going to be cool. You said we could paint it blue, right?"

"Light blue," she reminded him. She didn't want a dark-looking tomb for her son's bedroom.

"Can I get a Spiderman Fathead?" he asked of the life-size removable wall decal he'd been asking for ... for what felt like forever.

"Of course– Oomph."

Amber had shoved her elbow into Tanner's side as he answered without asking her.

She'd been saving to buy it and had already decided the superhero

would be on L.J.'s wall when he returned from his trip in a few weeks.

"We'll see," she said, ruffling his hair. She wanted the gift to be a surprise.

"Stop spoiling him," she muttered under her breath to the guys.

Just because they owned a hugely successful nightclub in Manhattan and could afford whatever they wanted didn't mean she would take advantage. She already felt guilty for how much they were doing for her now, paying for this house and her classes. But she desired to make a better, more secure life for L.J., and borrowing money allowed her to get her degree in education and hopefully a minor in business.

She'd already been taking classes part-time at home in Florida, and she'd needed the ability to complete her studies more quickly and obtain a job that gave her summers off for her son. The guys had offered their financial help for a while. She'd just been too proud, reluctant, and scared to accept.

"I'm hungry." L.J. interrupted her thoughts and reached for her bag, which she'd yet to remove from her shoulder.

"Of course you are." She gave him the oversized purse she'd stuffed with treats and bottles of water, enough for a growing boy to be satisfied any time he asked.

He knelt down and began digging through the bag, settling cross-legged on the floor so he could have his snack.

She looked at him and grinned at how his light brown hair fell over his forehead the way his daddy's used to do. She didn't need to wonder if Levi would have loved his son. He would have adored the boy who looked so much like him and, of course, his uncle Landon.

"How about I order in some sandwiches," Jason suggested, even as L.J. had already dug into some chips.

"Sounds good, man. I'm starving, too," Landon said.

"I want turkey!" L.J. looked up from where he sat on the floor. "And mayo. And a pickle. And a soda. I can have a soda, Mom, right?"

She sighed, not in the mood for a soda-or-water argument. "Sure. And say please," she reminded him.

He blinked and nodded. "Please!"

"Amber, what do you want?" Jason asked, his fingers hovering over the phone.

"Whatever you're getting for L.J. is fine for me, too."

While the guys stood by Jason and studied the app on his phone, adding in their orders, Amber glanced at her son, who looked up at his

uncles adoringly.

She'd miss her little man while he spent a few weeks with Landon's parents traveling. He was growing up so fast but this separation was necessary. If she was going to go back to college in the fall as well as hold down a job and raise her boy, she needed to get her feet wet with summer classes while she was on her own.

She'd moved from her hometown in Jacksonville, Florida, to Linton, Connecticut, in order to be closer to the Bennetts, giving them a chance to bond with their grandson, and it would be equally good for L.J. to have more family around since she'd left her parents down South. Last year, her mom had been diagnosed with late-onset multiple sclerosis and her mother and father had their hands full taking care of her mom's increasing symptoms.

Amber had then found herself at a crossroads. She could remain in Florida, continue her job as the manager of a local clothing store, taking part-time classes and hiring babysitters for L.J. when needed, or uproot their lives entirely. She'd gathered her courage and opted for change.

So here they were in a small college town in Connecticut, close enough to the Bennetts that they could help out while she was in school or working, and only an hour from the guys.

Now that she'd made the move, her emotions veered all over the place, from excitement over her new life to nervousness because she was starting classes in a few days.

"Mom! They're here!" L.J. was standing by the window. Turning, he ran for the front door.

"Wait for me!" She'd tried to teach him not to open the door until a grown-up was with him, but she sensed his excitement about seeing his grandparents. It had been a long while since their last visit in Florida.

She caught up with him as he bounced on his feet by the door and she pulled it open.

"Grandma! Grandpa!" L.J. called out, finding himself swept into their waiting arms.

From the day she'd discovered she was pregnant, she'd been embraced by Levi's grieving parents.

"Come in!" she said to the couple who'd always treated her like a daughter despite the fact that she hadn't been married to their son.

Carrie and Samuel walked in, each kissing Amber on the cheek. "I see your surprise helpers arrived?" Carrie asked with a chuckle.

"Hi, Mom, Dad," Landon said. He strode over and hugged his

parents.

"We can't tell you how happy we are to have you two nearby. I know it's a huge adjustment but it's going to be wonderful," Carrie, an attractive brunette, said, her hazel eyes glowing with happiness.

It was no wonder they had such good-looking sons, Amber mused.

"Of course, my wife said it best," Samuel said, also beaming with pleasure.

Amber was so happy to know she and L.J. weren't a burden to Landon's parents, that they were giving them something to enjoy and look forward to as well.

"We *would* like to get an early start and miss later-afternoon traffic on the way to the city," he said.

"We just ordered food. Can we add anything for you?" Jason asked.

Carrie shook her head. "We ate before we came over. How about we wait until L.J. has his lunch and then we get going?" she asked her husband.

"Sounds like a plan," Samuel agreed.

An hour later, they'd all eaten their sandwiches, caught up with each other, and it was time for the Bennetts and L.J. to get on the road.

"Mom, I'll be home later tonight. I'll see you all tomorrow. You have the key to my place, right?" Landon asked.

She nodded. "I still think we could just stay in a hotel."

"Nope. There's no reason you can't stay with me. I have the room," he said of his three-bedroom in Tribeca. He'd found a renovated warehouse that had been turned into an oversized apartment near Club TEN29, their place of business. "I mean, we have the space," he said with the grin he always had when mentioning Vivi, his wife.

"Okay, then. We'll see you when you get home tonight or in the morning," Samuel said.

Amber knelt down so she was face-to-face with her little boy. "You're sure you're ready for this trip?"

"I can't wait to see the Empire State Building and the Statue of Liberty and eat New York City pizza with Uncle Landon!" he said with a small fist pump that had her chuckling along with holding back tears. It was going to be a long few weeks, and they'd never been separated before.

But she wouldn't dim his excitement and anticipation by expressing her anxiety or fears. He'd be fine, and knowing that, so would she. "Okay then, give me a big hug and a kiss. Then we'll get your suitcase

out of my car and we'll put it in Grandma and Grandpa's SUV."

L.J. put his skinny arms around her and hugged her tight, something she cherished because she knew the time was around the corner when he wouldn't let his mom pepper him with the kisses she did now.

"Go run to the bathroom before you get on the road," she told him.

Standing, she faced Carrie and discovered the other woman staring at her with an understanding expression on her attractive face. "He'll be fine. We'll keep him so busy he won't have time to be sad or upset. And we'll have him call and FaceTime every day or whenever he wants in between."

Amber forced a smile. "I think he's handling this much better than me," she said, managing a laugh.

"Such is a mother's lot in life. But they say if you can send your child off happily without you, you've done your job. And you're doing an exceptional one. Especially since you're doing it alone." Carrie placed a hand on Amber's cheek. "Enjoy your summer, honey. Get used to classes and working and he'll be home before you know it."

Samuel cleared his throat. "Are we ready?" he asked, obviously uncomfortable with the two women's emotional reactions.

"I'm finished!" L.J. cried, running out of the bathroom and skidding to a halt by his grandfather, grasping the man's hand.

"Perfect." Amber smoothed a hand over her flowy top that covered her leggings. "Let's switch his bag to the back of your SUV and you can get going."

The guys had cleaned up the sandwich wrappers on the floor and thrown everything into a huge garbage bag in the kitchen.

"I'll get your bag," Landon said, following L.J. out to the cars.

While the guys waited inside, she watched as L.J. seat belted himself and she found herself waving goodbye from the driveaway, no longer holding back tears since he couldn't see that she was crying.

Tanner came up behind her. She hadn't heard him come outside, she'd been so focused on her son. Always the most silent of the three, he wrapped an arm around her and spoke, his voice a low rumble. "He'll be fine. And so will you."

She sniffed. "I know." And she held on to the thought that a big reason for both this move and the trip was to let him learn more about his father by spending quality time with Levi's parents and his twin

brother, all of whom had been so good to her over the years.

The moving van arrived a short time later, and she had no more time to dwell on missing her son. She directed the movers with the furniture, watching as they put the labeled boxes in their proper rooms and the guys got to work helping her put things away for both herself and L.J. They accomplished much more than she would have alone.

During the chaos, Carrie called to tell her they'd arrived safely in Manhattan and were going out for dinner later. Knowing she had nothing to worry about, she turned her focus to her new house.

Although she still had some boxes left, she was in much better shape than she'd anticipated, thanks to her friends. The guys left and she spent the night alone in her new house, learning the new creaks and sounds and getting used to her new normal.

The next day, she worked all day on the unpacked boxes, and when dinnertime came around faster than she'd expected, she decided to go into town to pick up something to eat while getting to know the area where she now lived.

She considered this summer a chance to find herself again, the woman she was beyond L.J.'s mother. She'd missed out on learning about herself before she became a parent. She figured a return to college, the milestone that had changed her life to begin with, would be the perfect way to start over.

\* \* \* \*

Shane Warden pushed his chair back from his computer, rose to his feet and stretched, his back aching from all the hours he'd put in at the desk in his office. If he didn't know better, he'd never believe he'd gone to the gym this morning to work out. But he had. Then he'd showered, come back here, and had gotten into the zone on his research, losing track of time, skipping lunch and working through the afternoon. Now, almost dinner hour, his stomach was grumbling and he was way overdue for a long walk and some food.

He strode through campus, the sight of students sporadic, as summer session didn't lend itself to kids hanging out on the lawns and in the student union. But the Circle, a cul-de-sac with a variety of restaurants and eateries, was open year round, and he decided to head there for dinner.

As he walked, he opened his phone and skimmed the progress he'd

made on the paper he was working on. Another couple of years and he hoped to move into a tenured position, something he would have thought impossible a few years ago. Shaking his head before he went *there*, he refocused on the words on the screen, a deep dive into a paper dealing with advanced quantitative economic theory and…

He bumped into someone, jolting himself and causing his phone to fall to the ground at the same time he reached out to steady whoever he'd crashed into. His hands wrapped around soft flesh and obviously feminine arms. A floral fragrance reached his nostrils, and he found himself breathing in for a deeper whiff of the tantalizing scent.

"I'm sorry!" the woman said as he helped stabilize her before letting her go and retrieving his cell.

"My fault. I was reading on my phone." He looked up and found himself staring into arresting light blue eyes surrounded by blonde hair that had been pulled up into a messy bun on top of her head, with sexy stray strands falling around her face.

"And I was looking at the directions on my screen. I'm new to the area," she explained, biting down on her full lower lip.

"Where are you headed?" He hoped she was going his way despite the fact that she was, in fact, walking in the opposite direction.

"The Circle. I'm looking for restaurants. A place to eat dinner but I think I got turned around or something. I'm not very good with maps," she said, her cheeks flushing an attractive shade of pink.

He blinked and tried not to look like the cat who'd swallowed the canary when he'd just gotten his wish. They were going to the same place.

He subtly took her in, a petite but nicely figured woman, wearing a pair of black workout leggings and a white and lavender top that draped around her body, giving him a hint of her curves that he enjoyed.

"How about you walk with me? I'm headed in that direction myself. I'm Shane, by the way."

"Amber. And that would be awesome. Left on my own, I'd probably end up on the opposite end of campus."

He chuckled. "Not everyone has a good sense of direction. So where did you move to?" he asked, making conversation.

She hesitated before answering. "A small cul-de-sac on the outskirts of the school," she said vaguely, which he understood. She didn't know him at all, and he shouldn't have asked something so personal.

They started toward the Circle, and he pointed out the library and

the businesses that surrounded the campus, consisting of large companies that tended to donate to the school. Those who lived in and around the area weren't solely college employees.

"Are you meeting anyone for dinner?" he asked, surprising himself with the question.

She shook her head.

"Want some company? I can familiarize you with the area a little," he offered.

She looked up at him as they walked. "Sure. I wouldn't know which restaurant is good, and I'd planned to sit outside and read. Company would be nice."

He was selective about dating and for good reason. But Amber wasn't a young student, she was a woman close to his own age. Besides, he justified to himself, she'd just moved to town, which explained why he hadn't run into her before now, and he was just doing a good deed by sharing a meal and telling her where to find things in her new town.

Although she was hot as hell to look at, he wasn't going to do anything beyond share this one meal. Even if he was more attracted to her than any woman he'd met before.

# Chapter Two

Amber hadn't looked twice at a man in more years than she cared to remember. Oh, she'd dated when she could, her mom watching L.J., but anyone she'd gone out with had freaked out at the mention of her having a kid or never called her again. Lately, she'd been too busy being a mom and keeping her head above water financially and emotionally to worry about meeting anyone. But she was looking now because Shane was a very attractive man.

They'd settled into an outside table and chairs with hamburgers and French fries in front of them. She took a sip of her soda, aware of his heated gaze on the purse of her lips around the straw. They certainly shared an immediate attraction, she thought, dropping her stare to the food in front of her.

She didn't have to look at him to be aware of his handsome face covered by a scruff of beard, warm brown eyes, and what looked like soft, kissable lips. She squirmed in her seat, unaccustomed to her body's reaction to the man. Any man. It had been so long since her sex pulsed in delicious response to the opposite sex.

Had she used her battery-operated boyfriend? For sure. But even those moments were few and far between with a little boy in the house. But this man with his nice body, his short-sleeve tee shirt pulling tight over his muscular frame, had her thinking about doing other things in her bed. Adult things she hadn't experienced in far too long.

"So the campus is a circle with roads situated like spikes that lead to different areas and buildings," he said.

His statement brought her out of her surprisingly sensual musings, and she met his gaze, doing her best not to blush. She hoped.

As he described the town, she was drawn by the rasp of his husky voice. "You turned down the wrong street the first time," he said, an amused tilt to his lips.

Clearing her throat, she nodded. "Picking the wrong street would explain things. I've also been a little distracted."

And she wasn't just talking about being preoccupied right now with thoughts of him. And her vibrator. *Oh, good God*, she thought to herself. *Just stop! Focus.*

Forcing her mind back to the mundane, she went on to explain. "The movers just dropped the boxes off that need to be unpacked, and my son left to spend a few weeks with his grandparents. I'm not used to being without him." Glancing up at him, she met his curious gaze.

"You have a son?" He blinked and she realized he had long, thick lashes, the kind she had to use mascara to obtain.

"I do." Maybe she was testing him, tossing this bit of information out when they were just having a friendly dinner. But she'd rather know than find herself interested in the man only to discover he was just like every guy she'd dated before him. Not that she was dating him. Oh, my God, this man had her so internally flustered.

Still, her son not only came first, he was everything in her world, and any man in her orbit needed to know it. "He's ten and he's a great kid," she couldn't help but add with a grin.

"Are you married?" Shane asked bluntly, his gaze scanning her fingers, no doubt in search of a wedding ring or telltale tan line.

She shook her head.

"Divorced then?"

She didn't mind the questions. She'd opened the door, and of course he was curious, but people did tend to judge her. There'd been the moms at the preschool, where she was the youngest one dropping off her little boy, which happened when you got pregnant at the age of twenty. They'd stared and whispered as if she'd done something wrong.

She pulled her bottom lip between her teeth, catching the way she'd nearly succumbed to awkwardness at the truth of her life. Instead she squared her shoulders and owned who she was. "No. I'm a single mom."

His eyes opened wide. "Kudos to you. My mom raised me alone, and I know how hard it must be for you. Forgive me for saying so, but

you must have had him when you were young."

"I did," she murmured and took a bite of her burger instead of explaining further. Her life was complicated, her past painful, and she wasn't going to elaborate with a stranger.

He leaned in closer and she caught a hint of delicious-smelling aftershave. "I didn't mean to strike a nerve."

"You didn't." She began to shake her head and decided to tell the truth. "Well, maybe you did. People can be judgmental. But clearly you're not, so we're good. Now can you tell me more about the shopping around here?"

His gaze settled on hers for a long moment before acknowledging her subject change with a nod of his head. "There's an Acme on the west side of campus, and if you go farther into town, there's a Stop & Shop. For the rush things you might need, there's a store on campus that sells everything from college gear to quick snacks and basic toiletries. And for real shopping, you get on 95 and head south to the mall." He followed up that summary by picking up his drink and taking a long sip.

She grabbed her cell and typed shorthand information about everything he'd said into her note app. "Well, that helps. A lot. Thank you."

"You're welcome."

They ate, finishing up the remainder of their meals in companionable silence until her phone buzzed and she glanced down.

Carrie's text showed on her screen. *Shower time. L.J. will FaceTime you in about thirty minutes.*

She glanced at Shane. "I need to get going. My son is going to FaceTime with me soon, and I don't want to miss the call."

"I get it. You're a good mom." He smiled at her, the beauty in his expression taking her breath away.

"Thank you. I try to be."

Because they'd ordered and brought their trays outside, she started to gather things together.

"I've got it," he insisted.

"Okay ... well, thank you for getting me to the right place. And for dinner." He'd paid despite her protests.

"You're welcome."

A pause ensued, the first truly awkward silent moment since they'd met. She didn't know what to say, and he seemed equally uncertain.

Would he ask to see her again? Take her number? She realized they hadn't even exchanged last names.

And she wasn't even sure if she wanted to get involved with a man now. Although her best friend from Tampa, Layla, insisted it was time Amber tried dating again, she wasn't ready. Considering she'd just moved to a new state, a new guy was the last thing she thought she needed.

And since Shane, despite the occasional intense and lingering looks her way, didn't seem inclined to make a move, she decided to wrap things up. "Well, thanks again and it was nice meeting you."

Feeling like a dork, she waved a hand in the air, turned, and walked away, hoping she was headed in the right direction this time. And doing her best not to turn around and look back to see if he was watching her.

\* \* \* \*

Shane watched the sexy sway of Amber's hips as she walked away, damning himself for letting her go without exchanging numbers. Despite the fact that he knew it was for the best. With the summer session beginning, he had two months to work on his paper in between teaching Intro to Economics as a substitute for a fellow professor, a friend who was on sabbatical.

Shane had always thrown himself into his work, determined to be successful in a way his father had told him he'd never be.

His father, and he used the term loosely, was a lawyer at a major Boston law firm, who'd divorced Shane's mother when he was five years old and married the partner's daughter in the firm where he worked, starting a new life and a new family. Leaving Shane's mother to raise her son essentially on her own.

Sure, there was alimony and child support, but his mom had been a single parent, there for Shane when he was sick, picking him up after school, attending every major event in his life when his father hadn't.

Yet despite being a mostly absentee parent, Zachary Warden, a top corporate attorney, had expected his only son to follow in his footsteps if Shane wanted him to pay for college. Shane's decision to become a college professor had been a disappointment to Zachary, one he'd never let Shane forget. Not even when he'd graduated summa cum laude from Yale with an MBA and a minor in economics. And his father hadn't paid for Shane's education.

Instead, Shane had taken loans and worked his way through college, determined to live life on his own terms, preferring to bury himself in academia rather than legal briefs or corporate mergers. He enjoyed teaching students and watching them succeed. Earning tenure would be the final step he needed to ensure the future he was working toward.

Succeeding was important to him and not to prove something to his old man, with whom he had no relationship to speak of. He had a goal and he was determined to reach it. Tenure and job security meant everything to him, and he'd nearly had his dreams derailed thanks to a student who reported him for coming on to her when he'd been an adjunct professor at another school.

Not only hadn't Shane made a pass at her, she'd approached him in his office, practically stripping before he could stop her. He'd turned her down. Not only because of the no-student-teacher-fraternization policy but because he'd had no interest in the younger girl. Even after he'd been proven innocent thanks to another student, who'd done the right thing and told the truth about her friend's retaliatory behavior, the incident had left a bad taste in his mouth for how his fellow professors had treated him during the scandal. They'd ostracized him until he'd been exonerated. He didn't need colleagues like that.

Seeking a new start, he'd come to Linton when a friend here told him of a job opening, and he hadn't regretted the move. Though he'd dated on occasion — he was a normal man, after all — he'd always been careful to choose women who weren't involved with the school. Women who were busy with their own careers and weren't looking for a man who would shower them with attention. Shane didn't have much time to give. Still, it had been awhile since he'd been with anyone, his paper and his teaching taking up all of his time.

Hell, he hadn't thought of a woman *that* way ... until bumping into Amber. And as he watched her go, he couldn't help but be filled with regret for letting her leave without any way of getting in touch with her again.

\* \* \* \*

Amber woke up, her stomach a jumble of nerves, as she readied herself for her first college class in ten years. She dressed in jeans and a pair of sandals, a silk sleeveless top with decorative roses completing the outfit. Drawing a deep breath, she ate her oatmeal and downed much-needed

caffeine before walking over to her backpack, where she rechecked that she had everything she needed.

Instead of the used laptop her mother could barely afford like she'd had the first time, she now packed the top-of-the-line laptop the guys in New York had bought her and insisted she couldn't return, along with a notebook because she was still a handwritten note taker at heart, pens … and courage. She needed a big heap of that.

She'd spent the weekend unpacking the most necessary boxes and trying to start making this new house her home, beginning with pictures of L.J. and his dad, along with those of Landon, Tyler, and Jason holding L.J. as a baby. Her mind often went to the man with whom she'd shared a meal and the new feelings he'd inspired.

Those enlightening sensations in her body had her thinking that maybe Layla was right and she should use her time alone this summer to put her toe back into the dating pool. She didn't think she was ready for the new world of online apps and swipe right or left, but a man she met the old-fashioned way? While walking on campus?

She wished she'd had the courage to ask for Shane's phone number. Maybe if she ran into him again she'd suggest they go for pizza. Her treat this time.

As she was about to walk out the door, her phone chimed, indicating her FaceTime was trying to reach her. She pulled the phone from her bag and answered, happy to see L.J.'s smiling face.

"Hi, Mom!"

"Hi, sweetie! How are you?" she asked, picking up her keys from the counter and swinging her pack over one shoulder.

"I'm good! I just wanted to wish you good luck. Grandma reminded me you had your first class today."

She laughed as she stepped out into the heat of the summer morning and locked up behind her, keeping her eye on her son's face. "What are you up to today?"

Glancing down the street, she followed the directions she'd looked up this morning, more certain she had the right way this time.

"We're going to the Empire State Building!" He let out a loud cheer and she laughed.

Samuel called for him from another room. "Gotta go, Mom."

"Bye, honey. Love you."

"Love you, too!" He disconnected them and the screen went blank.

She rushed along the path to her classroom, and as she came closer,

she looked around and was forced to accept the one thing she'd avoided thinking about while going through the enrollment process and making the choice to return to school. That she would be significantly older than everyone around her.

Now, as she took in the girls in their cropped tops and tight denim shorts, frayed at the edges, she came face-to-face with reality. She was out of place and didn't belong here. Making friends would be nearly impossible. Swallowing over the lump in her throat, she pushed any negative thoughts aside. She was here to create a better life for herself and her son, not make friends her own age.

Today's class was an intro to economics, something she needed for the business minor she desired. Unfortunately she struggled with math classes and didn't expect even the most basic to be simple or easy.

She arrived at the classroom and walked inside the big lecture hall. Despite the fact that it was summer session, an intro class obviously pulled in a large number of students. She chose a seat in the middle, not too far up front but not in the way back, either. People filled up the seats around her.

Reaching into her backpack, she pulled out her notebook and pen. She'd take out her computer if she felt the need later on. She could sense the minute the professor walked into the room because a hush descended and the chatter stopped.

She opened to a fresh page and glanced at the front of the room just as the professor strode up to the podium, freezing at the sight of Shane standing in front of the classroom. She'd never looked at her professors' names, knowing they wouldn't mean anything to her. And in the rush of moving in and unpacking, she hadn't had time to pay attention to little details.

Hands on the podium, he cleared his throat and began to introduce himself. It had never dawned on her that he might be a professor at the school, although it probably should have. To her, he'd been a hot guy she'd met on her walk to get dinner.

She glanced up, taking in his professor look and demeanor. He was more serious and buttoned up than he'd been the other night, wearing a white collared shirt and a dark sport jacket over a pair of dress slacks. He appealed to her on a visceral level, looking sexy yet smart, his hair combed neatly back, his expression serious as his gaze scanned the class.

She realized the moment he recognized her, his eyes opening wide. She hesitated, then raised her hand in a small wave only to have him

school his features into one of bland disinterest. Her stomach twisted in embarrassment, and she lowered her arm and studied the blank page in front of her.

Thanks to the wash of humiliation, she found it hard to pay attention at first, and by the time she'd recovered, he was asking questions and calling on students.

Too late, she realized there'd been an assignment, and if she'd logged on and checked her emails, she'd have known. Already behind, she fidgeted in her chair and tried to keep up. But as he went over the basic definition of economic theory, *opportunity cost is the value of the next highest value substitute use of that resource*, she knew she was in trouble. Math confused her. This completely bewildered her.

She swallowed hard and prayed he wouldn't call on her. He'd been jumping around on his class list, not going alphabetically, and at some point, she would be up. Another five minutes dragged by, with her scribbling down notes she didn't understand.

"What is the definition of microeconomics?" he asked. "Ms. Davis?"

She glanced up and slowly raised her hand to let him know where she was sitting. Although he might have already guessed by her first name if there were no other Ambers in the room.

"Umm … I'm not sure. I didn't realize there was an assignment for the first day." Her cheeks flamed with mortification.

He narrowed his gaze. "Microeconomics focuses on how individual consumers and firms make decisions, such as how they respond to changes in price. Now, this class might be an introductory one but it isn't a joke. If anyone thinks otherwise, you can visit the registrar and drop the course." After that reprimand, which she took as aimed at her, he moved on to other items on his agenda to discuss for today.

Upset with how her first day had gone and embarrassed that she'd come across as uncaring and disrespectful to her professor – to Shane – she couldn't wait for the class to end. Of course, the minutes dragged, until finally he ended the session.

"The syllabus and my office hours are in the email I sent," he reminded them, his gaze landing briefly on hers. "See you on Wednesday."

She swallowed hard and collected her things, aware of the rustle of noise around her as the other students did the same and rushed out of the room.

She wondered if she owed him an apology or explanation or if she should just show up better prepared next time. Not that the subject matter would lend itself toward her understanding it easily.

Lost in thought, she zipped up her backpack and rose to her feet, stepping into the aisle and bumping into…

"Shane. I mean Professor Warden." She stumbled over how to greet him. "I wasn't watching where I was going. Again."

"It seems to be a theme," he said, his voice a low rumble.

She glanced around the room, noting they were alone. "I haven't been to class in ten years. I just moved here from Florida this weekend, and I sent my son off with his grandparents for the first time. I should have checked my emails. I thought I was prepared and I wasn't. Math really isn't my thing, and this is all confusing but it won't happen again," she said, knowing she was rambling, repeating things he already knew about her in her rush to make him understand.

"Amber, relax." His hand came to rest on her shoulder, and she felt the heat straight through to her core. Her gaze flew to his, and she caught the flare of heat in his chocolate eyes before he removed his hand and banked the fire so quickly she thought she'd imagined it.

She breathed in deep and inhaled the now familiar scent of his cologne, which struck a chord inside her and made her even more aware of him as a man and not the teacher in charge of her class.

"It's a difficult class. You can always drop it now and take it in August when you've had more time to settle in," he said.

She shook her head, refusing to back down from something just because it was challenging. "I can do it … or are you trying to get me out of your class?"

The idea dawned on her and wouldn't let go. As awkward as she felt, maybe he was equally uncomfortable. Because he'd enjoyed having dinner with her, too?

Meeting his gaze, she waited for his reply.

\* \* \* \*

Shane knew he'd been an ass, first ignoring her wave, then calling on her when he knew she was as thrown as he was by finding out he was the professor of her class. The look of shock on her face said it all. In his attempt to convince himself he could handle having her as a student, he'd been harder on her than he normally would have been on day one.

"No, I'm not trying to get rid of you," he semi-lied. No doubt it would be easier for him if he didn't have to look into those pretty blue eyes every day or hide his obvious attraction to her behind the podium. "I just thought maybe, given everything going on in your life at the moment, postponing a difficult class might be in your best interest."

She straightened her shoulders, and his gaze was drawn to the swell of her breasts beneath her colorful top.

"No. I made a mistake but it won't happen again."

"Okay," he said, admiring her determination. "We'll see if you can handle the work."

She tipped her head to the side, taking a step closer to him. So close he inhaled her citrusy scent and his cock grew hard.

"Just like we'll see if you can handle having me in your class." She pinned him with a knowing gaze, clearly having decided she had him off-kilter.

She was right.

He blew out a long breath. If he'd had second thoughts about not getting her phone number, those had ended the minute he'd laid eyes on her in his classroom. Ironically he now had access to her phone via his students' information list.

"I just thought we could get a slice of pizza or something. Get to know each other better." Those blue eyes studied him with definite interest.

Interest he reciprocated, and he swallowed hard, tempted beyond belief to take her up on her offer. But the past, propriety, and common sense prevented him from acting on what he wanted. No way would he have a relationship with a student. Not even one obviously close to his own age.

"This can't happen, Miss Davis," he told her, his tone firm, using her last name to put much-needed distance between them.

She stared at him as if trying to decipher what was going on inside his head, pursing her delectable lips in thought.

"I don't think I'm imagining the chemistry between us," she said. "But that *Miss Davis* comment explains everything. Student-teacher. Forbidden. Got it." She lifted her backpack higher on her back. "I'll see you on Wednesday, Professor."

She turned away and walked out of the room, his gaze on her ass as she left.

Biting back a curse, he headed back to the front to gather his things,

hating how he was forced to go against every gut instinct he possessed by ignoring their attraction. He wanted to get to know her better. He was curious about how she'd come to be a mother so young, wondered what had happened to her baby's father, if he was still in her life, and why she'd decided to go back to school now.

Basically he wanted to discover everything about her, and that included learning the curves of her body that she tried so hard to hide with her flowing clothing. His hands itched to slide beneath her colorful top and run along her bare skin. He was dying to close the space between them when they were alone and seal his lips over hers and find out if she tasted as delicious as he thought she would.

For a man who had never wanted more from a woman than a good time, who'd never gotten serious about anyone he'd dated, the desire he felt for all things about Amber shocked him.

Why the hell did it have to be the one woman he couldn't have in any manner, shape, or form?

# Chapter Three

Over the next couple of weeks, determined to conquer her economics class, Amber pulled herself together and worked hard on every assignment, quiz, test, and question posed by *Professor Warden*. She did her best to put the idea of dating him out of her mind and focus on her studies. Neither one was going the way she'd hoped.

She couldn't stop thinking of him as Shane, the sexy man with whom she'd shared dinner ... and the guy she wanted to kiss. She'd even gathered her courage and put herself out there with him, only to be shot down. Surprisingly, she wasn't hurt by the rejection, because she really did believe his being her teacher was behind his unwillingness to date her. She still gave herself credit for making the overture.

Levi was the last man she'd truly been interested in sexually as well as emotionally. When she was a young woman, he'd been the love of her life. It was only as she'd grown up that she realized they hadn't shared enough for that to be true. She hadn't known him as well as she wished she could have if he'd been given more time in this world. She'd been young and sex had been new and exciting, but she was hardly experienced.

And the men who'd come after? The select few she'd gone to bed with before they'd discovered she came with child baggage and run for the hills? Those men hadn't exactly let her explore her sexuality all that much. The attraction she'd felt for her past flings wasn't the kind of instant, sizzling, all-consuming desire she felt for Shane Warden.

She had a feeling going to bed with him would be an out-of-this-world experience. She only wished she could find out if her imagination lived up to reality. She wanted that so badly she was willing to overlook the fact that she'd had a baby and her body wasn't the thin, lithe one she'd had when she was in college the first time.

As she realized her mind had drifted back to Shane the man once more, she acknowledged she really wasn't doing a good job of putting him in the professor box. But if she was going to accomplish her mission, earn her degree, make her son proud, and provide him with the best life she possibly could, she had no choice but to focus on her studies. She needed to at least pass her Intro to Economics class, and she was struggling. Badly.

But she had an exam tomorrow she needed to pass, so after FaceTiming with L.J., who was having a blast in the Big Apple, catching up with Carrie and Samuel, and then having her weekly check-in with each of the guys in New York, she made herself a cup of coffee and settled in to study.

* * * *

Shane sat in his family room, grading the most recent test he'd given to the class, and groaned when he came to Amber's exam. No matter how he looked at it, she was one point short of passing. Although for most students, he'd chalk it up to a bad exam result, upload the grade, and move on, he pored over her test, trying to figure out what the issue was so he could help her, because she really was trying hard to succeed.

She was doing the work, reading the assignments, participating in class, and asking all the right questions when she had a problem. Clearly she was eager to learn and was doing everything she could … on her own. Either her study techniques were an issue or the subject matter just didn't make sense in her brain. Not everyone excelled in every course, but if she really needed this as a prerequisite, she had to pass the class.

He noticed, too, that she'd joined a study group, which was a positive step, except that group included a student, Dan Markham, Shane had had before in a math class. Dan didn't struggle in the class the way Amber did, but he was averaging a B- and he wasn't happy. In Shane's past with Dan, the boy had issues with any grade less than an A and had a tendency to blame the teacher and not accept responsibility himself. Not that Amber would know that. It wasn't his place to say

anything to her, either. Shane had hoped that Dan and the others would be able to help Amber, that they could all help each other, but that didn't seem to be the case.

He'd have to talk to her about her grade after class today. Without a significant change, she was at risk of failing the entire course, and there was no way she could pass the final. With the right help, however, there was still hope. Although he told himself he'd go to this extreme for any of his students, in his heart, he knew he was digging deeper because this was Amber … and he felt a connection to her even if he had kept his distance.

He'd stand at the front of the room, trying to concentrate on the subject matter, which he knew inside and out, or on the other kids in the room, but his gaze always came to rest on Amber. Yes, she was older than the others, but she was persistent and he admired her diligence. She'd sit and type in her notes, occasionally resorting to a notepad and pen, always paying attention.

He knew when she was frustrated by the cute crinkle of her nose and realized when she'd caught on to a concept by the bright light in those striking blue eyes. While taking exams, she twirled her hair around her finger, pulling her bottom lip between her teeth while trying to figure out the answer. And when she was antsy, she crossed and uncrossed her legs, nice long legs he admired, even when covered by jeans or leggings.

He had it bad for her, and it wasn't easy to focus on what mattered most. All his students. His job. Tenure.

Fuck.

He didn't sleep well that night and arrived at class just in time to start the lecture. He waited until the last five minutes to hand back the exams, not meeting Amber's gaze as he slid the paper onto her desk.

After striding back to the front of the room, he turned to look across it. "You can reach me in my office if you have any questions," he said, then reminded them of his office hours. "That's it for today." He paused, then said, "Miss Davis, would you stay after for a moment?"

Everyone scrambled to grab their things and leave the room. Only then did he allow himself to look at Amber and catch the sheen of frustrated tears in her eyes thanks to that test result.

\* \* \* \*

Great. So not only did she have another failing grade but now she had to face Shane in her humiliation, Amber thought. She swallowed past the lump in her throat, wondering not for the first time since starting this class if she'd made a mistake in coming back to school. Maybe she was too old. Maybe the subject matter was just too much for her. If she couldn't handle it now, when she had no other responsibilities at home, what was she going to do when L.J. came home and demanded most of her time?

She had no one to talk to, either. The Bennetts, her mom, the guys were all cheering her on and believed in her. Even L.J. had told her this morning how proud he was of her. She smiled at the thought of her little man. She missed him so much, but he was having the summer of his life, and she knew she'd made the right decision starting school alone and letting him spend time with his family.

She'd told Layla she was struggling in economics, but her friend's joking answer had been to ask her hot professor for *extra help*, and that just wasn't happening. Shane had made it clear he was off-limits to her. But now he wanted to talk, probably to suggest she drop the course, even now, so late in the semester. The room had emptied out, and she heard the sound of footsteps coming up the aisle.

Looking up, she glanced into his concerned gaze. She still had a hard time thinking of him as *Professor Warden*.

He strode over to her and settled into the closest chair, shocking her when he placed his hand over hers. "Hey."

Sparks flew at the simple touch, her entire body alighting with sudden life and need. She didn't have to wonder if he felt the energy between them, too. He ripped his hand away from her so fast her head spun, and he was right to do so. She couldn't allow herself to focus on sexual tension when she had this failing grade glaring at her from her desk. But the scent of his cologne surrounded her, mocking her attempt to keep things purely innocent and professional.

"Amber?" he asked, his voice gruff with what she thought was the same desire pulsing inside of her. "What can I do to help?"

She shook her head. "I don't know. I'm doing everything I can but nothing is enough."

"How are your other classes going?"

She blinked back her earlier tears. "Fine. Good, actually." The realization helped center her. "It's just this one that's giving me fits."

Understanding lit his expression. "So it's not school that's hard for

you, it's economics."

She grimaced. "Right. And I wanted to minor in business, so I need this intro class for any course that comes after it."

"What about a tutor? Maybe some one-on-one instruction will help," he said.

"Are you offering?" The words were out before she could censor them.

A heightened flush hit his cheeks, and even that hint of color was sexy. She could imagine the same ruddy hue on his cheeks when they were in the middle of a hot make-out session or when he was deep inside her while in her big, lonely bed.

He opened his mouth to reply and she spoke first. "I was kidding," she said before he could reprimand her again. "Can you recommend someone to tutor me?"

He nodded. "Let me ask around, see who's available in the summer, and I'll get you a couple of names."

Gratitude rushed through her. "Thank you. I don't want to quit, but I know I can't do this on my own." And though he couldn't offer his own help, he'd come up with a solution she hadn't thought of herself. "I appreciate the suggestion."

He smiled. "I'm glad you like it. Now let's hope it works."

They rose at the same time, and she took a step back, unsteady on her feet. He reached out a hand to steady her, pulling her forward, and suddenly she was in his arms, her head tilted backward, his mouth millimeters from hers.

"Dammit," he muttered gruffly, and as if unable to hold back from kissing her any longer, he closed the distance and sealed his lips over hers.

She'd dreamed of this moment many times in the last few weeks, but reality superseded fantasy. He wrapped her in his body heat as his tongue swept into her waiting mouth. She moaned and leaned into him, her long-dormant senses coming alive with the sensations he awoke inside her.

Their tongues touched, tangled, and delved deep. Gripping his shoulders in her hands, she lifted herself onto her toes so she could get closer. He tasted like the mints she'd seen him pop during class, a fresh hint along with his unique masculine flavor, and she couldn't get enough.

She wanted more, more of his taste, more of his scent, more of

him. He wrapped an arm around her waist, hauling her against him, her hips grinding against his, her sex coming into direct contact with the hardness of his erection. He was big and thick and her body softened, desire pulsing through her. She'd known she wanted him. She hadn't known how much until now.

A loud creaking noise sounded, followed by the slam of the lecture hall doors.

She glanced around but nobody had entered the room.

"Shit." He pushed her away as if she were toxic and stepped back into the aisle. "Shit," he repeated, running a hand through his hair. "This shouldn't have happened."

"But it did." And she couldn't say she regretted it.

"It can't happen." Panic laced his voice. "Never again."

She narrowed her gaze, knowing she hadn't mistaken the desire between them or the fact that it had been mutual. "Why not?"

"For so many reasons, but the main one is that I'm your professor."

"Is it against school rules for a student to get involved with a teacher?" she asked.

His brow wrinkled adorably. "Not in writing. Although many schools do have things spelled out, not all do. However, I cannot allow for any hint of impropriety to taint my professional reputation. Been there, done that," he muttered under his breath but loud enough for her to hear.

"Can you explain?" She wanted to know everything about him, and if he'd dealt with any kind of scandal, that would help her understand his reticence to get involved with her now.

He groaned. "At my last university, a student claimed we had an affair. In reality, she was pissed I'd turned down her advances and decided to get back at me. Damn near ruined my career." He paced up and down the aisle as he spoke. "I realize we're the same age; however, there are so many issues with what's happening between us I couldn't begin to name them all. But I can't afford anyone to think I'm giving you special treatment, using my position of authority to push you into a sexual relationship... Dammit!" The pacing continued.

"So you admit there's something between us?" she asked hopefully.

He spun to face her, a scowl etching his features. "That's what you took from my concerns?"

A hint of a smile lifted her lips. She couldn't help it. She was excited he felt something for her. "No," she said softly. "I understand it all, and

for that reason, I'll stay away … until class ends." Then she wanted to get to know him.

He already knew she had a son and wasn't running away because of L.J. Which meant he was a good guy, something she'd already figured out. So she wanted to see if they could form some kind of relationship, as hard as it would be to find time to see one another once her son came home.

He raised an eyebrow, obviously surprised by her easy acquiescence. "What's the catch?"

She laughed. "The catch is I want to get to know you in another way."

"What's that?"

"The old-fashioned way. You can talk to me at night on the phone. You can text me. I want to see if we have things in common besides"— she gestured between their lips—"that."

Somehow she'd left him speechless.

"Please let me know about a tutor as soon as possible," she said, her tone somber.

"I will."

"And *Professor Warden*? You have my number."

# Chapter Four

Despite the opening Amber had given him, Shane kept his distance. He'd been burned too badly once before by a nonexistent relationship with a student to indulge in any sort of real one. No matter how drawn he was to the bubbly blonde.

And in the last few weeks, he'd seen a more radiant side to Amber's personality as she grew more comfortable both in his class and with the material. He knew from Professor Anne Slater, who was tutoring Amber, that she was grasping the material thanks to the individual attention dedicated to the subject. She also had made some friends in class, her study group, which showed him the lighter side she kept hidden beneath the busy mom or harried student. He often saw her laughing, revealing a more carefree side he wished he could get to know better.

Every time he caught a glance of her smile, his dick reacted. *Remember that kiss?* it seemed to ask him. *Don't you want a repeat?*

He frowned and refocused on the papers in front of him, but the information blurred, and when his cell rang, he was grateful for the reprieve.

"Hello?" he asked without really looking at the number.

"Shane? It's Margo. Your step— I mean it's Zachary's wife." She'd clearly been about to say *stepmother*, a term he'd never been open to or welcomed.

Still, she'd tried. She'd never been the stereotypical bitch he'd

expected, just the second wife his father had left his family for. It'd been hard to welcome her, especially when his own father hadn't bothered much with him and yet had been such a stubborn ass when it came to how Shane chose to live his life.

"Hello, Margo. How can I help you?" he asked, his standard answer for her rare phone calls. And they were rare.

"It's your father. He ... he had a heart attack," she said, her voice cracking.

Despite their fractured relationship, panic ran through Shane's veins. "Is he ... is he okay?"

"He is. The doctors are optimistic, though they want to run a few tests."

Relief flowed through him. After all, the man was an ass but he was the only father Shane had.

"But he's asking for you," Margo said. "Can you come visit? Tomorrow would be best because they are running tests today."

Shane ran a hand over his eyes and groaned. "I'll be there." He didn't have class in the morning and they were only located an hour away. But why in the hell did his father want to see him?

And how did he feel about it? His father had either left him to his own devices or stepped in when he didn't approve of Shane's choices. He'd never once asked to see him for no apparent reason. True, a brush with mortality could spark a man's deepest fears, but Shane didn't see his father reaching that deep into his soul, and apologies weren't in his vocabulary.

"Thank you. I'll let Zachary know. I'll text you the hospital information and I'll see you tomorrow," she said before disconnecting the call.

He opened a beer and walked to the kitchen window above the sink and looked out over his lawn. The neighbors were sitting on their deck, a drawback to this house as there were no trees as a barrier giving him privacy.

Deciding not to go outside, he sat down on the sofa in the family room, took a sip of his drink, and stared into the empty room. He needed someone to talk to, someone he thought would understand his past and mixed emotions about visiting his sick father. There was no way he'd burden his mother with this news, and he hadn't made any friends here close enough to unload this kind of crap on.

Which left the only person he really wanted to see anyway. The

same woman he'd been avoiding unless he saw her in his classroom. The one he'd steadfastly refused to text or call despite the open invitation for him to do so.

He wanted to talk to Amber.

* * * *

Soon after Amber's conversation – and kiss with Shane, though she wasn't thinking about that now – she'd received an email with two tutor names and nothing else written in the note. Ignoring the pang of disappointment that he wasn't going to discuss anything personal, she'd jumped on the opportunity, texting both tutors and setting up a meeting with a female assistant professor who replied to her first. Knowing she had a plan set Amber's mind at ease about the class. She felt certain with one-on-one help she could get up to speed enough to pass and put Intro to Economics behind her.

Unfortunately she couldn't do the same for Shane or that kiss. She'd been reliving the moment while awake and daydreaming and in her sleep at night. But he'd made his intentions or lack thereof clear, and she wasn't going to chase after a man who wasn't interested in her. She understood his reasons for not wanting a public relationship, but she'd offered him a way to get to know each other without anyone else being aware. And he hadn't acted on it. So she'd thrown herself into her schoolwork.

Thanks to the tutoring, over time, her grades slowly inched up. She'd never be an economist, but she was going to get more than a D in this class. She'd consider a C a major accomplishment. When Shane handed back quizzes and assignments with her better grades, she saw the gleam of approval in his gaze and the pleased expression on his face. He still didn't get in touch with her the way she'd hoped, and after a few weeks went by, she came to accept that he was going to keep his distance and she needed to respect his wishes.

In between studying, she'd finished unpacking her house, finished decorating L.J.'s room, and had fallen into a comfortable routine, speaking to L.J. every evening and texting with him in the mornings before she went to school on the days she had class. She'd also joined a study group and met with them twice a week, and though the information she'd learned there hadn't helped before tutoring, once she had a grasp on the material, she felt more comfortable contributing and

gaining information there.

Because of the difficulty she had in economics, she put aside the idea of getting a part-time job until the fall, when she knew she'd be more comfortable with the classwork and be able to dedicate work hours when needed. All in all, things were going well.

She'd just finished dinner and put her dishes in the sink when her doorbell rang. She wiped her hand on a dishtowel, placed it on the counter, and went to answer it.

A glance through the curtains shocked her. "Shane!" She opened the door and he brushed past her and stepped inside, the scent of his cologne immediately surrounding her.

"What are you doing here?" she asked.

He winced at the question. "Abusing every privilege and right I have to your personal information by showing up on your doorstep because … I need you."

At the admission, which seemed reluctantly pulled from him, her pulse skipped a beat. "What's going on?" She shut the door behind him.

"My father had a heart attack," he said, and when she really looked at him, the pain etching his features became obvious.

"Shane, I'm sorry." She reached out and placed her hand in his. "But I'm not sure why you need *me*?"

Of course she felt bad that his father had a health issue, but what did that have to do with her?

His intent gaze bored into hers, and she sensed something had definitely shifted.

"Why do I need you? Because I haven't been able to get you out of my head since the day we met. Because I watch you from the front of the class and have to pretend I'm not completely turned on by every move you make. Because I want to know every little thing that makes you tick and then learn some more. And because when I got the call about my father and thought about who I wanted to share my deepest pain with, only you came to mind."

She drew a startled breath, completely taken off guard by his honest admission. "But … when you didn't call or text, when you ignored me except for calling on me in class, I thought you weren't interested in me that way."

A wry yet sexy smile lifted his lips. "I'm a damn good faker when I need to be. So there's just one thing I need to know for now."

Her heart beat out a rapid rhythm inside her chest. "What's that?"

"Do you still want me the same way?"

She didn't need to think about her answer. "I do."

Although everything that had concerned him before still stood between them, he was here now, and she had no problem acting on her feelings. She moved toward him at the same time he lifted her into his embrace, wrapping her arms around his neck at the same moment his lips came down hard on hers.

Pausing mid-step, he allowed them the time to kiss, to drop the barriers and pretenses that had held them apart, and let them come together now. His words had stripped the defenses she'd built thinking he didn't want her. She was open to anything he desired from her now. This was her summer of new beginnings and explorations, and where better to start than with the man who desired her as much as she did him?

Threading his fingers through her hair, he tugged on the long strands, her head tilting, giving him complete access to her mouth. His tongue slid inside and he took control, gliding his lips over hers, nipping at her bottom lip and sucking on her tongue until her sex pulsed with unfulfilled need.

"Bedroom?" he asked.

"At the end of the hall." He carried her through the house and stepped inside, making his way to the bed and easing her down onto the mattress.

Standing over her, he hooked his fingers into the waistband of her leggings and pulled them down, taking her panties along with them. Eyes darkened, he studied her for a long while until she squirmed under his intent gaze. Then he lifted the edges of her top and slid it over her head, leaving her in just a bra, her bottom half bared to him completely. Her cheeks burned with discomfort, concern about the shape of her body rising to the surface.

"What's wrong?" he asked, obviously noticing the sudden stiffening of her muscles. He stroked a hand down her cheek. "You're beautiful and–"

"I'm not," she blurted out. "I have a stomach and stretch marks. I had a baby. I'm not anything like the women I'm sure you're used to." She bit down on her bottom lip and met his gaze, her entire body trembling with a combination of embarrassment and worry that she'd ruined everything between them with her sudden burst of insecurity.

"Shh." He slid one finger from her throat to her sternum, his gaze

hot on hers. "I'm not interested in any other women. There hasn't been anyone in a long while, and the only person who has my attention is you."

"But—"

"But nothing. I already know you've had a baby and I don't care. All I see are your beautiful curves." He traced the scalloped edge of her bra, dipping his finger beneath the lace and tweaking her nipple with his fingers.

She moaned and her thighs spread almost of their own volition, wanting him to touch her *there*, too.

"That's it," he murmured. "Trust me to make you feel good." He flicked his fingers in the front clasp and her bra slid down her arms. And he tossed the garment aside.

Before her brain could come back online and worry some more, he bent his head and pulled a distended nipple into his mouth, and she saw stars behind her eyes and delicious sensations traveled straight to her sex. Dampness settled between her thighs, and a warm pulsing feeling aroused her even more. He played with her breasts, first one then the other, giving them equal attention and making sure to stimulate her to the point where she was squirming on the bed, her hips gyrating, reaching to fill the desperate ache he inspired.

He kissed her, swirling his tongue around and around hers at the same time he eased one finger inside her. She moaned at the feeling, her inner walls clasping around him, and though it had been a long time for her, she knew she could take more. She needed more.

"I want you, Shane."

"And you're going to have me." He bent one of her legs, placing her foot on the mattress, and then the other, exposing her to him completely. Pumping one finger in and out, he added a second, and she arched her hips in an attempt to pull him deeper into her.

He dropped to his knees, removed his fingers, and suddenly his mouth was on her sex, his tongue gliding up and down, eating at her with a gusto that surprised her. In her brief experiences, no man had ever been that eager to go down on her before. Had they done it? Sure, but had they spent the amount of time Shane did, licking, sucking, and nipping at her sensitive flesh? God no. And she loved every second.

Building, pulsing sensation pooled between her thighs, and she was so close she could almost reach the climax she so desperately wanted. She rubbed her sex against his mouth, and he chuckled, the sound

vibrating into her as he began to lick her clit, then nip at the tight bud. Suddenly she soared, the orgasm just out of reach slamming into her like a freight train.

"Shane," she moaned, moving her hips back and forth against his greedy mouth until the glorious waves of pleasure subsided, her legs collapsed, and she fell back against the bed, her body still tingling.

The next thing she knew, she heard the sound of him ripping into a condom. Levering herself up on her elbows, she realized he'd stripped off his clothes and was naked, amazing in his bare masculinity. He was well built and sexy, a pleased look on his face, his mouth glistening with her juices, and her sex pulsed as she realized that fact.

A glance at his thick cock and she had a moment's hesitation, wondering if she could take him, and then his hands were on her thighs and his heavy erection poised at her entrance.

His dark brown gaze met hers as he eased into her, starting slow, then, finding her wet, he thrust all the way home.

"Shane." His name seemed to be the only word she was capable of uttering because she felt him everywhere inside her.

"Hold on, beautiful."

She blinked back tears at the endearment because she hadn't been this close to a man … ever. Sexually, she had been, but what she already felt with Shane was more than the brief encounters she'd had after Levi. She didn't know how or why she could feel so much so soon, considering they didn't know each other well, but he obviously cared about her emotions and concerns. He was trying to make her feel desirable and she did.

She so did.

And when he began to move inside her, his serious gaze never leaving hers, her world shifted. He pumped his hips, his thick cock thrusting deep and pulling out again, her nerve endings feeling like sensitive live wires. Even though she'd already come once, from the throbbing awareness in her body, she could definitely climax again.

"I want you to come with me," he said, as if reading her mind.

She blinked up at him, his gruff tone an indication of how close he already was. He slid a finger over her clit and she responded with a drawn-out moan. "Again," she urged him. "Don't stop."

He pressed down and worked his finger in circles, all the while pumping into her. She felt the waves, and before she could process what was happening, she flew. She came hard, her entire being his to master

as he continued to work her clit through her orgasm, lightening his touch as she came down from the high.

And then he thrust harder and deeper, again and again. Sweat dripped down the side of his face, his expression taut as he came on a long, drawn-out groan of complete satisfaction.

\* \* \* \*

Shane's legs shook and he barely refrained from collapsing onto Amber's sexy body. He managed to hold himself up as he returned to reality and glanced down at the woman he'd just — well, he hadn't fucked her. And he wondered if he knew her well enough to have made love to her. Either way, something monumental had occurred between them.

"Can we use your shower?" he asked.

She nodded, her eyes heavy-lidded, as he helped her to a sitting position and, once again, lifted her into his arms.

He enjoyed carrying her, he thought, as he slid her to her feet in the pretty white bathroom.

She pulled towels out of a small linen closet behind the door and he turned on the shower. Together they stepped into the walk-in and rinsed each other off with a citrusy soap that smelled like Amber. He was going to smell like her, he mused, and he'd have to shower in the morning before going to visit his father.

Something he did not want to think about.

"So tell me about your dad," she said as she poured soap onto her hands and began soaping him up from his ankles up, a wicked gleam in her eyes as she spent a prolonged period of time re-arousing his cock.

It didn't take long, either. But instead of staying there so they could play, she pinned him with her gaze as her slick hands ran up his sides. "You mentioned your mom was a single mother, too, but you never said anything about your dad."

He groaned, knowing he'd have to tell her. That he'd wanted to confide in her all along. "My father left us when I was five. He'd been having an affair with the partner's daughter in the law firm where he worked. Ultimately, he married her and they had two daughters."

Amber winced. "I'm sorry."

He was long accustomed to that source of hurt. "As for my mom? She was and is great. An amazing mom who did everything herself. The

only good thing I'll say about my father was that he didn't shirk his financial responsibilities to us. He wasn't there for me at all, but he paid child support and alimony. We didn't want for anything. But..."

She maneuvered him under the water so the stream could rinse off the soap, and when he was clean, he began to wash her, already accepting the fact that this wasn't going to be about sex. He soaped up her legs, moving his hands up her calves, knees, and thighs, letting out a grunt when he slid his hands over her sex but kept going because he knew she wanted to talk and get to know him.

"But?" Amber pushed, proving him right, although her eyes had flared when his fingers slid over her pussy.

"But when it came to college, he'd only agree to pay if I went to law school like he did."

She narrowed her gaze. "Seriously? Why did he even care if he had nothing to do with you for most of your life?" She sounded indignant on his behalf and he appreciated the show of support.

He rolled his shoulders because he'd never figured his father out. "Beats me. Because he likes control is the best I can come up with. Anyway, I told him to keep his money, took loans, and put myself through school." He soaped up her breasts, her arms and then placed her under the steady stream.

"Where?" she asked.

"Yale."

Her eyes opened wide. "He should be proud. What an ass," she muttered.

"Yeah. But he's still my father, he had a heart attack, and he's asking for me."

"Are you going?" Amber asked.

"I am." He wasn't feeling a sense of duty as much as the pull of a child to his parent.

She nodded in understanding, then quickly washed and conditioned her hair before shutting off the water.

They dried off and then, wrapped in towels, made their way back to bed. He could leave but he didn't want to go, so he climbed in beside her and pulled her against him.

She sighed and snuggled against him and of course his cock began to perk up again. But he was well aware of the fact that just because they'd had sex didn't mean he knew her as well as he wanted to. He was drawn to her, though, and for now he was going with that.

"What about you? Tell me how you ended up a young, single mom."

\* \* \* \*

Amber knew it was only fair she talk about herself. "I was a sophomore in college, dating a freshman named Levi Bennett, and I guess it happened. Looking back, we weren't as careful as we should have been." She bit down on her lower lip.

"Where is he now?" Shane asked.

She drew in a difficult breath. Despite how many years had passed, it was never easy to recall what had happened to L.J.'s dad, and she dreaded the day when she had to explain the circumstances to her son.

"He died in a hazing incident at school. To hear his twin and best friends tell it, the night was brutal. He suffered a lot and so did they. But I didn't know I was pregnant. I didn't find out until a few weeks after he died, and though I was in the middle of grieving, I knew I wanted to keep Levi's baby." She leaned back into the hard body behind her, taking comfort in the wrap of his arms around her.

"You loved him."

She managed a smile, if only for herself. "As much as I was capable of at that age. And I was lucky. My parents accepted my circumstances and let me come home. They helped me raise L.J. And he has Levi's parents and twin brother and two godfathers."

"He's a lucky boy," Shane said.

She nodded. "His uncles, real and pseudo, they feel responsible because they were there that night. They offered to pay for my school and this house, and though I said no for a while, I finally realized if I didn't take this step and leave Florida, I wasn't doing justice to L.J. or the life he deserved. The guys have been great, although I really hope to pay them back one day."

"What's your relationship with his *uncles*?" he asked, a hint of what sounded like jealousy in his tone.

"They're like my brothers."

He exhaled a long breath, the rush of warm air hitting her shoulder. Then he slid his hand around and cupped her breast in his palm.

Next thing she knew, he'd flipped her over, reached for his jeans to grab a condom, and slid into her, making her feel utterly owned as he took her for a hard ride.

Early the next morning, Shane woke her with a kiss. "I've got to get going."

She rolled her head to the side. "Are you going to be okay alone?"

"Are you offering to come with me if I'm not?"

She chuckled. "Funny."

He stared into her eyes as he spoke. "I'm not kidding. Want to take an hour's ride? I could use the company as well as the support."

She sat up, pulling the covers with her. "You're serious."

He nodded.

"Okay then. No class today. Study group doesn't need me. I can call in sick. Sure. I'd be happy to come," she said, and she wondered what she was getting herself into.

# Chapter Five

On the drive to the hospital, Shane and Amber talked more about their childhoods, how she'd managed raising L.J., and he learned a lot about her son.

According to Amber, he was a sweet boy with a good disposition, easy to get along with, hated baths, showers, and anything to do with water. On the plus side of that, he was a good listener, so she merely had to remind him and nudge him a time or two to get him to clean up at night. He liked superheroes and baseball. He also loved to read and was ahead of his grade. His favorite books were *Harry Potter*, and he was looking forward to making new friends in school this year.

Shane hoped to meet her son soon, which was saying something, considering he'd never have thought he'd be interested in a woman long-term, never mind getting to know her child.

Now he was focused on his immediate concern, dealing with his father. He strode into the hospital with Amber by his side, following the directions Margo had texted to him, walking down the hall where his father's room should be located.

From a distance, Shane saw his dad, Margo next to him, slowly making his way toward them, his father's hand on an IV pole as he walked.

"Incoming," he said, gripping Amber's hand, and she glanced up at him.

"That's your father?" she asked.

He nodded.

They met up with the other couple in the middle of the hall. In his hospital gown and slippers, his face pale, expression drawn, his dad looked much older than his years. Margo, too, looked exhausted, her dark hair pulled back, no makeup, as if she'd been at the hospital since his father had been brought in.

"Shane! Margo said she'd called and you were coming but I wasn't actually sure," Zachary said.

"I'm here. Hello, Margo." Shane tipped his head at his stepmother, the awkwardness between all of them a tangible thing. "Dad, Margo, this is Amber. Amber, my father, Zachary, and his wife," Shane said stiffly.

"It's nice to meet you," Amber murmured.

"Same." Margo smiled at Amber, her entire demeanor welcoming, while Shane could feel his father studying Amber, assessing her.

"Zach, you should get back to your room. The nurse said a short walk," she reminded him.

"Sure. Son, walk with me," Zachary commanded.

"If you could point out the waiting room?" Amber asked before Shane could comment. "I'll grab a cup of coffee if there is one."

"I'll show you," Margo said. "I'd like a cup myself. I'll be right back," she assured her husband.

Amber sent Shane a reassuring smile, and though it grated, Shane stayed with his father, not wanting to upset him while he was in the hospital.

They slowly headed back to his father's room in silence, and Shane waited until he resettled himself in bed before walking over and speaking. "So you're okay?" Shane asked.

"I haven't gotten yesterday's test results back yet but I think so. It's just going to be a lifestyle adjustment." Zachary shifted in the bed, getting more comfortable.

"So no more steaks and whiskey?" Shane pulled up a chair and sat down.

"Bite your tongue." His father's mulish expression was typical.

"Well, I'm sure things will have to change, and Margo will make sure you're here for a while."

A long while, hopefully, because his father wasn't old at all. He'd just turned sixty last year. Margo had thrown a party. Shane had made sure he was too busy to attend.

"So who's the woman you brought with you?" his father asked before Shane had a chance to delve into why Zachary had wanted to see

him.

Smiling at the mention of Amber, Shane glanced at his father. "A good friend." He had no intention of involving a man who couldn't care less about him most days of the year in his private life.

His father narrowed his gaze. "Tell me about her."

Shane shrugged. Talking about Amber wasn't a hardship. "She's smart, going back to school to make a better life for herself and her son."

"Seriously? You can do better than a single mother looking for someone to take care of her."

Shane blinked, any hope he'd harbored deep down that this heart attack had softened his father gone in the second it had taken for that shit to spew from his mouth.

"First, I said we were friends."

"And I saw the grin on your face the minute I mentioned her."

Shane pushed himself to a standing position. "Okay, I came because Margo said you asked for me, but if you're going to be your usual pompous, arrogant self, I'm out of here."

Insulting Amber was off the table. Shane admired all she'd done with her life in the face of difficult circumstances. He was falling hard for her, and though he had to hide it publicly for now, he wasn't letting her go. Especially not because his father didn't approve. He couldn't give less of a shit what Zachary thought.

"Wait." Zachary paused, then added, "Please."

Folding his arms across his chest, Shane met his father's gaze. "Why did you want to see me?"

His father's expression faltered, and suddenly he looked more … humble, if Shane had to pick a word. "When I had the heart attack, I was lying waiting for the ambulance and a lot of my mistakes flashed in front of my eyes. Things I'd done wrong, especially with you."

Shane wasn't exactly shocked his father had had a revelation when he was scared and thought he might die. But how he'd reacted to Amber? The man hadn't changed. He waited for Zachary to talk more before he passed full judgment.

"I wasn't a present father."

"To put it mildly."

A muscle ticked in his father's jaw. "I wanted a fresh start, and I thought if I threw money at your mother I was doing right enough by you. I was wrong."

Shane swallowed hard. "I'm grateful Mom didn't have it harder than she already did, raising me alone. But you were wrong. A boy misses having a father."

Something Amber's son would surely go through, Shane suddenly realized, his heart hurting for the little boy. Although she'd said he had a solid support system, uncles, grandparents. That ought to help. And if he met and liked Shane, he could be there for him, too. A more local, present male influence. Once again, he was shocked the man who'd never thought he had the time for anything more than his work and his future goals was thinking about Amber and her son as more than just a summer fling.

"Shane. Are you listening? I said I know and I'm sorry," Zachary said.

"But you still have your opinions. And those don't jibe with the way I live my life. What you said about Amber is just one example. You don't even know her and you found her lacking and assumed she'd be using me."

His father nodded. "You're right. But you don't expect a zebra to change its stripes overnight, do you?" He tried to make a joke of it but Shane wasn't laughing.

Frowning, he shook his head. "No. But I can't say it's going to be easy to have a relationship after all these years."

"I'm just asking if we can try."

He wasn't about to argue or upset the man who'd just had a heart attack. As much as he resented his father, a small part of him, the little boy who'd missed a father at his ball games and graduations, wanted more than one birthday phone call a year with him. "We can try," Shane agreed.

Just then, a knock sounded on the door and Margo walked into the room. "Okay if I stay?"

"Sure, honey. Come in," Zachary said.

Margo walked over to the bed and sat on the edge. "Did you two have a good talk?"

Shane nodded. "We did."

"I spent some time with Amber. She's a sweetheart," Margo said.

With a grin, Shane couldn't help but agree. One thing his father was right about, he couldn't help his reaction at the mention of Amber. She had him wanting things he hadn't imagined in his future before he'd bumped into her on campus.

Now all he had to do was get through the end of the summer semester and they were free to explore what could really be between them.

\* \* \* \*

Amber sensed Shane's need to think on the ride home from the hospital, and she allowed him the silence he needed. If he wanted to talk, she was here to listen. He surprised her when he pulled off at an unfamiliar exit.

"Where are we going?" she asked him.

"I think we need a nice late lunch, don't you?"

Her stomach rumbled at his suggestion. "Yes, as you can hear." She patted her belly and laughed.

"I know of a place off this exit. A colleague mentioned it at a faculty meeting. We're here. We might as well give it a try."

She nodded in agreement. "Sounds good to me. What kind of food?"

"American. Burgers, chicken, that sort of thing. I think they also have an outdoor terrace where we can eat if you don't think it's too hot."

"I'd love to sit outside."

"Good." He didn't speak again as he drove to the restaurant.

She glanced at his still-serious profile. He was clearly uptight about whatever had happened with his dad. She had to admit the man hadn't been friendly to her, but she'd chalked it up to illness. Margo had been sweet and she'd enjoyed the few minutes she spent with her, although she understood why Shane had his issues with his father's wife. Amber's parents had a happy marriage, and she couldn't imagine what he'd lived through as a child.

After a short drive off the exit, he pulled into the lot. A large framed building with a wraparound porch sat behind it. Shane helped her out of the car and led the way up three steps to the hostess stand.

On their request, they were seated outside in a private corner where no one was around them. They each ordered a glass of iced tea and studied the menu and placed their orders, a Niçoise salad for her, a grilled chicken sandwich for Shane.

Finally, she couldn't take the silence any longer. "Are you okay?"

He braced his arms on the table and met her gaze. "It's hard admitting my father's an asshole. Always was, always will be. Yes, he had

an epiphany and knows he didn't do right by me, but it hasn't changed who he is deep down. And that's tough to swallow."

She reached across the table and put her hand in his. "I'm really sorry."

"Thank you." He nodded, stroking his thumb over her skin. "The thing is I'd made my peace with who he is. I just hated having it thrown in my face again."

She bit down on her lower lip. "Do you want to talk about it?" she offered.

He answered with an abrupt shake of his head. "It's fine. I'll eat a good lunch with fabulous company and put it behind me."

His more relaxed grin put her at ease. "Sounds like a good plan to me."

She picked up her drink to take a sip just as her phone chimed and she recognized the sound. "Sorry, it's L.J. on FaceTime." She hated to ever not accept her son's call.

"Take it," he said. "And maybe you could introduce me? As your friend?"

He sounded eager to meet her son, and a warm feeling wrapped around her heart. She hit the accept button and her little boy's face showed on the screen.

"Mom! We went to the Statue of Liberty!"

She grinned at his excitement. "That's so cool. Did you see the whole city?"

"It was amazing."

"Are you going to the beach this weekend?" Carrie and Samuel had been taking him to the Hamptons on the weekends to a house they'd rented for the summer, and during the week they were staying with Landon and touring Manhattan.

"Probably. I hope my friend Andrew is there. He's from a place called Long Island."

"That sounds great, honey." She glanced across the table at Shane, her heart in her throat.

She'd never had reason to introduce a man she was seeing to her son. For one thing, she'd be careful before bringing someone into his life who would only disappear again a few weeks or months later, and for another, no man had been that interested.

Swallowing hard, she gestured for Shane to sit in the chair beside her. "Speaking of friends, I want you to meet a friend of mine. This is

Shane Warden, honey. I met him this summer." No reason to explain to her ten-year-old that Shane was her professor.

She turned the phone so Shane could see her brown-haired little boy. "Hi, L.J. I'm Shane. Your mom has told me so much about you."

He lifted his hand in a shy wave.

"Say hi to Mr. Warden, honey. I mean Professor Warden."

"Shane is fine. I hear you're having fun with your grandparents in New York."

L.J. nodded. "Next week we're going to a Yankee game!"

Shane grinned. "I also heard you love baseball. Maybe we could play some catch when you get home. I could dust off my catching mitt."

An excited light hit her son's brown eyes. "That would be awesome!"

"I'll look forward to it. Here's your mom." He fully turned the phone back to her.

She had to fight back the lump in her throat and the tears forming in her eyes. This man, he'd barreled into her life or she'd barreled into his and turned her world upside down. He made her feel things long forgotten, and now he was including her son.

She swallowed hard. "Hi, honey. I need to go. I'm sitting in a restaurant." At least no one was around her or she wouldn't have taken the call and disturbed their lunch.

"Okay. I love you, Mom."

"Love you, too, baby."

"I'm not—"

"You'll always be my baby," she said before he could finish. Laughing, she said goodbye again and they each disconnected the call.

She drew a deep breath and met Shane's warm gaze.

"Well, that went well," he said.

"It did." Acting on impulse, she leaned forward and kissed him, expressing everything he made her feel without using her words.

His tongue slid against hers, the moment quickly heating up, the kiss going on, arousal settling low in her belly, desire pulsing between her thighs.

He placed a hand on her leg and broke the kiss, his dark eyes meeting hers. "We really need to get back to your place."

"We so do."

He straightened in his seat. "But there's something we need to talk about first."

With her mind still hazy from his warm lips on hers, she wasn't thinking all that clearly. "What is it?"

"Where we go from here. At least for the next two weeks while class is still in session."

She froze, knowing the wonderful feelings she'd experienced since he'd shown up on her doorstep were about to disappear. Temporarily, she hoped, but it hurt. Still, she was adult enough to understand and handle it.

She straightened her shoulders. "I get it. We can't be seen together." But was he going to disappear from her life as if their time together had never happened? "What are you thinking?" It was his job on the line. No matter how her heart felt, because she knew she was falling hard for him in a very short time, she could handle a few weeks apart. She had to.

"I need every possible angle of professionalism covered. To start with, nothing changes in public. I'm the professor, you're the student."

She nodded in understanding.

"And for the final exam, I'm going to have my teaching assistant proctor the exam. I'm going to assign random numbers to each student and grade anonymously. If anything ever gets out about us, nobody can say I favored you at all."

"Makes sense." She paused. "You've really thought about this."

"The whole trip here. My time with you is precious." Taking her hand, he held it up to his face. "I don't want us to risk anything or have anything taint our future."

She blinked, shocked by the tears that suddenly fell from her eyes. "Future?"

He met her gaze, staring into her eyes. "I know it's fast. I know we have a lot to learn about each other, but that's what I want. The chance for a very real future."

"I want that, too."

"Good. Then let me do everything I can to protect it."

She nodded. Because she'd never wanted anything more.

\* \* \* \*

Was there really such a thing as *the one*? Because Shane sure as hell was certain Amber was it for him.

The whole way home from the hospital, his focus wasn't on his sick

father but his attitude towards Amber. He'd be damned if he'd tell her the rude things his father had said. Instead he would do everything in his power to get through the next two weeks and move on with their lives.

He dropped her off at her house and walked her to her door, stepping inside.

"Can you stay?" she asked.

"I wish I could but I think we need to just say goodbye." Before she could react, he stepped closer, easing her against the wall. "But don't think it isn't hard for me. Don't think I don't want you. I'm just trying to be smart." He'd been weak the last two days, giving in to his need for her, but they needed to walk a fine line from now on.

She stroked her hand down his cheek, her gaze soft on his. "I understand. There will be plenty of time after class ends."

He braced a hand on the wall behind her, dipped his head, and closed his mouth over hers, devouring her, his entire body consumed with desire. His cock throbbed against the rough denim of his jeans, and he rubbed himself against her. Moaning, she threaded her fingers into his hair and held him in place, rocking her hips against his.

Dammit, he was too close to saying fuck it and taking her to bed. But if he did that, he wouldn't want to leave in the morning. There would never be a good time to part ways, and eventually they'd get caught by someone and his worst nightmare would happen all over again.

With regret, he stepped back, leaving the warmth of her body, and she released her hold. "Go, Shane. Just leave now."

He nodded, drawing in a rough breath. "Bye, beautiful. I'll talk to you soon."

She smiled but he caught the sheen of frustrated tears. Forcing his heavy legs to move, he headed out to his car and closed himself inside. He laid his head on the steering wheel and groaned. Doing the right thing shouldn't feel so damned wrong. He consoled himself with the fact that the next two weeks would pass slowly but they would pass. And then nothing could stop them from being together.

# Chapter Six

With the economics final coming up, Amber increased her tutoring to twice a week. She didn't want to risk failing and having to take the course all over again. In addition, she invited her study group over to her house for an extra session. She sensed she wasn't the only one struggling, and she thought another couple of hours talking about the material would help.

She was grateful the other students didn't hold her age against her as a reason not to include her. And though she had a wealth of life experience they didn't, she enjoyed their company.

They showed up around seven and she had put out chips and soda. As usual, the girls came together. Tamara Acker, Bonnie Green, and Rhonda May arrived arguing over whether or not a guy Amber didn't know was interested in Rhonda as something more than a friend. The guys, two of them, Dan Markham and Jeff Rhodes, came late. Also as usual.

The discussion about said guy's interest in Rhonda continued even after the study group guys showed up.

"What do you think, Amber? If a guy flirts, is he interested?" Rhonda, a pretty brunette, asked.

She crunched on a baked chip before answering. "Depends if he's a natural flirt with everyone. I'd have to know his personality before I could answer that."

"You see? And he is a flirt with most girls," Rhonda said to Bonnie and Tamara. "It's not just about me."

"Except the way he looks at you is different," Tamara argued.

"Agreed." This came from Bonnie.

"So, two against one," Amber mused. She'd never gone for the overtly flirtatious ones. Both Levi and Shane had that intense focus in common. Once they saw what they wanted, they just knew. They didn't need to flirt with the world.

Speaking of Shane, he hadn't disappeared on her. In the week since he'd dropped her off after the trip to the hospital to see his dad, he texted her nightly to talk and they really were getting to know each other a lot more. Not just superficial things like he preferred vanilla to chocolate, though he did, but that his mother lived twenty minutes away and he wanted Amber to meet her before school started again in September. He was neat, not fastidious; she liked a clean house as well. And he was pretty good at sexting, as she'd learned a day or two into their nightly *talks*.

"Amber? Where did you drift off to?" Dan asked.

She blushed and shook her head. "Sorry. I was thinking about my son," she lied. "He was supposed to call earlier and didn't."

Dan frowned. "Well, we said we wanted to get started. Unless you're feeling like you don't need us now that your grades have gone up?"

She blinked at his somewhat annoyed tone. Of everyone in the room, she liked Dan the least. He had an attitude that rubbed Amber the wrong way, and he definitely preferred when other people didn't do well in class and he did.

"I'd hardly call C's a solid enough grade," Amber said, hating how defensive she sounded. "Of course I need all of your help. I suggested this meeting, didn't I?"

"Shut up, Dan," Tamara said. "Amber has responsibilities you can't understand."

Now Amber felt bad about lying regarding her thoughts, but Dan didn't have to be such a jerk. Still, they'd taken her into their group, making it worth putting up with his bullshit that included bragging about how he was going into his father's financial firm after he got his MBA. Like everyone, he had years of college and then business school to get through first.

The rest of the night passed without incident and they parted ways, but they'd see each other in class on Monday.

Seven more days until the final.

Seven more days until she could see Shane in public and act on her feelings.

She could handle a week.

After locking up for the night, she headed for the bathroom, washed off her makeup, brushed her teeth, and changed into her favorite silk nightshirt.

She'd just climbed into bed when her phone rang and her body immediately responded, knowing it was Shane on the other end. "Hi," she said on a breathy whisper.

"Hey there. How was study group?" he asked.

"Productive." She didn't like to mention the other students to him since they were in his class. No reason to let him know what an ass Dan was. He would be out of her life soon enough.

"Are you in bed?" Shane asked, his voice low and gruff.

She shifted on top of the covers. She hadn't crawled underneath yet. "I am. How was your day?"

"Busy. Buried in research."

"And you love it," she said.

"I do."

She'd come to realize he was most at home in his office at work or in the house he was renting, researching and getting lost in his economic theories ... that she despised, and that was putting it mildly. Good thing they had other things in common. They both loved dogs but neither had time for a pet, at least right now, neither loved to cook but they both knew how since they didn't want to starve and she had another mouth to feed.

But she hated his taste in pizza toppings and they had to order half and half. Pepperoni made her want to gag and he hated mushrooms. She could live with that, she thought wryly.

She yawned, the sound coming out of her mouth before she could control it. "Excuse me," she said, laughing.

"Someone's tired."

She stretched out on her queen-size bed. "I had a long day studying, but I'm a little worked up with all those theories and things in my head. I don't know if I'll be able to fall asleep so fast."

"I have the solution for calming your mind." He chuckled, the sound low, deep, and sexy.

She squeezed her thighs together, knowing exactly what he had in mind. Sometimes he sent her sexy text messages, and other times he

talked her through what he'd do to her if they were actually together. "Yeah? Tell me more."

"Well, I know if I were there, I'd use my mouth to make you come before filling you deep with my cock. Seeing as how we have to wait for that, I'll just have to give you an orgasm another way. That'll take your mind off of math and theory and put it exactly where it belongs. On feeling good. On me."

"I can do that," she murmured.

"What are you wearing?" he asked.

"A silk nightshirt and underwear."

"Mmm-hmm. Okay pull those sexy panties down your legs and expose that sweet pussy for me." His voice rumbled low in her ear.

Doing as he asked, she placed the phone beside her, put him on speaker, then hooked her fingers into her underwear and wriggled them down her thighs, pulling them completely off. They'd only be in the way. "Done."

"You know what to do now, don't you?"

Her breath hitched at his gruff voice, her finger automatically going to her clit. She was already wet with arousal, and she ran her fingers through the moisture and moaned aloud at the delicious waves rippling through her.

"Good girl. Do what you like best. What you're going to teach me next time we're alone together."

She began to move her finger in circles, the tip sliding repetitively over her sensitive clit. Normally it would take her a long time to come if she was alone, but in the last week, with Shane instructing her, whispering naughty things in her ear, it wasn't difficult at all.

"Shane," she said on a low groan.

"Keep going. Do you want to know what I'm doing?" he asked.

She closed her eyes, unable to withstand the sensations and focus on anything around her. "Yes." She arched her hips and pressed down harder.

"I've got my hand around my cock, my eyes are shut, and I'm imagining you, working yourself until you come."

At the admission, she realized his breathing had picked up and taken on a rougher sound. He was obviously pumping himself with his hand, his body as primed and ready as hers was.

On that thought, she whimpered and squeezed herself harder. Stars flickered behind her eyes and everything around her exploded in bright

lights and wondrous sensation. "Shane!"

"I love that you scream my name when you come. God, yes. Fuck, Amber."

She heard the words, her name, and knew he'd reached his orgasm as well, and her body gave another little tremor before her legs fell to the mattress and she lay trying to catch her breath.

"Damn, if this is what you do to me over the phone, I can't imagine the next time we're together."

She couldn't help the smile that lifted her lips.

"Are you okay?"

"Yeah."

"Gonna sleep okay now?" His voice sounded raspy and so close, as if he were by her side. But his arms weren't around her and she was alone.

"I will but I miss you." The words came naturally and without thought, making her realize she was in so deep with this man.

"I miss you, too. Another week."

"Seven days. We've got this," she said as much to herself as to him.

"And then we've got each other."

On that very pleasant thought, they said good night and she rolled over, her body satisfied and her thoughts on Shane as she drifted off to sleep.

* * * *

The last economics class fell on the day before the final exam. Amber didn't think she'd ever feel ready, but she knew she'd done all she could to get herself to the point where she could walk into that room with some confidence.

Shane was going over the more difficult concepts when she heard the low buzz of her cell phone in her bag. She'd forgotten to shut it off before walking into the lecture hall, but he didn't seem to notice.

A quick glance told her it was Carrie, who rarely texted, so Amber peeked at the message. *EVERYTHING IS OKAY but L.J. had a little accident. Five stitches in his leg. Wanted you to know but promise he's FINE.*

Panic and worry rushed through her. She believed Carrie and trusted her to take care of her son, and if something really serious had happened, that text would have said to call her immediately. But to Amber, stitches were a big deal.

It meant her boy's first trip to the emergency room, his first time getting sewn up, without his mom there. Worried and needing to talk to L.J., she gathered her things and, without a glance around her, rushed out of the room. Without waiting, she dropped her things right outside the door and pulled out her phone.

A second later, Carrie's face was on the screen. "He's fine, Amber. I promise you."

Tears fell from her eyes. "I believe you. It's just that I'm not there."

Carrie's expression was soft and understanding. "He was a champ."

"What happened?" Amber asked, leaning against the wall outside the classroom.

"He didn't listen and ran to give Samuel the pair of scissors. I'm sorry, honey. I feel terrible and responsible."

Amber shook her head. "No! It could have happened while I was there, too. I know he's in good hands. Can I talk to him?"

"Samuel took him to the ice cream shop across the street from where we're staying Uptown. I really felt like we were intruding on Landon's privacy after so long."

Amber smiled in understanding. "Would you have L.J. FaceTime me as soon as he gets back?"

"Of course. Are you ready for your exams?" Carrie asked.

"One down, a paper turned in, and one more to go." Amber didn't mention that it was the hardest one. She didn't want anyone to know how much she'd struggled.

"Well, good luck and we'll talk soon. And don't worry."

Easier said than done, but Amber didn't want Carrie to feel worse than she already did. They disconnected the call just as the class ended and the students streamed out of the lecture hall.

Realizing she'd taken her backpack but left her small purse on the floor by her chair, she waited for everyone to leave and headed back inside. She saw her little bag on the floor and bent down to grab it.

When she rose, Shane was by her side. "Is everything okay? You bolted out of your seat and scared the shit out of me."

She managed a smile though she still felt shaky and was beyond upset. "I'd left my phone on by mistake. Carrie texted me. L.J. fell and needed stitches. She said he was fine but I needed to talk to her."

His gaze was one of complete understanding. "And? He's okay?"

She bit down on her lower lip, which had begun trembling. "He is. He was running with a pair of scissors." She shook her head and

muttered, "Boys."

Shane raised a hand and slid his palm behind her neck. "Did you speak to him?"

"No. He went for ice cream with his grandfather."

Shane's low chuckle reassured her somewhat. "If he's up for ice cream, he must not be in too much pain. I'm sure they numbed the area first."

Tears began to fall from her eyes unexpectedly and Shane swore, then pulled her into his arms. "Shhh. He's fine. You're just upset because you weren't there for him."

"How did you know that?" she asked.

"Because I know you." He slid his fingers through her hair, and she let her emotions free, sniffling into his white dress shirt beneath his jacket. She liked that he always dressed for class, taking even summer session oh so seriously. Her professor, she mused, her thought taking her off guard.

Hers.

She wanted him to be hers, because in the short time she'd known him, she'd fallen in love with everything that was Shane Warden. But she wasn't ready to tell him. Not while they were still in professor-student limbo.

"You okay now?" he asked.

She nodded, wanting another minute in his safe, secure arms.

That was her mistake.

"I knew it." Dan stood by the last row of seats, his phone in his hand, aimed at them. "I knew you didn't raise your grades on your own."

"What the hell?" Shane, who had already separated himself from Amber, strode up the aisle toward the smug punk. "What are you doing?" he asked him.

"Proving what I suspected. That she fucked her way to a passing grade."

"But... No. I didn't! I had a tutor. I–"

Shane held up a hand, cutting her off. "Don't bother arguing with him," he said in that authoritative voice she remembered from the first day of class. "I'll deal with this. Amber, you can leave."

She blinked but the tears fell anyway, the entire emotion of the last few minutes catching up with her ... along with the fear that Dan's accusation could cost her everything.

* * * *

Amber paced back and forth in her house. It was the not knowing how Shane was handling Dan that both concerned and frightened her. She'd come home from the incident shaken, but L.J. had FaceTimed her almost as soon as she'd walked in the door, so she'd had no choice but to put on a bright smile and talk to her son.

Instead of expressing pain or being upset, L.J. had been eager to show her his stitches. He had ice cream stains on his face, and he was chatty as ever, allowing her to breathe, at least about him. She duly lectured him about the dangers of running with scissors and not listening to his grandparents but figured he'd been punished enough by the hospital experience. She had no doubt the stitches and numbing had hurt him badly. She winced at the thought but forced deep breaths into her lungs. He was fine.

Was Shane?

This was his worst nightmare, the one thing he'd gone out of his way to avoid happening ... and she'd caused it. She'd remained in his arms despite the risk. She'd let them get caught by someone who clearly had issues either with her or anyone he felt threatened by, though why he'd targeted Amber made no sense.

She rubbed her hands over her arms and tried to concentrate on studying for tomorrow's test while she waited to hear from Shane. It wasn't easy ... and he never called.

He did return her text with a generic answer. *Don't worry. I have it handled. Will talk to you after the test. Good luck.*

Handled how? Don't worry why? What was going on? The not knowing was killing her, but she understood he wanted her to focus on the exam, and she needed to do just that. Unfortunately she tossed and turned all night.

The next morning, she dragged herself to the test, tired, cranky, and concerned about how she'd handle the exam on little sleep and the worry clawing inside her.

Had he gotten in trouble and blamed her? Was that why he was waiting to talk to her until after the test? She walked into the lecture hall expecting to see Shane. Although she knew he wanted the teaching assistant to proctor the exam, she thought he'd at least speak to the class first or wish them luck.

His absence made it even more difficult to concentrate, but she knew how much rode on her passing. Every higher-level class in business required this entry-level course first. She wanted to set a positive example for L.J., wanted to prove to Landon, Jason, and Tanner that their faith in her was well placed. That lending her money for school hadn't been a mistake.

Across the room, Dan glared at her, and she didn't know what to make of his attitude. He'd gotten the upper hand, after all. He could report Shane to the dean and… No. She couldn't think about that now. Later. Later she'd see what had happened.

Pushing every thought aside but economics, she drew a deep breath and settled in to work.

\* \* \* \*

Shane paced the hall outside the dean's office, waiting to be called in. Yesterday, after being caught by Dan, instead of letting the kid go and having yet another student make a mess of Shane's life, he'd taken control of the situation. He'd marched Dan and his damned cell phone and the recording of Shane holding Amber in his arms straight to the dean's office.

*"Show him," Shane said to a shocked Dan. "Show Dean Frost what you have on your phone."*

*Sputtering and unsure what Shane's end game was, Dan hit the play button and the video of Shane and Amber came up.*

*Dean Frost watched, an unhappy expression on his face, and Shane's gut twisted hard.*

*"I see," the man said, then turned his gaze on Dan. "And why did you film this?"*

*"Because she obviously slept her way to a good grade! It's not fair. The rest of us have to work for what we get," Dan said, his cheeks red with anger and frustration.*

*The dean stared at him. "You do realize this isn't the first time you've come to me with accusations about a student cheating."*

*That was news to Shane. He had issues with Dan's unhappiness with bad grades, but he hadn't known others did, too.*

*"But … this time I have proof." Dan gestured to the phone on the dean's desk.*

*"That remains to be seen." The older man folded his hands across his chest as he stared Dan down. "You, however, have issues with everyone but yourself. After the last time you accused Jeanne Clark of cheating, which she hadn't done – there were*

*cameras in the classroom — I kept an eye on grades. You're struggling, young man. And you blame everyone but yourself. One more incident and I'll have no choice but to expel you. You can't go on accusing others with no consequences."*

*Fury lit Dan's features and he stormed out of the room.*

*The dean then turned his gaze to Shane. "I know the boy's father. I suppose it's time we have a talk," he said on a sigh. "As for you, would you care to explain?" He gestured to the phone, which remained on his desk.*

*Shane blew out a long breath, gathering his thoughts. The dean knew Shane's history and he understood this video looked bad. But he hadn't broken any school rules. And he'd covered himself regarding the test and grades.*

*He'd gone on to explain that Amber had a frightening situation with her son and he'd merely been comforting her. However, he admitted to having a relationship with her. One that he'd put on hold until class was over. He gave the dean the name of Amber's tutor and asked the man to talk to the woman and find out how long she'd been working with Amber. Then Shane listed everything he'd done to keep the final exam fair and impartial.*

*"I can understand why you'd be careful, given your history," the man said. "What exactly is going on with you and this student?"*

*"Woman," Shane corrected him. "She's a full-grown adult who decided to go back to school."*

*"Aah. I hadn't realized."*

*Shane nodded. "But you need to know I intend to pursue a serious relationship with her now that class is over. And if you have a problem with that, if I need to choose between my job and Amber..." Shane's heart nearly beat out of his chest as he drew a deep breath.*

*He'd been up most of the night contemplating this conversation and what was more important to him. And no matter how much he wanted tenure, no matter that he knew if he blew it at another school, his fault or not, he wouldn't get a third chance, he came to the same conclusion.*

*"I choose Amber."*

*The man's expression was bland, his eyes not giving away a damned thing as he said, "I'd like the night to consider the situation."*

So Shane had gone home alone. Not wanting Amber to worry about the fact that a decision would be made about his career, he hadn't called her. If he spoke to her, he didn't trust himself not to tell her everything, and she needed to focus on passing the test. So he'd texted her back, told her everything would be okay, and left the details until today.

Right now she was taking the exam.

And he was awaiting his fate.

"I was up much of the night," Dean Frost said.

*Join the club*, Shane thought.

"As you know, you haven't broken school rules, but I do have to look at the ethical considerations of you dating a student."

"A former student of mine as of yesterday," he felt compelled to remind the older man.

Dean Frost nodded. "Yes. And she is an adult, as you said. Although there is the argument to be made that any of our students over eighteen are adults. I'd be setting precedent."

Shane thought he was going to throw up. His career, everything he'd worked for, was about to disappear before his eyes.

"However, the fact that she is not a young woman but an adult with experience behind her does help your cause. As does the fact that you stepped aside while class was going on. You covered the exams, made them impartial, and handled things with impartiality."

His hard stare didn't allow Shane to read his final thoughts at all. He stood, hands clenched, shoulders tense, and waited.

With a frown, the dean said, "I can't say I like it or that it's going to make things easy on us going forward … but you would also have a case against us for unlawful termination if I fired you. Which I don't want to do. You're a good professor. A solid addition to the faculty. And you got a raw deal twice, first at your last school and now again here. I knew Dan was a loose cannon, and I did nothing to prevent him from causing trouble again."

"So where does this leave us?" Shane asked.

Dean Frost extended his hand. "It leaves you with your position intact, Professor Warden."

"Thank you, sir." Relief filling him, Shane clasped the other man's hand. "I appreciate your understanding."

To Shane's surprise, Dean Frost smiled, dropping the stern formality he'd held on to throughout their meeting. "I met my wife when I was eighteen. It was love at first sight. I'm not going to deny you what's obviously true love."

Shane grinned. Although he hadn't said the words to himself, he knew it was true. Why else would he be willing to give up his job for Amber?

"So what are you waiting for?" Dean Frost asked. "Go get your girl."

# Chapter Seven

Amber finished her exam, too afraid to hope. Yes, she thought she passed. But did she get a C? C-? D? It was anybody's guess. She needed the D to pass the class, and she really believed in her heart it was possible. But even with that huge concern off her shoulders, she wasn't free of worry because she still didn't know what Shane's *Don't worry, I have it handled* text meant.

She stepped into the bright sunshine and looked around. If she'd hoped to see Shane, she was disappointed. There were plenty of happy students whose final test of the summer had ended but no Shane.

She made her way home, taking the long way, needing to walk and clear her head. L.J. was coming home tomorrow with his grandparents, and real life was about to descend on her. She was so excited to see her baby, but she knew it meant more responsibilities, more routine, more schedules. She'd have to find ways to find time to see Shane ... if he still wanted to see her after what had gone down with Dan.

By the time she arrived on her street, she decided she was going to Shane's house to talk to him and find out what was going on. Except she didn't need to.

Shane sat on her doorstep waiting for her.

With trepidation, she met him at the bottom of the porch. "Hi."

"Hi. How was your test?"

"You're a hard teacher, Professor Warden. But I think, I hope I passed."

A pleased smile lifted his sexy lips. "I asked Eric to grade them this

afternoon," he said of the teacher's assistant. "They should be posted by morning."

She blew out a deep breath. "Good. Another night tossing and turning." She smiled wryly. "Don't worry, I expected to have to wait to find out."

She pulled her purse in front of her and looked for her keys, extracting them from her bag. "Want to come inside?" Her heart pounded in her chest, the fear of not knowing what was going on consuming her.

"Sure." He smiled at her but she still didn't know where they stood.

After letting them into the house, she closed the door behind them and turned to face him. "I can't take it anymore. What happened with Dan?"

"I took him to Dean Frost myself and showed him the video. Dan has a history of reporting people for cheating when he doesn't do as well as he'd like in a class. The dean wasn't pleased with him. I don't think he's going to be my problem anymore. As for us..."

"Oh, my God. Is he angry? Am I in trouble? Are you?"

He shook his head and tried to breathe deeply and evenly.

"Then what did he say?"

Shane's serious expression made her stomach twist with uncertainty.

"At first he asked for the night to think, which was why I didn't want to explain things last night. I didn't want to leave you hanging the night before a test. Well, any more than you already were." He shook his head, a wry twist to his lips.

She twisted her hands in front of her, nerves getting the best of her. "And this morning? What did he say?"

"Before I tell you what he said, you need to know what I said. In no uncertain terms, I told him that if it came down to a choice between my job and you, I chose you."

"You did *what?*" She got light-headed. "I need to sit down."

Chuckling, he wrapped an arm around her waist and led her to the nearest sofa in the family room, easing her onto a cushion and sitting beside her.

He clasped her hand in his. "I'm serious. I know it's early days, but I know what I'm feeling for you and it's not casual. It's not something I'm going to walk away from."

"But your job, your career ... tenure."

"I'd have dealt with losing it if I had to… Luckily I don't have to. Dean Frost is a smart man. He was able to discern the differences between us and me and an eighteen- or nineteen-year-old student. And regardless, I didn't violate any school rules or policy. Although I have a feeling that might change going forward, but it won't affect us." His hands tightened around hers.

She swallowed hard, trying to come to terms with what he'd done. "You risked your career … for me."

Meeting her gaze, his expression softened. "For us. I risked being terminated for *us* because I believe what we could have is too special to let go."

Her heart thudded in her chest. "I think so, too," she whispered, almost afraid to jinx what they shared.

"So we're in agreement? We're together?" He moved closer, as if her answer was a foregone conclusion. Which, of course, it was.

"Yes!"

He rose, pulling her to her feet.

Happy tears in her eyes, she grinned, took a few steps, and jumped into his arms, wrapping her legs around his waist and trusting he'd catch her. Then she pressed her lips to his.

She kissed him and all her worries fled, replaced with hopes and dreams she thought she'd given up on. After the kiss, which was long and beautiful, she drew back.

"L.J. is coming home tomorrow," she told him. Although he was saying all the right words, she felt compelled to remind him of her real life. The one he hadn't experienced yet.

He met her gaze, all the while holding her tight. "And I can't wait to meet him."

"Really?"

He tilted his head to the side. "Really. Haven't I done everything possible to prove that to you?"

She nodded. "You really have. Now can we go to bed and let me prove to you how much I appreciate you?"

He strode out of the family room, down the hall, and into her room. Laughing, he tossed her down on the bed and stripped her out of her clothes. She did the same to him and they came together, skin to skin.

Pressing her cheek against his, she closed her eyes and breathed in deep, feeling his chest rise and fall beneath hers. "I love you," she said,

the words tumbling out. "I mean—"

"I love you, too, so you'd better not mean anything else."

She let out a puff of air. "Well, no. I don't. I just thought maybe it was too soon or I shouldn't have said it yet…"

"It's soon. I get that, but if we feel it, what's wrong with saying it?" He slid his lips over hers and his thick erection pulsed against her belly.

At the feel of him hard against her, her legs opened and his cock came to rest at her entrance. "Amber." He let out a groan.

"I'm on birth control for other reasons. And you know I haven't been with anyone in a long time. I've had an annual exam and I'm clean. I want to feel you bare inside me."

He visibly swallowed hard. "I wouldn't put you at risk. I'm fine, too."

His cock seemed to throb in response and she grinned. "Then what are you waiting for?"

He slid into her and everything inside her settled. Her world seemed brighter. Everything that was uncertain fell into place.

Long after she climaxed and he came right along with her, she lay in his arms, happy and complete.

* * * *

The next morning, after a breakfast of scrambled eggs and bacon, made by Amber and Shane together, he was dressing after a shower, stuck in his clothes from the day before. His gaze fell on a long tube leaning against the wall.

Amber strode out of the bathroom, makeup complete, dressed for the day in a pair of jeans and a tank top, looking fresh and sexy. "What are your plans for the day?" she asked him.

"I was going to go home and change. Then I hoped to come back and meet L.J.?" He heard the hope in his voice. But how could they become closer, more like a family, if he didn't first meet and spend time with her son?

"Sounds good! I want you two to meet." She braced her hands on his shoulders, leaned down, and kissed him.

"Hey, what's that?" He pointed to the rolled tube he'd noticed earlier.

She grinned. "A Spiderman Fathead. L.J. wanted a life-size superhero on his wall. I thought I'd surprise him when he came home,

but I didn't anticipate how big it actually was. I can't put it up by myself."

"Then let's do it. He's going to be home soon, right? So let's hurry and put it up."

Her eyes lit at the idea.

For the next thirty minutes, they struggled getting the life-size decal onto the wall behind the head of the bed, but between the two of them, they managed.

"You do realize it's going to have to come down when I paint the room blue?" she asked, a little out of breath from their work.

He groaned. "We'll deal with that when the time comes—"

The sound of the doorbell cut him off.

"Who could that be? It's too early for L.J. They said they were leaving around eleven and would be home by lunch." She headed for the front door and Shane followed.

Amber peeked through the side narrow window and let out a shriek of excitement, unlocking the deadbolt and yanking the door open.

"Baby!" She knelt down and pulled a brown-haired boy into her arms.

He hugged her back but very quickly began squirming to escape her hold.

"I think you'd better let him go," a muscular dark-haired man with a scruff of beard said from behind him.

Shane knew immediately from photos he'd seen this was L.J.'s father's twin. His Uncle Landon.

Amber released her hold but her gaze never left her son. "You'd better believe I expect more hugs later."

"Mooom!" He groaned her name. "I have to go to the bathroom!" he said and took off at a run.

Shane chuckled, drawing the other man's attention to him. "Who are you?"

"Landon, don't be rude!" Amber held up a hand against his chest. "Landon Bennett, this is Shane Warden. Shane, this is L.J.'s uncle," Amber said, eyeing the man warily.

Shane extended his hand and Landon took it, shaking hard.

Okay, he got it. The man was protective of Amber and L.J. Well, he'd damn well better learn he came second to Shane now. "Nice to meet you."

"It's early for you to be here," Landon said pointedly.

"And you're ridiculous! I'm a grown woman. You have no say in what I do. Although in this case I better warn you, you're going to be seeing a lot of Shane, so I'd appreciate it if you got to know him and didn't just act like an ass on first meeting."

"Mom! Five bucks in the swear jar," L.J. said, rejoining them.

She sighed. "I unpacked it and it's in the kitchen. You can watch me add money later." She ruffled his hair. "I swear you grew a couple of inches. We need to set up a measuring wall here."

Landon grinned. "He's certainly eaten enough to have a growth spurt. Which reminds me, we stopped for breakfast on the road."

Clearly the reprimand had been forgotten. Shane didn't need Amber fighting his battles for him. He could win L.J.'s uncles over on his own, but he appreciated her coming to his defense.

"Why did you leave so early?" she asked.

"Your boy couldn't wait to see you." Landon chuckled.

"L.J., why don't you take your suitcase into your room." She gestured to the bag with wheels that Landon had placed inside the door.

"Okay." He pulled the luggage along, and as they watched him go, she met Shane's gaze with a knowing grin.

"Cool! Mom, you got me the Fathead!"

She laughed. "I'm going to talk to him for a few minutes. Can you behave while I'm gone?" she asked Landon, who was still eyeing Shane warily.

"Go ahead, we'll be fine," Shane assured her. He wanted a word with the other man.

He waited until Amber disappeared, deliberately not watching her sexy ass, before he turned to Landon. "I get it," he said before the other man could speak. "You're protective. You're worried. You don't know me, don't trust me, and you don't live nearby."

The other man cocked his head to one side. "That about sums it up."

Shane held up his hands. "I love her and she loves me."

Landon let out a snort. "In one short summer?"

Shane ignored him. He'd heard from Amber how quickly Landon had fallen for Vivi. The man had no room to judge them. "In the meantime, I'd appreciate it if you cut me some slack. Get to know me before deciding how you feel about me. And know I'd cut off my arm before I'd hurt them."

Arms folded across his chest, Landon studied him, his expression

shifting a bit at Shane's last comment. "You said them. So you understand they're a package deal. L.J. isn't some kid you can push aside so you can fuck his mom."

Shane's blood boiled at the careless words. "One," he said through clenched teeth, "don't talk about Amber like that. She's worth a lot more than a fuck," he muttered. "And two, it pisses me off you'd jump to that conclusion. I know L.J. is her world. I only want to be part of them. Not come between them."

Landon scrubbed a hand over his face. "Fine. You pass. But I'll be watching you. Jason, Tanner, and I will all be keeping an eye out. Just because we're in New York doesn't mean we're not involved in their lives."

"I'd expect nothing less," Shane said. "I'm glad she had the three of you all these years."

"We're not going anywhere."

Shane shook his head and let out a low chuckle. "I didn't think you were."

"Everything okay in here?" Amber asked, returning from L.J.'s room.

"Perfect." Shane wrapped an arm around her waist and kissed her cheek.

"Good. Landon, are you staying for the day?" she asked.

He shook his head. "The club needs me. I just offered to take the ride so Mom and Dad could go straight home. They said they'll call you later so you can work out a schedule for when school starts."

She shot him a grateful look. "Thanks for everything." She hugged him and he returned the gesture, but even Shane could see it was all platonic ... even if he did look exactly like his twin brother had.

He let out a relieved breath he hadn't been aware of holding.

A few seconds later, Landon had said his goodbyes and walked out to his car. Amber shut the door to the house.

"Where's L.J.?" Shane asked.

"Doing his best to unpack. There are no dirty clothes, thank you, Carrie," Amber said with a grateful smile.

"Want me to go so you can spend some time alone?" he offered.

She wrapped her arms around his waist and shook her head. "I'd like my two boys to get to know each other. Unless you want to go home and change?"

He chuckled. "It can wait."

She stared up at him with those big, beautiful blue eyes. "We're a lot to handle," she said nervously.

"I can't wait to do it. I know the juggling of schedules won't be easy, finding time alone won't be simple, but I know what I'm getting into. And I'm all in."

She reached onto her tiptoes and brushed her lips over his. "I'm so glad. You changed my life, Shane Warden."

"Same, Amber Davis. And I couldn't be happier."

# Epilogue

It was a day to celebrate. Amber received her combined bachelor of arts degree – with her minor in business - and her master's in education, and Shane had earned tenure at the end of this school year. At the New York uncles' insistence, they'd all come to Manhattan for a celebration at the nightclub, which they'd opened on a Sunday afternoon just for this special occasion.

With his arm around Amber and L.J., now a lanky teenager beside them, Shane walked into Club TEN29, aptly named after the date Levi Bennett had passed away. But the club was now a happy place, one where people came to have fun and celebrate. The owners, L.J.'s uncles, had all come around and accepted Shane's presence in Amber's and L.J.'s lives. They'd moved in together when Shane's lease ran out, and since they were always at Amber's anyway, they'd decided to live together then.

Although he'd been ready for more, he knew Amber wanted to finish school. She liked to put all her focus on one big thing at a time, and a wedding would have thrown her off her studying game, no matter how small they might have made it. And with the guys finding their wives, the size of their pseudo-family had expanded.

The party was small, just close family and friends. Amber's parents had flown up from Florida, for which Shane was grateful as their presence played into his plans. He waited until the end of the day, after presents had been opened and a lot of food eaten.

Even Shane's father and stepmother were there, something Shane's

mom had no problem accepting. Many years had passed, and she was long over their marriage and years together. In the time since his heart attack, Zachary had made an attempt to be part of Shane's life and he'd reciprocated warily. Now things were decent between them all.

Amber, wearing a pretty pink dress and gold heels, stood by his side. Knowing there was no time like the present, Shane cleared his throat. "Excuse me," he said. "I'd like to say something."

The murmurs and conversation quieted down and all eyes were on him. He slid a hand into his suit jacket, which he wore because the party had been dressy and he'd wanted this day to be special and one to remember.

Amber turned to him, questions in her wide blue eyes.

"First I want to thank the guys, Landon, Jason, and Tanner, for the fabulous party, and Faith, Scarlett and Vivi for helping."

A small round of clapping followed.

"I also want to thank them for giving a college professor a chance with this woman here. I know if they'd put their foot down, it could have made Amber's choices much more difficult." In the years since that awkward meeting with Landon at Amber's front door, they'd all become good friends.

"I can make my own decisions, you know," she said beside him.

He nodded. "I also know you would not have wanted to argue with your family. I'm glad they didn't make you." He tipped his head at the three men who stood with their hands around the respective women in their lives.

"Thank you, Carrie and Samuel, for treating me like I'm part of the family. It means the world to me."

The couple smiled at him.

"Thanks to Lydia and John for raising such a fabulous woman and to my mom for being my rock."

She brought her hands to her heart and blew him a kiss.

"Finally, L.J., thanks for sharing your mom with me. And thank you for giving me permission to do this." He reached into his pocket and pulled out the ring he'd bought a long time ago. He'd just been waiting for Amber to be ready. Then he dropped to one knee.

Amber gasped. He knew she'd expected a graduation and congratulations party ... not this. "Amber, from the second you bumped into me on campus—"

"Umm, I think you bumped into me," she said with a grin.

"From the second we bumped into each other and I looked into your eyes, I think I recognized the other half of my soul. I just wasn't ready to admit to myself I was ready. We all know it didn't take long for me to fall for your laughter, your warmth, and your poor, poor economics skills."

The tinkling of laughter warmed him inside.

"I fell for your son the minute he smiled at me. And we became a family. Now I just want to make it legal and tie you to me forever. Amber, will you marry me?" He held out the round diamond with pavé stones surrounding it.

"Yes! A million times, yes."

He slid the ring onto her hand and then her lips were on his. They kissed too briefly and then he stood up grinning like a fool, Amber pulled tightly against him.

Shane barely heard the clapping around him. All he could focus on was the woman in his arms. The boy beaming with approval beside them. The family that was now his.

* * * *

Also from 1001 Dark Nights and Carly Phillips, discover Take the Bride and His to Protect.

Sign up for the 1001 Dark Nights Newsletter
and be entered to win a Tiffany Key necklace.

There's a contest every month!

Go to www.1001DarkNights.com to subscribe.

**As a bonus, all subscribers can download
FIVE FREE exclusive books!**

# Discover 1001 Dark Nights Collection Seven

THE BISHOP by Skye Warren
A Tanglewood Novella

TAKEN WITH YOU by Carrie Ann Ryan
A Fractured Connections Novella

DRAGON LOST by Donna Grant
A Dark Kings Novella

SEXY LOVE by Carly Phillips
A Sexy Series Novella

PROVOKE by Rachel Van Dyken
A Seaside Pictures Novella

RAFE by Sawyer Bennett
An Arizona Vengeance Novella

THE NAUGHTY PRINCESS by Claire Contreras
A Sexy Royals Novella

THE GRAVEYARD SHIFT by Darynda Jones
A Charley Davidson Novella

CHARMED by Lexi Blake
A Masters and Mercenaries Novella

SACRIFICE OF DARKNESS by Alexandra Ivy
A Guardians of Eternity Novella

THE QUEEN by Jen Armentrout
A Wicked Novella

BEGIN AGAIN by Jennifer Probst
A Stay Novella

VIXEN by Rebecca Zanetti
A Dark Protectors/Rebels Novella

SLASH by Laurelin Paige
A Slay Series Novella

THE DEAD HEAT OF SUMMER by Heather Graham
A Krewe of Hunters Novella

WILD FIRE by Kristen Ashley
A Chaos Novella

MORE THAN PROTECT YOU by Shayla Black
A More Than Words Novella

LOVE SONG by Kylie Scott
A Stage Dive Novella

CHERISH ME by J. Kenner
A Stark Ever After Novella

SHINE WITH ME by Kristen Proby
A With Me in Seattle Novella


*And new from Blue Box Press:*

TEASE ME by J. Kenner
A Stark International Novel

# Discover More Carly Phillips

*Take the Bride*: A Knight Brothers Novella
by Carly Phillips

**She used to be his. Now she's about to marry another man.
Will he let her go ... or will he stand up and take the bride?**

Ryder Hammond and Sierra Knight were high school sweethearts. Despite him being her brother's best friend, their relationship burned hot and fast...and ended with heartbreak and regrets.

Years later, she's at the altar, about to marry another man.

He's only there for closure, to finally put the past behind him.

But when the preacher asks if anyone has a reason the couple shouldn't wed, she turns around and her gaze locks on his.

Suddenly he's out of his seat.

Objecting.

Claiming.

And ultimately stealing the very pissed off bride and takes her to a secluded cabin.

He wants one week to convince her they're meant to be, to remind her of the fiery passion still burning between them.

When their time together is up, will she walk away and break *his* heart this time, or will he finally have the woman he's wanted all along?

\* \* \* \*

*His to Protect*: A Bodyguard Bad Boys/Masters and Mercenaries Novella
by Carly Phillips

Talia Shaw has spent her adult life working as a scientist for a big pharmaceutical company. She's focused on saving lives, not living life. When her lab is broken into and it's clear someone is after the top secret formula she's working on, she turns to the one man she can trust. The same irresistible man she turned away years earlier because she was too young and naive to believe a sexy guy like Shane Landon could want *her*.

Shane Landon's bodyguard work for McKay-Taggart is the one thing that brings him satisfaction in his life. Relationships come in second to the job. Always. Then little brainiac Talia Shaw shows up in his backyard, frightened and on the run, and his world is turned upside down. And not just because she's found him naked in his outdoor shower, either.

With Talia's life in danger, Shane has to get her out of town and to her eccentric, hermit mentor who has the final piece of the formula she's been working on, while keeping her safe from the men who are after her. Guarding Talia's body certainly isn't any hardship, but he never expects to fall hard and fast for his best friend's little sister and the only woman who's ever really gotten under his skin.

# About Carly Phillips

Carly Phillips gives her readers Alphalicious heroes to swoon for and romance to set your heart on fire, and she loves everything about writing romance. She married her college sweetheart and lives in Purchase, NY along with her three crazy dogs: two wheaten terriers and a mutant Havanese, who are featured on her Facebook and Instagram. She has raised two incredible daughters who put up with having a mom as a romance author. Carly is the author of over fifty romances, and is a NY Times, Wall Street Journal, and USA Today Bestseller. She loves social media and interacting with her readers. Want to keep up with Carly? Sign up for her newsletter and receive TWO FREE books at www.carlyphillips.com.

# More Than Sexy

Sexy Series Book 1
By Carly Phillips
Now Available

**One protective alpha male...**
**Plus one hot curvy blonde...**
**Equals an insta-love they can't deny.**

Billionaire nightclub owner Jason Dare doesn't stand a chance. From the moment he lays eyes on the luscious blonde stuck on the side of the road and realizes she's in danger, he goes from playboy to bodyguard.

Faith Lancaster's sweet body won't come to any harm on his watch. And watch Faith he does. He can't take his eyes off her. Jason will stop at nothing to keep Faith safe. Even if it means moving her into his apartment and letting her into his once private life.

Hiding from her past, Faith has spent the last year building her candy business into a profitable company while keeping to herself and staying under the radar ... until she meets the delicious Mr. Dare. Alpha and irresistible, he awakens desires she has long denied. It doesn't take her long to succumb to his charms and fall hard for the man.

They both have their reasons for keeping things casual but when Faith's past catches up with her, can Jason finally claim the woman meant to be his?

\* \* \* \*

## Chapter One

With happy hour being celebrated loudly around him, Jason Dare stood on a balcony above the bar area and surveyed his domain, Club TEN29, a nightclub in Tribeca, an ode to the past and a reminder that the future wasn't guaranteed. Despite the fact that his two partners were here, as were members of his actual family, he still felt very much alone.

Although solitary was a state of being he chose for reasons only he and his partners – men he considered his brothers – understood,

sometimes it wasn't easy, especially since they were very much in demand. As owners, they were becoming well known here and had had extremely positive press, and that made him a target – for those who wanted an in with the occasional high-brow guest, and for women with dollar signs in their eyes and hopes to snag a wealthy man. Jason didn't engage. He was ultra-selective with the females he brought to his bed.

His life was the club, his partners, and his large family. He kept his circle close and *minimized his risk of loss* as best he could. That mantra defined him, extending into his love life, as well. After his father had blown his family sky-high, after he'd almost lost his sister to cancer when she was a child, after losing his partner Landon's twin and Jason's best friend back in college, he didn't, couldn't get close to people and risk more loss.

He didn't get emotionally involved. Ever. A woman couldn't expect anything more than the occasional hookup when it was convenient, but he enjoyed those moments of connection with the females he did allow into his bed. He had enough darkness in his life that when he let go, he wanted to enjoy and have fun.

"Jason, this has been an amazing night!" his sister, Sienna, said, throwing her arms around his neck and planting a kiss on his cheek.

He chuckled and smiled at her glowing face.

Her husband, Ethan Knight, grinned as he pulled her off him and into his arms. "She's been liberal with the alcohol." Ethan explained her exuberant enthusiasm. "Her first time out since having the baby." He held his wife tight against him.

"I had fun! And now we're going home to f–" Ethan placed a hand over Sienna's mouth, sparing Jason from hearing about his sister's love life. Jesus.

He shot the man a grateful look.

"And on that note, we're leaving. We just wanted to say goodbye," Ethan said with a smug grin on his face.

"Thanks for coming." Jason extended his arm and shook Ethan's hand. "And give that little bundle a kiss from her uncle Jase."

Accepting this man as his sister's husband had been an adjustment, one Jason was still making, considering Ethan had knocked up Sienna before anyone even knew they were together. They now had a baby girl named Lizzy, who Jason adored, and Ethan was a member of the family. More people for Jason to worry about. He watched them leave, acknowledging his sister was in good hands with the other man.

His gaze turned to his closest friends since their time together in college, now equal partners in Club TEN29. They stood huddled together around the bar with some of their repeat customers. Tanner Grayson was the night manager, and Landon Bennett was the head of Entertainment and Appearances, Brand Deals, and Promotions. After Landon's twin died, he'd pulled into himself, while Tanner had spiraled, and it was only by sheer determination that he'd dragged himself out of the angry place he'd gone to and the trouble he'd gotten himself into.

Jason held the position of CEO. Together they were a solid mix of personalities and work ethic in a club that was merely two years old but becoming prominent in the night scene. They made sure Club TEN29 provided a memorable experience for everyone who stepped inside. There was no task too menial they wouldn't handle personally if the need arose.

But Jason wanted *more* for their singular club. They had a stage on which customers danced but it wasn't fully utilized, and although they'd put a lot of money into ads and promotions, they weren't growing as fast as he would like. He just hadn't figured out in which direction they needed to go in order to break out the way he wanted. Since Tanner and Landon thought things were fine as they were, Jason needed a fully fleshed-out plan before presenting it to them for a vote. Which was why he was meeting his cousin Gabe later on tonight. To hash out some ideas.

Gabriel Dare owned Elite, also a nightclub but one that operated on a scale Jason couldn't imagine, one where people paid over five figures for a table and A-list celebrities visited often. They had clubs all over the world, including on the island of Eden, an exclusive invitation-only resort near the Bermuda Triangle.

He wanted to think things through before he met up with Gabe, and he couldn't make decisions here, where the music blared and people partied. As much as Club TEN29 was home, Jason needed a break.

After clearing his departure with Tanner and Landon, Jason headed out into the cold air. He pulled his wool jacket around him and headed to his car. Despite it being impractical in the city, he liked having his Jag at his disposal.

Once he was enclosed in the luxurious interior and the heated seats and warmth began to surround him, he relaxed. He turned on some music and decided to drive around a little before heading to his cousin's. This area of the city wasn't the grid of ease that was Uptown Manhattan,

and he wound his way through the smaller streets, taking in the shops that lined them.

Because it was cold, not many people were out, so when he came upon a lone van parked in front of a run-down apartment building, with two women standing alongside it, he slowed down. When one of the women bent over, her cute ass peeking out from beneath the edge of her down jacket, he noticed. And when she kicked what he realized was a flat tire in frustration, he came to a complete stop, then parked his car in front of hers.

As he climbed out and got a look at the curvy woman with waves of blonde hair, full lips, and a startled expression on her pretty face, currently clutching the lug wrench in her hand like a weapon, he realized his night was about to get much more interesting.

\* \* \* \*

Faith Lancaster loaded the last of her marshmallow pops into the back of her company van, adjusting the baskets, taking care to space the items far enough apart that nothing would get ruined or crushed. She'd spent all day in her small apartment kitchen, making and wrapping her treats with the intention of dropping off baskets to nearby stores along with her business cards. She planned to request they leave them on the counter for their customers to sample, hoping to drive business to Sweet Treats, her candy store located off the beaten path.

Kelsey Johnson, the culinary school intern Faith had hired to help, joined her after working in the shop all day. Before she and Faith could climb into the car, Faith noticed her flat back tire and groaned.

The deflated tire mocked her and all the time she'd spent creating and preparing. Although she could have handed them out during the day, she'd ended up spending all afternoon cooking and creating, deciding to work from home instead of the shop, and now it was early evening. But she knew the area she wanted to hit up had open stores with people browsing for the evening. A used bookstore, a coffee shop, and a few other boutique-type stores that would hopefully help out a fellow business.

She should have known better than to drop a big chunk of change on an old beat-up delivery van with no known history, but desperation made a woman do stupid things. And Faith, although she'd come a long way, had been desperate when she'd arrived in Manhattan with a new

name, a limited amount of funds, and a dream of opening her own candy shop.

She glared at the flat on the back tire, wondering why luck just wasn't on her side. She'd had a rough go of it for a long time now, and she'd thought she was coming out on the other side at last. Now this.

"Kelsey, can you grab the lug wrench in the back? Just be careful not to knock over the candy. I'll deal with checking out the spare once I see if I can even get the lug nuts off." Assuming this old van even had a spare.

Kelsey, a pretty girl with brown hair and bangs, met Faith's gaze, eyes wide. "You can change a tire?" the twenty-one-year-old asked.

Faith managed a laugh or else she might cry in frustration. "I'm going to try."

When Faith was young, her dad, before abandoning Faith and her mother and older brother, had been a car fanatic. *Always have a lug wrench in your car, baby girl. It'll save you any time you have a flat.* Not that a ten-year-old knew anything about changing tires, but Faith had hung on her daddy's every word until one day he hadn't come home. After that, Faith had given up on learning about cars, but she knew what she had to do from a class she'd taken in high school.

Accepting the lug wrench from Kelsey, she knelt down by the tire once more. When all her strength wouldn't turn the nut and she tried all four of them, she groaned, rose to her feet, and kicked at the tire in annoyance.

"Pretty sure that won't help," Kelsey said, just as Faith muttered an obscene curse thanks to the pain shooting through her foot.

She was in so much agony, she barely registered the car stopping, then pulling into the open spot in front of her van until a large man approached them, making her aware they were two women alone on an empty street in the dark.

Using the wrench as her defense, she held it up in front of her. "Don't come near us."

"Relax." He stepped to the side until he was underneath a streetlamp, the glow illuminating his features. "Do I look like a killer to you?"

She studied him, a handsome man with dark brown hair, in a wool coat with his tie visible. "Ted Bundy was handsome, too."

He grinned and her heart skipped a beat. My God, he was good-looking. A dimple beside that amazing smile winked at her, and body

parts she'd thought long dead came to life.

"Thank you ... I think?" he said with a shake of his head. "Or not. Look, you obviously need help." He strode past her, ignoring her weaponry, and knelt down by the tire. "What about roadside assistance? Did you call?"

She glanced at his obviously expensive coat, had noted his suit beneath and brand name shoes. "Umm, does this old hunk of junk look like it comes with roadside assistance?" She shot him a look of disbelief. "Some of us can't afford luxuries and AAA is definitely a luxury."

From somewhere behind her, Kelsey, who had been silent, laughed out loud.

When he didn't immediately reply, Faith braced her hands on her hips and studied him, wondering why he'd stopped in the first place. "Listen, I appreciate the fact that you tried to help, but I'll figure something out."

He slowly rose to his feet. "Do you have a spare? You must if you were trying to take this one off."

"I assume I do, underneath all the baskets I just loaded into the back." She heard the frustration in her voice and fought back an inkling of defeat. She wasn't going to fall apart over a flat tire and ruined plans.

"You assume?" He shook his head and strode around to the back end of the van, glancing inside and muttering a curse.

"There's no obvious spare in here, so we'll have to unload all this to see what's underneath. What is all that anyway?" he asked.

"Candy. Homemade."

"Interesting." He raised his eyebrows, his gaze going from the sweet treats in the back to her face before he spoke. "Jason Dare," he said, extending his hand.

"Faith Lancaster." She placed her hand in his, and the heat of his skin sizzled against her palm.

"Nice to meet you, Faith." He curled his fingers around hers and lingered longer than was necessary for a handshake. Long enough for her body to tingle with awareness before he released her.

"And this is my intern, Kelsey," Faith said.

The other woman smiled at him but didn't shake his hand.

"What do you do for a living?" Faith asked in a husky voice she barely recognized, her entire body still hyperaware of that one brush of his skin.

"I own a nightclub. Club TEN29. Have you heard of it?" he asked.

She shook her head. She never went out to party at night, so what would she know about the club scene? But this man looked like he fit into it, with his sexy tousled brown hair that he probably paid a fortune to get cut so it fell just that way.

"Oh my God! My friends and I have been dying to go, but there's always such a long line to get in," Kelsey said, her excitement tangible.

She'd been so quiet, Faith had almost forgotten she was there.

"Well, here's my business card," Jason said, putting his hand in his coat pocket and coming out with a few cards. He handed one to Kelsey, who was bouncing on her feet in excitement. "Just show it to security and they'll let you right in or, at the very least, call me."

"Oh my God, thank you!" she practically squealed.

His gaze settled on Faith's face. "Now, let's see to that spare."

* * * *

If Jason had to peg the type of woman he liked, tall and willowy would describe most of his hookups, yet he couldn't stop staring at the full-figured, curvy blonde with the porcelain skin and full lips who created candy, of all things.

"Let's move the baskets back to the apartment," Faith said, breaking the spell that had woven between them as they stared at one another, both clearly struck by something bigger than themselves.

"I'll take some." Kelsey walked between them and started to work.

Together they unloaded the candy, which Faith and her assistant brought back upstairs to what he assumed was her apartment while he did something he hadn't done since college.

It was a miracle he knew how to change a tire.

For sure, his father, Robert Dare, hadn't taught him, as he'd rarely been around. Maybe he'd taught Jason's half brothers from a woman nobody knew about how to handle the things a man should know. Shaking off that painful memory, Jason called his cousin Gabe and let him know he would be late before throwing his jacket into the back of his car, rolling up his sleeves, loosening his tie, and getting down to his task.

While he worked, Kelsey called an Uber to take her home and one showed up quickly. Apparently Faith, having taken one of his business cards, had decided he was a legitimate businessman and safe to be alone with.

It didn't take long to get the tire off the van, and on examination, Jason realized it had been deliberately slashed, and that bothered him.

"How's it going?" Faith asked him.

"No problems, unless you count the fact that someone deliberately cut your tire." He glanced over his shoulder.

Faith had frozen in place, her eyes wide, her concerned expression clearly telling him she was upset.

"It's probably some of the kids in the neighborhood," she finally said, visibly forcing herself to relax. "They congregate around here late at night, and I haven't looked at the van since the day before yesterday."

He wasn't sure whether or not he believed her, and he tucked her reaction away to dissect another time.

She wrapped her arms around herself, appearing uncertain for the first time since he'd met her. And a fierce feeling of protectiveness rushed over him, one he'd previously experienced only for people he cared about, yet he didn't know this woman at all.

"So what are you doing with all the candy?" he asked as he worked on the tire, eager to take that stricken look off her face, change the subject, shake off the weird emotions she provoked in him, and maybe get to know her at the same time.

"I own a store called Sweet Treats," she said. "I want to build my business, so I made baskets of my signature item, and I was going to go around to the local businesses and ask if they'd put the candy and my business card by the register."

"What makes your candy stand out?" he asked.

"Other than how good it is?" she asked cheekily. "It's handcrafted and made with love. If I grow enough, I'll have to bring in outside-made candy to fill the cases, but that's for another time. Meanwhile, I know I'm a small shop and it'll be hard to get my name out there, but if I can dominate the area around my store based on the one thing I offer that's different than anyone else, then maybe word of mouth will work in my favor."

He listened to her words and his hand stilled on the last lug nut. Everything she said made sense.

Her words *dominating the area and standing out* jumped out at him. "That's it!" he said, excitement filling him because her words had hit on the one thing missing from Club TEN29. Something unique to them, and suddenly he knew just what he needed to discuss with Gabe.

"What's it?" she asked.

"You've come up with a brilliant idea, Faith Lancaster. And it just might help me with my business, so thank you." He turned the wrench one last time and rose to his feet, his legs stiff from crouching in one position for so long.

"Happy to help." She shrugged, obviously confused, but that was okay because he wasn't. He finally had direction.

He looked down at his hands, now completely covered in dirt and grease.

Faith glanced at his blackened skin. "Oh! Come upstairs and wash up. It's the least I can do for you after you saved me."

He didn't want to get into his car covered in filth, and she seemed okay with him now, so he nodded. "I'd appreciate that."

He followed her inside and up two flights of dark stairs. He immediately didn't like where she lived. From the description of the guys hanging out front late at night to the lack of lighting in the walk-up, it screamed danger. But who was he to judge? Yet it bothered him. He wouldn't let his sister live here.

By the time they walked into the small apartment, he was frowning, but one look at the cheerful décor and his mood lightened. This was a woman who made the best of any situation, he realized, taking in the white curtains and the old furniture with bright pink throw pillows covering the cushions. A matching fun pink rug sat under a beat-up coffee table covered in well-read books.

"You like pink," he mused, coming up beside her. "And candy." She even smelled sweet and delicious. "Are you fun, Faith?"

Her cheeks turned an adorable shade of … pink. "I can be, in the right situation."

He wondered what that right situation might be, because he'd definitely like to have fun with her. The kind between the sheets. Before his dick could react to that thought, he asked, "Where's the bathroom?"

She led him to a small partly open door and gestured for him to go inside. "There's a tiny linen closet behind the door. Take a towel and get yourself cleaned up."

She stepped away and headed back to the main area of the apartment.

He glanced over to where the small kitchen was visible through a pass-through. The candies were neatly stacked on the Formica countertops.

"So about those treats. Did I earn myself one?" he asked, joining

her.

She blinked in surprise. "Why didn't I think of that?" She rushed to the kitchen, returning with a pop and handing it to him.

He bit into it once, then twice, quickly swallowing the sweet, delicious candy. "Mmm. Damn, these are good. S'mores flavor?" he asked.

She nodded, a grin on her face. "It's like a taste of home," she said softly.

Sensing this meant something to her, he wanted to know more. "How so?"

She sighed. "My mom and I used to make candy all the time when I was growing up. She always wanted to open a store in our small town, but she didn't have the ability. Things were ... out of her control. And she needed to work to take care of me and my brother. But this was her favorite recipe and it reminds me of her."

"What happened?" he asked. "If you want to talk about it."

"She died recently." Faith blinked and looked away.

Recognizing raw pain, he changed the subject. "Well, your candy is delicious and I hope you succeed," he said, treating her to a warm smile, realizing their time together was coming to an end.

"I have a meeting I need to get to," he said. But he wasn't ready to leave.

"Oh, right." She rushed over to the kitchen and returned with a basket in her hand. "Take this. As a thank you. You're a Good Samaritan, Jason Dare."

He accepted her gift, their skin brushing as it exchanged hands. A shot of electricity jolted up his arm and went straight to his cock. Something about this woman got to him, from her gorgeous face and curvaceous body to her strength and the hint of occasional fragility beneath. He knew with everything in him he ought to stay away. From the fact that her tire might have been slashed to the fact that she didn't radiate one-night-stand type of woman to him, he should say goodbye and walk out the door.

"Have dinner with me." He blurted out the words before he could think them through.

She stared at him in surprise, those pretty lips pursing in thought, green eyes huge. "Umm ... I really don't think it's a good idea. I have too much going on right now and I don't date and ... well, we shouldn't." She sounded sad, as if she didn't want to say no.

He rolled his shoulders, deciding it was for the best even if he didn't like being turned down by her. "I understand."

She stared at him for a heartbeat. "Well, thanks again."

He inclined his head. "You can thank me by locking your door and being careful out there." Her slashed tire stayed with him, bothered him, even.

Sure, this was New York City and not the best neighborhood, so it really could have been done by someone who considered vandalism a good time. He'd probably have gone with that theory, too, if not for her slightly panicked reaction she'd tried to hide.

"Don't worry. I'm a big girl and I can take care of myself," she said, striding toward the door. "But I'll take your advice."

He stepped out the door she'd opened for him. "Bye, sweetness," he said. "It was nice meeting you, Faith Lancaster."

She wrinkled her nose at the nickname.

"Would you prefer candy girl?" he asked, chuckling at the blush on her cheeks as he walked away.

# Discover 1001 Dark Nights

COLLECTION ONE
FOREVER WICKED by Shayla Black
CRIMSON TWILIGHT by Heather Graham
CAPTURED IN SURRENDER by Liliana Hart
SILENT BITE: A SCANGUARDS WEDDING by Tina Folsom
DUNGEON GAMES by Lexi Blake
AZAGOTH by Larissa Ione
NEED YOU NOW by Lisa Renee Jones
SHOW ME, BABY by Cherise Sinclair
ROPED IN by Lorelei James
TEMPTED BY MIDNIGHT by Lara Adrian
THE FLAME by Christopher Rice
CARESS OF DARKNESS by Julie Kenner

COLLECTION TWO
WICKED WOLF by Carrie Ann Ryan
WHEN IRISH EYES ARE HAUNTING by Heather Graham
EASY WITH YOU by Kristen Proby
MASTER OF FREEDOM by Cherise Sinclair
CARESS OF PLEASURE by Julie Kenner
ADORED by Lexi Blake
HADES by Larissa Ione
RAVAGED by Elisabeth Naughton
DREAM OF YOU by Jennifer L. Armentrout
STRIPPED DOWN by Lorelei James
RAGE/KILLIAN by Alexandra Ivy/Laura Wright
DRAGON KING by Donna Grant
PURE WICKED by Shayla Black
HARD AS STEEL by Laura Kaye
STROKE OF MIDNIGHT by Lara Adrian
ALL HALLOWS EVE by Heather Graham
KISS THE FLAME by Christopher Rice
DARING HER LOVE by Melissa Foster
TEASED by Rebecca Zanetti
THE PROMISE OF SURRENDER by Liliana Hart

COLLECTION THREE
HIDDEN INK by Carrie Ann Ryan
BLOOD ON THE BAYOU by Heather Graham
SEARCHING FOR MINE by Jennifer Probst
DANCE OF DESIRE by Christopher Rice
ROUGH RHYTHM by Tessa Bailey
DEVOTED by Lexi Blake
Z by Larissa Ione
FALLING UNDER YOU by Laurelin Paige
EASY FOR KEEPS by Kristen Proby
UNCHAINED by Elisabeth Naughton
HARD TO SERVE by Laura Kaye
DRAGON FEVER by Donna Grant
KAYDEN/SIMON by Alexandra Ivy/Laura Wright
STRUNG UP by Lorelei James
MIDNIGHT UNTAMED by Lara Adrian
TRICKED by Rebecca Zanetti
DIRTY WICKED by Shayla Black
THE ONLY ONE by Lauren Blakely
SWEET SURRENDER by Liliana Hart

COLLECTION FOUR
ROCK CHICK REAWAKENING by Kristen Ashley
ADORING INK by Carrie Ann Ryan
SWEET RIVALRY by K. Bromberg
SHADE'S LADY by Joanna Wylde
RAZR by Larissa Ione
ARRANGED by Lexi Blake
TANGLED by Rebecca Zanetti
HOLD ME by J. Kenner
SOMEHOW, SOME WAY by Jennifer Probst
TOO CLOSE TO CALL by Tessa Bailey
HUNTED by Elisabeth Naughton
EYES ON YOU by Laura Kaye
BLADE by Alexandra Ivy/Laura Wright
DRAGON BURN by Donna Grant
TRIPPED OUT by Lorelei James
STUD FINDER by Lauren Blakely
MIDNIGHT UNLEASHED by Lara Adrian

HALLOW BE THE HAUNT by Heather Graham
DIRTY FILTHY FIX by Laurelin Paige
THE BED MATE by Kendall Ryan
NIGHT GAMES by CD Reiss
NO RESERVATIONS by Kristen Proby
DAWN OF SURRENDER by Liliana Hart

COLLECTION FIVE
BLAZE ERUPTING by Rebecca Zanetti
ROUGH RIDE by Kristen Ashley
HAWKYN by Larissa Ione
RIDE DIRTY by Laura Kaye
ROME'S CHANCE by Joanna Wylde
THE MARRIAGE ARRANGEMENT by Jennifer Probst
SURRENDER by Elisabeth Naughton
INKED NIGHTS by Carrie Ann Ryan
ENVY by Rachel Van Dyken
PROTECTED by Lexi Blake
THE PRINCE by Jennifer L. Armentrout
PLEASE ME by J. Kenner
WOUND TIGHT by Lorelei James
STRONG by Kylie Scott
DRAGON NIGHT by Donna Grant
TEMPTING BROOKE by Kristen Proby
HAUNTED BE THE HOLIDAYS by Heather Graham
CONTROL by K. Bromberg
HUNKY HEARTBREAKER by Kendall Ryan
THE DARKEST CAPTIVE by Gena Showalter

COLLECTION SIX

DRAGON CLAIMED by Donna Grant
ASHES TO INK by Carrie Ann Ryan
ENSNARED by Elisabeth Naughton
EVERMORE by Corinne Michaels
VENGEANCE by Rebecca Zanetti
ELI'S TRIUMPH by Joanna Wylde
CIPHER by Larissa Ione
RESCUING MACIE by Susan Stoker

ENCHANTED by Lexi Blake
TAKE THE BRIDE by Carly Phillips
INDULGE ME by J. Kenner
THE KING by Jennifer L. Armentrout
QUIET MAN by Kristen Ashley
ABANDON by Rachel Van Dyken
THE OPEN DOOR by Laurelin Paige
CLOSER by Kylie Scott
SOMETHING JUST LIKE THIS by Jennifer Probst
BLOOD NIGHT by Heather Graham
TWIST OF FATE by Jill Shalvis
MORE THAN PLEASURE YOU by Shayla Black
WONDER WITH ME by Kristen Proby
THE DARKEST ASSASSIN by Gena Showalter

*Discover Blue Box Press*

TAME ME by J. Kenner
TEMPT ME by J. Kenner
DAMIEN by J. Kenner
TEASE ME by J. Kenner
REAPER by Larissa Ione
THE SURRENDER GATE by Christopher Rice
SERVICING THE TARGET by Cherise Sinclair

# On behalf of 1001 Dark Nights,

Liz Berry, M.J. Rose, and Jillian Stein would like to thank ~

Steve Berry
Doug Scofield
Benjamin Stein
Kim Guidroz
InkSlinger PR
Dan Slater
Asha Hossain
Chris Graham
Chelle Olson
Kasi Alexander
Jessica Johns
Dylan Stockton
Richard Blake
and Simon Lipskar

Made in the USA
Columbia, SC
28 March 2020

**DATE DUE**

| OhioLINK | | |
|---|---|---|
| MAR | | |
| MAY 14 '99 FAC | DEC 01 REC'D | |
| APR 29 REC'D | NOV 30 2002 | |
| | DEC 2 6 2002 | |
| NOV 30 REC'D | | |
| OhioLINK | MAR 07 REC'D | |
| MAR 0 1 REC'D | MAY 12 2008 | |
| DEC 22 2000 | MAY 2 2 2009 | |
| DEC 21 REC'D | JUL 0 7 REC'D | |